WHITEOUT

Whiteout

How Canada Cancels Blackness

GEORGE ELLIOTT CLARKE

Véhicule Press

Published with the generous assistance of the Canada Council for the Arts and the Canada Book Fund of the Department of Canadian Heritage.

 Canada Council Conseil des arts
for the Arts du Canada

Canadä

Cover design by David Drummond
Set into type by Simon Garamond
Printed by Marquis Imprimeur

Dépôt légal, Library and Archives Canada and the Bibliothèque national du Québec, second trimester 2023

LIBRARY AND ARCHIVES CANADA CATALOGUING IN PUBLICATION
Title: Whiteout : how Canada cancels Blackness / George Elliott Clarke.
Names: Clarke, George Elliott, author.
Description: Includes bibliographical references.
Identifiers: Canadiana (print) 20230200826 | Canadiana (ebook) 20230205240 | ISBN 9781550656077 (softcover) | ISBN 9781550656138 (EPUB)
Subjects: LCSH: Black people in literature. | LCSH: Race in literature. | LCSH: Canadian literature—
Black authors—History and criticism. | LCSH: Canadian literature—History and criticism. | LCSH: Black people—Canada—Social conditions. | LCSH: Black people—Canada—Intellectual life. | LCSH: Canada—Race relations. | CSH: Canadian literature—Black Canadian authors—History and criticism. CSH: Black Canadians—Social conditions. | CSH: Black Canadians—Intellectual life.
Classification: LCC PS8101.B6 C53 2023 | DDC C810.9/352996071—dc23

Published by Véhicule Press, Montréal, Québec, Canada
www.vehiculepress.com

Distribution in Canada by LitDistCo
www.litdistco.ca

Distributed in the US by Independent Publishers Group
ipgbook.com

Printed in Canada on FSC certified paper.

For Geraldine Elizabeth Clarke (1939–2000)
& William Lloyd Clarke (1935–2005):
Adepts, Believers, African Baptists

Escape the writing of an irreconcilable history.
—RAED ANIS AL-JISHI, "Standard Girl"

When I begin screaming,
I am more beautiful.
—LORELEI LEE, "Boat Show"

Screams dissolve into,
the politics of Poetry.
—BÄNOO ZAN, "Non-Narrative"

CONTENTS

PREFACE

THOUGH THESE DOZEN essays are written by a black professor, they are not the magisterial commentaries of a scholar. In fact, I confess that I am an interloper in the Academy. There were many who thought that someone of my ilk—or my complexion—did not belong among the professoriate, and saw through my pretensions, and ensured that I would have no support as a graduate student at Queen's University, in Kingston, from 1990 to 1993. Their hope was that I'd drop out or slyly *t'ief* my doctorate and then disappear to craft poetry, screeds, diatribes, squibs, bulletins, and notes, here and there, but never ever become a pedagogue and researcher. They knew that I was a phony, a fraud, a trickster, and that my research essays would never be more than cartoonish bumf about unimportant subjects like Black poets and white racism. So, dear reader, you will find in these essays a writer who is only accidentally a scholar, only somehow a stowaway in the Ivory Tower, and so you should feel reassured that I have written nothing herein that is either jargon-packed or dryly clever. I likely lack such tradecraft.

Although I have edited all of these essays—to prettify language, to clarify statements, and to diversify evidence—I have tried to refrain from giving them holus-bolus makeovers. One new addition to these essays is a "Bridge"—at the end of each—to help move you from one essay to the next: to establish a degree of continuity.

The earliest essay dates back to 1996, and the latest (a book review) to 2020: that marks the passage practically of a quarter-century. In that span of time, nomenclature has shifted. Back in 1991, I could write *Native* and *First Nations*; by 2001, *Aboriginal* had become the politic usage; now, in 2021, it is *Indigenous* that seems most appropriate. Of course, *Black* and *black* have been in and out of fashion and back in fashion (due to George Floyd's martyrdom in Minneapolis, Minnesota, in spring 2020). However, the question of capitalization remains unresolved. I don't tend to capitalize it when it seems casually to represent race—as in *black people*, but I do capitalize it when it is meant to designate a cultural or political trait: *Black English* and *Black Canadian*. However, my own preference is to use *African-Canadian* and/or *Africadian* (when I refer to Black Maritimers). Out of my fealty to the thought of Nahum Dimitri Chandler, I also employ *Negro* here and there. Please note that I deploy these terms—all of them—in a range of circumstances, where I let poetic feel—more than political sentiment—determine the diction.

Despite the newfound appetite for expanded Black Studies programs and the hiring and promotion of black professors, to me, African-Canadian history militates against any sustained optimism. I am not cynical but realistic. Black protest movements win lasting change when they reject all efforts to win their acquiescence via photo-ops and parliamentary apologies.

George Elliott Clarke, Point Pelée, Ontario
December, 2021

White like Canada

ON BECOMING CANADA's first black member of Parliament, in 1968, Lincoln Alexander pointedly declared that he would not speak on behalf of blacks. Eleven years later, in May 1979, Haitian-born Jean Alfred, a Parti Québécois member of Quebec's National Assembly, sparked a row when he told a meeting of the now-defunct National Black Coalition of Canada that he was more interested in the cause of Quebec's independence than in the call for national black unity. Today, there are three black members of Canada's governing Liberal Party and one black opposition party member in Parliament, but there is still no national spokesperson or leader for Canada's half-million people of African heritage.

This lack of racial solidarity has something to do with the scarcity of nonwhites in Canada: people of colour—such as Africans, Asians, and First Nations people—account, collectively, for only 12 percent of the Canadian population; blacks themselves make up only 2 percent. Then again, the counting of African-Canadians is more an exercise in semantics than in statistics: according to a 1997 McGill University study, almost half of the black people in Canada do not identity themselves as such on census forms, choosing instead "British" (the tendency of Jamaican Canadians) or "French" (the practice of Haitian Canadians). Whatever the numbers, though, Canada's coloureds are an almost invisible presence in the country at large. Because most of them live in the largest cities—Toronto, Montreal, and Vancouver—one can travel huge tracts of the second-largest country in the world and seldom lay eyes on another person of colour.

Yet the vagueness of black identity in Canada does not merely reflect the relative paucity of souls. Rather, it is emblematic of a larger crisis of Canadian identity. It is difficult enough to figure out what it means to be Canadian, let alone African Canadian. The positive content of Canadian identity is unclear; as one wag has it, one is merely "as Canadian as possible...under the circumstances." English Canadians—whether black, white, yellow, red, or brown—agree only that they are not Americans. (French Canadians know themselves to be French, but with an American streak. They like to have their French bread *and* their french fries, too.) What both English and French Canadians know is that they are better than Americans. Northrop Frye once defined a Canadian as an American who rejects the American Revolution; I think that's close to the nub of the matter.

The general incoherence of colour-based identity in Canada permits Canadian whiteness to exist, then, as the ethereal force. Left pretty much to its own devices, the white majority in Canada exudes a kind of ideal whiteness, ready for export. All my life, I've considered Canada to be a kind of discount warehouse where American networks and film companies go to purchase images of immaculate, politic whiteness. You want cool? Check out Mike Myers or Dan

Aykroyd. You need cerebral poise? Try Alex Trebek or Peter Jennings. You want family values? Here's Michael J. Fox. You want sex appeal? Take Pamela Anderson or Shannon Tweed. You're in the market for a sellable lesbian? Choose k.d. lang. You're searching for clean-cut action heroes? Hire William Shatner or Keanu Reeves. Weary of Alice Walker? Read Alice Munro. Sick of Babyface winning all the Grammys? Give one to Celine Dion. Bruce Springsteen too aggressive for your sensibilities? Listen to Bryan Adams. Polite, pacific, respectable Canadian whites are abundantly available for Americans who want to glorify whiteness without alienating African Americans.

The reality is less pleasant and a lot weirder. In a sense, Canada would not exist were it not for the irresistible boundary that America, quite unwittingly, provides. Canadians were the world's first anti-Americans: as political scientist Seymour Martin Lipset suggests, Canadians have never forgotten that two nations, not one, resulted from the American Revolution. While Americans laud the decision of the Thirteen Colonies to break away from Britain, they tend to forget that six colonies to their north remained loyal. Those six colonies evolved into Canada, a nation in profound philosophical disagreement with a southern neighbour it has always viewed as violence-ridden and cockroach-infested.

Canadian identity, such as it is, defines itself primarily in opposition to the United States. Canada is pristine, unpolluted wilderness; the US is decaying urban centres. Canada built a welfare state; the US built a warfare state. Canada is mildly socialist; the US is unabashedly capitalist.

Canadians are nice; Americans are trigger-happy. Canadians also claim to be uniquely sensitive to multiculturalism. Whereas the American paradigm for assimilation is the melting pot, Canada celebrates a gorgeous mosaic of peoples permitted to maintain their ethnic particularisms (so long as this permit does not hinder class stratification[1]).

The most significant difference between Canada and the US is, finally, that America has a race problem. In Canada, the party line goes, there are no racists save those who watch too much American television. Whenever some blatantly racist event transpires, the official response is to deny it. In 1991, after the fatal shooting—in the head—of Marcellus François, an unarmed black man, by Montreal police, Quebec premier Robert Bourassa lectured a group of black protesters that there was no racism in Quebec.

Like Bourassa, white Canada imagines itself to be congenial, hospitable, tolerant. There are plenty of white liberals in Canada but little white liberal guilt: Canadians generally do not believe that they have committed any racial sins for which they should atone. If anything, they are self-righteous in maintaining their innocence. The reception of Bharati Mukherjee's short story collection *Darkness* (1985) is a case in point. In the introduction to that book, Mukherjee claimed that Canadians were racist toward people from hot, damp climates; furthermore, she had the temerity to suggest that the US was more accepting. The white Canadian reaction? What an ungrateful immigrant!

This kind of thinking is not atypical. In April 1994, a mob of whites, convinced that they had spied a black fugitive, chased an innocent black man through the streets of downtown Toronto, until he was "saved" by the police, who took him into custody temporarily. The incident was ignored by the very media that had precipitated it. For weeks, the Toronto newspapers had circulated blurred photographs of a black murder suspect whose only recognizable feature was his dreadlocks. Suddenly, all young black men, with or without dreads, became monsters. Even Michael Valpy, a liberal columnist for the *Globe and Mail*, contributed to the public hysteria. Valpy linked "a growing tendency toward random violent crime" in Toronto to "young black people of Jamaican origin," whom he described as fomenters of "a culture of violence." He warned that "their dress, patois, and behaviour" are being "imitated by other young Canadians."

The incident prompted the socialist then-premier of Ontario, Bob Rae, to demand that Jamaica accept the return of "Jamaican" lawbreakers. The Jamaican prime minster replied, coolly, that the criminals in question were Canadian citizens—raised and educated in Canada, not Jamaica. Rae was properly embarrassed. The affair revealed the hollowness of Canadian claims to racial tolerance.

White Canada's faith in its innocence is equally evident in its cheerful reading of Canadian history. Canadians take pride in the fact that their country was the last "stop" on the Underground Railroad. One standard history of the country noted that Canadians can "claim the proud distinction for their flag...that it has never floated over legalized slavery." The claim is literally true, but only because Canada did not yet exist when the enslavement of Natives and Africans flourished on what is now Canadian soil. A 1995 poll conducted by the Canadian Civil Liberties Association found that 83 percent of Canadian adults did not know that slavery was practised in pre-Confederation Canada until 1834, when Britain abolished the institution throughout its empire (but with a white-"massa"-profiting delay in the West Indies). You would most likely find a similar ignorance regarding the existence of school segregation in Ontario and Nova Scotia (as recently as the 1950s); the $500 head tax that the Canadian government once slapped on all Chinese immigrants; and the numerous "Black Codes" enacted by various levels of government to control where Chinese, Japanese, Indigenous, and African citizens could work, live, be buried, and even, in some cases, vote. During the Second World War, Canada interned its Japanese (but not its Germans) and refused entry to Jews fleeing Nazi persecution. That Canada, like the United States, also served as a haven for Nazi war criminals has been a steady embarrassment.

These incidents pale in comparison to the sustained maltreatment of Canada's Indigenous peoples. Though much of the country was never ceded by treaty, First Nations people were nevertheless sequestered on tiny reservations that grew smaller as monied interests claimed oil and mineral deposits on the land. Centuries-old colonial policies have decimated Indigenous populations—or wiped them out altogether, as in the case of the Beothuk of Newfoundland.

In 1969, the federal government attempted to resolve its nagging "Native Question" with a "White Paper" that proposed the cancellation of the reservation system and the wholesale assimilation of Aboriginals into the white majority population. Natives responded with a "Red Paper," and the contemporary Indigenous rights movement commenced. Since then, in the courts and on the reservations, increasingly militant groups have attempted to settle land claims and institute self-government. In the summer of 1990, armed Mohawks barricaded sacred burial grounds that the village of Oka, Quebec, wanted to develop into a golf course. The resulting standoff ended when the Canadian Army rolled in with armoured vehicles to arrest the Mohawk leaders. At the height of the crisis, as Mohawk Elders, women, and children were being evacuated from the site, their convoy of automobiles was viciously stoned by a white mob as hateful as any group of archetypal Southern racists. The provincial police force, the Sûreté du Québec, looked on and did nothing.

The original "two solitudes" of Canadian nationalism—Anglo and Québécois—have never had a vision of Canada as anything but a white man's country. Immediately after Confederation in 1867, a group of young businessmen and professionals in Toronto united with literary patriots to form the first major Anglo-Canadian nationalist organization, Canada First. Its mission was to promote close relations with Great Britain and to create a national, pan-Canadian sensibility. In his *Pelican History of Canada*, first published in 1969, Canadian historian Kenneth McNaught asserts that one wing of Canada First elaborated "a mystique of northern superiority" and a "wayward faith in racial supremacy." For these Canada Firsters, "the population of the United States was not only increasingly mongrel, but was also prey to the debilitating effects of a more southerly climate. The northern races of Europe, especially the Anglo-Saxons, were the true custodians of constitutional liberty and martial valour."

In the 1920s, the Ku Klux Klan was popular on the Prairies (and empowered in Saskatchewan) but not in Ontario, due to the dislike of the provincial government for an alien, *American* organization. In Quebec, a xenophobic, ultranationalist secret society, L'Ordre de Jacques-Cartier, was founded in 1926. By 1941, it was being described as "le Ku Klux Klan du Canada français." In the 1930s, pro-Mussolini Quebec Catholics supported a fascist movement spearheaded by Adrian Arcand. As William Kaplan notes, Arcand's Parti National Social Chrétien, founded in 1934, "had as its emblem a swastika surrounded by maple leaves with a Canadian beaver appearing at the crown."

Though Canada has had a hard time defining a national identity, there is one symbol to which it has always been able to cling: geography. Voltaire notoriously dismissed the country as "nothing more than thirty acres of snow," and it's certainly true that the bleak topography of winter—polar bears and permafrost, tuques and tundra—has fired the imaginings of Canadian whiteness. The one inescapable fact of Canadian life—the inevitable, constituting myth of Canadianness—is the nation's frigid vastness. Québécois nationalist poet Gilles Vigneault's celebrated 1964 song "Mon Pays" goes so far as to declare that his nation "is not a country—it is winter."

Canada is a spartan, tough, *cold* country, testing the resolve of hardscrabble voyageurs and masochistic adventurers—a Wild West in subzero. Survival is an overbearing theme of white writing in Canada; it is also the title of Can Lit doyenne Margaret Atwood's influential 1972 book on Canadian literature. To bring the nation into existence, the white settlers must make common cause with an often white landscape. The primeval frontier and the white body become one. These lines from Patrick Lane's poem "Passing into Storm," published in 1974, encapsulate this viewpoint:

> Finding a white man
> in snow is to look for the dead
> ...
> He has left too much
>
> flesh on winter's white metal
> to leave his colour as a sign.
> Cold white. Cold flesh.

No matter that a black man, Matthew Henson, discovered Canada's spiritual heart, the North Pole. The presence of people of colour is whitewashed from these Canadian modernist landscapes. In the work of writers such as Atwood, Pierre Berton, Emily Carr, and Farley Mowat, as in the canvases of the Group of Seven painters, Indigenous people are sometimes reduced to props, and the land becomes the domain of troubled, conscience-stricken whites.

Still, non-whites have often served as a kind of phantom resource. Responding to criticism that she excludes urban life from her writing, Atwood confesses in her 1995 study *Strange Things: The Malevolent North in Canadian Literature* that she finds cannibalism more interesting than donut shops. In Atwood's first novel, *Surfacing*, published in 1972, the anonymous narrator "goes native" in order to express her separation from a patriarchal, consumerist, American-oriented society. Atwood was likely inspired by Archibald Belaney, also known as Grey Owl, a British naturalist who spent his life pretending to be a Native on the shores of Ajawaan Lake, in Saskatchewan. (Grey Owl lived the part: he married an Iroquois woman, Anahareo, and was accompanied by a giant beaver, Jelly Roll.) This hoity-toity primitivist stance is almost a compulsion in Canadian culture.

The soft and fuzzy prototypical Aryan nature of Canada has a dark, tortured soul. Québécois nationalists have dramatized their plight by calling themselves the "white niggers" of Canada.[2] An editorial in the *Vancouver Review*, a literary journal, recently suggested that Canadians should embrace "snow nigger" as an endearing term for a Canadian post-national identity. Were they identifying with the Jafaicans—scraggly white guys with dreadlocks, reeking of patchouli—who populate Vancouver? In fact, despite its marginal presence in the country, blackness has always played an overlooked role in the development of Canadian identity. As far back as the 1840s, white proto-Canadians like Thomas Chandler Haliburton took images from coon shows to popularize negative ideas of blacks and "backward" whites while advancing positive views of upper-class whites. More recently, one notes the exceedingly twisted case of convicted serial rapist and sex murderer Paul Bernardo. Although Bernardo and his killer helpmate, Karla Homolka, had moved from Toronto to St. Catharines to escape Toronto's immigrant (read: "nonwhite") population, Bernardo aspired to become a rap star.

Jean Baudrillard writes of film stars that they are "dazzling in their nullity, and in their coldness." The ghostly, cool, glimmering whiteness of the cinema is precisely that of white Canada. It is this original whiteness that sent forth Mary Pickford to Hollywood to become "America's Sweetheart" at the same time that *The Birth of a Nation* enshrined the Ku Klux Klan as the white knights of America. It is this same whiteness that members of the proto-fascist Canadian Airborne Regiment bore with them to Somalia, in 1993, where they beat, tortured, and murdered a Somali boy and had themselves photographed taking pleasure in the act. In 1997, the Canadian government closed an inquiry into the affair without examining an attempt by the defence department to suppress the homicide. As happens so often in the Great White North, racism was made to disappear.

[*Transition: An International Review,* no. 73, 1997]

～

Racism in Canada is the *-ism* that dare not speak its name. Why? Because, for Canadian Negrophobes, the Great Satan is the Great Republic, whose racisms are violently evident across any given news cycle. To avoid answering any charge of domestic racism, the white supremacist establishment wilfully relegates African-heritage citizens to the periphery of the national imaginary, whitewashing them out of the histories, rejecting their refugee claims, deporting them from its shores, or incarcerating them in marshy gulags. Canada considers what Fanon called "the fact of blackness" an aberration—a body too polar to the white majority to ever be dubbed "Canadian." The next essay broods upon the socio-political challenges of being African-Canadian and proposes ways for us to think ourselves out of the oppressive binaries of True North racism—and even anti-racism.

~

An Anatomy of the Originality of African-Canadian Thought

For Brycen Edward Clarke (1988–2013)[3]

SELDOM HAVE WE CONSIDERED the likely truth that African Canada represents the greatest, northernmost expression of the existence of African-heritage—"Negro"—beings on this planet.[4] Certainly, there are Negroes in Scandinavia and Russia and, I'll wager, in Iceland too. However, what distinguishes African Canada is the existence here of *communities* of black people, with many dating back a century—or two—or three. Arguably, Canada possesses a uniquely *Nordic* set of "Black" cultures, of "long" establishment (if hundreds of years count as long). We should think instantly of the enslaved woman Marie-Josèphe Angélique fleeing from burning Montreal, in April 1734, in deep drifts of snow; we should also recall fur trader Pierre Bonga, likely garbed in beaver and buffalo, trekking through Prairie blizzards on behalf of the North West Company c. 1802.[5]

If our *nordicité* marks African-Canadians—of whatever "rootedness"—as representing an unorthodox blackness—"souls on ice," our "tropics" more frosty forest than "triste"—we must also note the eccentric fact that we inhabit the world's largest monarchy (in geographic girth and heft). Moreover, anomalously, we African-Canadians accept, as our monarch, a white Anglo-Saxon Protestant who also presides over her own United Kingdom, an island and a few satellite isles that could be plunked down easily in the combined area of Newfoundland and Labrador. Yet, as otherworldly—or simply "weird"—as the Canadian Crown is, its very existence means that Black Canadians inhabit a space where privilege and hierarchy matter—as do the associate status indicators of ethnicity, "colour," religion, and pedigree.[6] Canadians think that, because they worship Tim Hortons donuts and hockey players, they are populists, if not republicans. But the truth is, they are stealth monarchists, and, thus, they tolerate a pecking order of entitlements. Succinctly put, this means cake for the rich, "Timbits" for the middle-class, and crumbs for the poor, the worst off being the First Nations and the next-worst-oppressed being "Visible Minorities" (i.e., Africans and Arabs and Asians and Latin Americans, but especially Africans). The Dominion of Canada is really a conglomeration of dichotomies—of distinctions among peoples and differences between groups—with the Queen beaming benevolently upon all—from overseas.

Although African-Canadians are tempted to conceive of Toronto as a displaced Trenchtown, or Montreal as a fur-trade Marseilles, or Halifax as a True North Harlem, or Vancouver as a pacific *Veldt*, the truth is, we are—our miscellany of melanin—quite alone amid the Diaspora. We are adrift, as it were, on an iceberg (of "black ice," natch), and no one can or will give us succour or rescue: neither Northern Europe nor North Africa. Then again, we are, all of us, no matter our genealogies and cultural allegiances, the products of imperial collisions, whether it was America versus Britain, or Britain versus France, or France versus Spain, or Spain versus America. (I do not forget the Portuguese and the Dutch either. The transatlantic slave trade was the first "Scramble for Africa," and it was prosecuted for the same reason as the later "Scramble": to enrich the participating European powers.) No matter the victors in these trans-oceanic contests, our ancestors constitute the *actual*, historical losers: their Churchillan "sweat, blood, and tears"—and semen and eggs—served to fatten Europe and its white-ruled colonies with foodstuffs, stimulate them with coffee and chocolate, set them groggy with rum, sweeten them with sugar, swell their ranks with "bastards" (kids grateful or ungrateful), and fill their purses with precious metals and paper profits. Slavery was a crude—and cruel—global system of labour exploitation and resource extraction, and practically every European nation that had a seaport was involved, if tangentially, and got to share in the spoils. (In his review of Walter Johnson's *River of Dark Dreams: Slavery and Empire in the Cotton Kingdom*, Michael T. Bernath observes that what Johnson terms "slave racial capitalism" underwrote an American vision "of global empire premised upon the commodification of cotton and the human beings forced to tend it."[7])

Thanks to African servitude and the slaughter of Indigenous peoples in the Americas and the theft of their lands and resources, the European empires—and their colonies—realized an economic "lift-off" that still benefits them today, a wealth and power further guaranteed by the armaments that their plunder has permitted them to heap up. Now, "Fortress America" and "Fortress Europe" set their gunboats upon and prepare their jails for the Third-World poor, who take to the seas in deadly voyages, desperate to have better lives—or drown in the attempt.[8] Gallingly, the Euro/American Empires, successful in having killed, conquered, and cashiered masses, now declare themselves exonerated from these crimes, wrap themselves in Constitutions, and dare to pontificate about human rights and the rule of law.[9] African Canada emerges out of these international hypocrisies and contradictions.

Indeed, it was due to four centuries of Black migration movements, compelled first by slavery and then by anti-slavery, anti-racism, or dreaming of improvement via immigration,[10] that African Canada coalesced. Shipped to these shores by imperial, slaving navies, but fighting back as Maroons or as runaways and rebels, or as abolitionists and pan-Africanists, and then voyaging or flying here to seek economic betterment as immigrants, or safe haven as refugees, African Canadians are inseparable from the global flux and flow of the African Diaspora.

Yet, the arrival of Black peoples to what is now Canada, from every corner and angle of the transatlantic slave trade, the abolitionist and anti-colonial and anti-apartheid struggles, plus the wars among empires and between colonies and empires,[11] means that the African-Canadian population (to use the singular deliberately) is heterogeneous, cosmopolitan, polyphonous, and multicultural (if not yet multitudinous). In short, we are radically diverse. We are even diversely diverse, given that we may feel aligned to a particular

Canadian province or region or city (especially if we have community or family of "long-standing" therein); we may also feel fealty to an originating "homeland" or culture and/or language; we may subscribe to a religion or branch of Christianity rooted in a "back-home" heritage; we may even carry a Métis allegiance connected not only to Africa and (perhaps) Europe but also to China and India (if one claims Caribbean descent), or to Europe and (perhaps) Lebanon and India (if one claims direct African descent), or to Aboriginal American peoples (if one's genealogy intertwines with those of First Nations here).

To claim an African-Canadian or Black Canadian identity, then, is to subscribe to a melanin-inflected and sometimes differently accented multiculturalism within the multi-racial, multi-ethnic, and multi-faith multiculturalism of the Canadian state.[12] Intriguingly, the only inhabitants of Canada more variegated than African Canadians are the members of First Nations. (This fact should encourage us to look to the Assembly of First Nations and—especially—the Idle No More movement as models for our own potential national political mobilization.)

Thus, while we share the African-American position of being— "visibly"—a minority group, but one of much less provenance, we differ from African Americans in having no constitutional, pop cultural, economic, legal, or political clout, especially when regarded nationally. While we share a Caribbean context of once-slavery and once-colonialism and continued fealty (for too many of us) to ye olde metropoles— London and Paris, along with, again, a population of plural cultures—we differ from Caribbean societies in our being

33

a minority too small to elect governments of—literally—our own complexion. So, while we can be influenced and inspired by African American, Caribbean, South American, and African ideas, ideals, aesthetics, ethics, theologies, and politics, we are—in the world's second-largest country—generally powerless to forward any specific Afrocentric agenda as public policy. Not only are our numbers too little to constitute a viable voting bloc in any city or province of Canada, we are also too diverse in our allegiances—ethnic and religious, political and cultural—to easily speak and act as one. In socio-political terms, our diversity can look adversely like division, and thus means that we are collectively more easily suppressed by those whose policy is their persistent empowerment and our perpetual oppression.

Nevertheless, the lack of a commonly embraced—*mass*—identity is a godsend for African-Canadian artists and writers, of all backgrounds, for it means that they are free to explore a multitude of *potential* identities. Similarly, on the personal, individual level, African Canadians can enter into interracial and multi-ethnic unions, of all sorts, and feel little *angst* (less than may be the case for African Americans), simply because an Afrocentric—or Black nationalist—option has less credence amid the multifarious Canadian population.

None of these feel-good truths means that Canadian, Anglo-Franco white supremacy—delivered with a smile, a handshake, and a kiss on both cheeks—is nullified.[13] In fact, the existence and persistence of Canadian white racism can be agonizingly disorienting for its Negro victims for two reasons: first, the official denials of the experience of racism—and of even its history[14]—may make victims doubt their own sanity; secondly, generally, there is no ready Negro coalition to which victims may appeal for assistance and support. In Canada, then, one can be born Black, marry white, and die confused, or struggle to build a career, be blocked in ascension (due to racist spite), and quit—or be fired—embittered, but not ever know—for sure— why one failed or faltered.

So the surreal or eccentric aspect of African-Canadian experience (or "Canadian experience"[15]—to riff on the oft-given explanation for a refusal to hire or promote a black/immigrant due to their supposed lack thereof) is that we face a racism that "dare not speak its name." It is a tentative racism, a speculative racism, a ghost racism, whose smile is that of the Cheshire Cat and whose trace is a subtle chill—like that which spectres float when they want their presence felt, not seen. Afrocentrists and anti-racism activists who seek, then, to rally like-minded and good-hearted persons to struggle against "institutionalized racism" must fight official doubt with socio-economic statistics. Even police shootings of unarmed black men—often just boys—can be put down as accidents, or deviations, or as a trained reaction "in the line of duty." In these instances, few police are prosecuted; few police chiefs apologize; infrequently, though, a few dollars get doled out to mollify grieving mamas.

Moreover, when explicitly racist events occur, they are cast as abhorrent but aberrant, or as bizarre, or as an American importation, and so the systemic racism that may underlie such occurrences is ignored. One example is the May 2005 revelation of the ugly treatment of black workers at "the Centre Maraîcher Eugène Guinois Jr. Inc., a 1,300 acre family-run vegetable farm in Ste-Clotilde de Chateauguay, about 45 minutes southwest of Montreal. As part of its workforce, the farm—which does about $8 million in business each year and has a total workforce in the neighbourhood of 250—employed about 100 black workers as day labourers. These workers commuted from the Montreal suburb of Longueuil. They were paid $350 per week" ("Rampant Racism"). The reports about their abuse belong to medieval Europe:

> Though the farm had a nicely equipped cafeteria, the black workers were not allowed anywhere near it. Instead they had to eat and change in a filthy shack that was never cleaned, had no running water and lacked heat. The building had four microwaves, but only one was functional and it was too dirty to use. The refrigerator was broken. The toilets had been condemned and the farm had set up chemical toilets outside the shack for the black workers to use.
>
> Graffiti appeared on the farm stating "here are our monkeys" and "blacks are pigs."
>
> One black worker who attempted to sit on a picnic table near the clean cafeteria was told to leave by the owner's wife because the area was for Quebeckers only. She told him to sit at a table closer to the chemical toilets. White workers had a white supervisor, black ones worked under a black supervisor.

Four Negroes complained about their deliberate dehumanization to the Quebec Human Rights Tribunal, and won, and thus their experience became news. They were awarded more than $60,000 in damages.

Significantly, however, the judge was reportedly "stunned" and "scandalized" by the blatant racism on the vegetable farm. "Judge Michèle Pauzé opened her decision with the statement: 'The events you are about to read happened here, in Quebec, in the years 2000 and 2001.'" Then, either the judge or a reporter editorialized, "Though the events happened in modern day Quebec, the racism and segregation seem out of place and more suited to the deep south of the United States in the pre-civil rights era" ("Rampant Racism"). As is typically the case, the *Canadian* white racism that the Blacks suffered was characterized, correctly, as outré, outlandish, and out-of-bounds and, incorrectly, as *foreign*. Rather than foreign, however, it was merely *proven*. Too frequently, the proven experience or existence of racism in Canada is cast aside as accidental or incidental, as a unique circumstance, unworthy of further inquiry. Even more usually, the racist occurrence remains unproven, a matter of guesswork and emotion, and evaporates quickly from popular consciousness (and conscience)—as if a mirage.

Then again, in Canada, *white supremacy* is a phrase that is seldom heard beyond freak news events of a cross-burning here (Hants County, Nova Scotia, 2010), a blackface minstrel show there (Campbellford, Ontario, 2010). Yet Canadian scholar Richard Fung holds that "white racism is the bedrock of identity politics of race."

"But, no matter," we might say. "Things will be better

for our children." It is the standard liberal prophecy (or bromide), and those who utter it will take solace in the truth that, statistically, more and more of "us" are (inter) marrying with more and more of lots of "others" and producing children whose classrooms now resemble not just the United Nations but also a kind of globalized Woodstock. This positive is most vivid in the largest Canuck cities, where most newcomers—of all tints and hints and accents—gather. Thus, in his article "Mixie Me," published in *Toronto Life* in 2013, journalist Nicholas Hune-Brown, "half Chinese, half English," recognizes that, "According to the 2006 census, 7.1 per cent of [Toronto-area] marriages were interracial." He continues on to cite a Statistics Canada prediction that, by 2033, "63 per cent of Torontonians will belong to racialized minorities." Hune-Brown also reads the numbers as showing that "more than half of second-generation visible minority immigrants who are married have partners outside their race; by the third generation, it's 69 per cent."

His prose is unclear as to whether these figures count only Torontonian Coloured people's marriages or whether they relate to all Canadians *de couleur* and their legalized romances. Still, he is correct that interracial couples who become parents will likely raise open-minded children, who will also marry "across racial lines...producing a myriad of mixie [i.e., mixed-race] babies." Not only should African-Canadians celebrate our own high rates of intermarriage,[16] we should also relish the 2006 Census disclosure that, as Hune-Brown reports, "mixed-race couples were young and urban and tended to be more highly educated: one in three people in mixed-race relationships had a university degree, versus just one in five people in non-mixed unions." Moreover, mixed-race couples are "in the black" (so to speak). In a 2010 article published in the *Toronto Star*, Nicholas Keung reports that "mixed couples, with a median family income of $74,670 a year, made $5,000 more than non-mixed couples, who earned $69,830." In contrast, those who wed within their own Black or Brown cohort earned, according to Keung, "just $53,710, the lowest of all groups," but "the highest earners, making $76,150, were couples in which a visible minority was married to a Caucasian." The future is rosier, the grass greener, and the kids a rainbow, for those who—"dreaming in Technicolor"—pursue colour-blind love and equal-opportunity procreation.

However, we should keep in mind that Canada has had a long history of mixed-race couples and offspring, who even enjoy Constitutional recognition,[17] and yet there is also a record of racist oppression.[18] I designate the Métis—the result of unions mainly between French fur-traders and First Nations women—whose dispossession, like that of "pure-blood" First Nations people, was so intense that two Métis (plus Native) rebellions rocked the nascent Dominion of Canada in 1869 and 1885–1886. Mixed-race status—*métissage*, hybridity—is no bulwark against victimization by white supremacist racism. (One remembers that the officially designated "Coloured" population, comprising persons of multiracial admixture, in apartheid-era South Africa duly endured state-sanctioned humiliations, deprivations, disenfranchisement, etc.) Many Métis—and Natives—and Blacks (for that matter) may "pass" as Caucasian, or come pretty damned close, but that fact does not ameliorate the white supremacist racism that their phenotypically Aboriginal or African (or Asian or Arab) brethren and sistren endure.

En tout cas, Black Canucks have coupled with, are coupling with, and will continue coupling and copulating with First Nations people (as well as Inuit and other "Amerindians"), Status[19] Métis, Asians (South, West, and East), and Europeans—West, East, South, and North—including (arguably) Jews and Arabs, and they will generate offspring with all, as well as from couplings between genitals of solely African (Negro) descent. For the most part, however, the children—"beautiful and content in…exotic, beige-ish glory"—will still mature in a society where, says Hune-Brown, "class…remains stubbornly tied to skin colour."

Recall my earlier reference to Canadian society being innately hierarchical: even interracial couples, without their knowledge and likely against their will, are ranked so that "Asian-white couples" end up socially preferred and wealthier than all other pairings, according to US data.[20] Hune-Brown believes that "it is easy to imagine a future in which upwardly mobile Asians and whites mix more frequently, while other minorities are left out of a trendy mixed-race future." Yet Hune-Brown admits that borderline whites do sometimes realize that "there are real social advantages that come when you edge yourself a little closer to whiteness." So, regardless of how much interracial "shagging" happens and how many multiracial children result, those who appear more black than they do white or Asian may yet find themselves subjected to bigotry, but with little audience for their complaints. Hune-Brown also finds that, "of all the many privileges that come with [Canadian] whiteness, being able to ignore race entirely is one of the most precious." So, being "beige" (and beautiful) is not necessarily enough to forestall one's being treated as "Black" (and "bad") by smug, smiling, Negrophobic white folks. Perversely, too, being "off-colour" is no proof that one is anti-racist. Brian Connolly, in his 2011 essay "Intimate Atlantics," asserts that hybrid figures "also animated the eighteenth and nineteenth centuries in the service of both white racial consolidation and national imperial expansion."[21]

Clearly, then, in Canada, Negro identities are all over the map, and even if Black children identify—or want to identify—with Africa, their own parents, especially if of British or French (or American) cultural affiliation, may not feel the same way. A 1997 McGill University study of African-Canadian responses to the 1991 Canadian Census found that 43 percent of African-Canadians were more likely to describe themselves as British (especially if culturally Jamaican) or French (the Haitian tendency) than to jot themselves down as "Black." In other words, almost half of the Black population in Canada prefers to think of itself as *not*.

This fact has policy implications. See, for instance, the 2001 Supreme Court of Canada decision regarding whether an African-American father, namely Theodore "Blue" Edwards, and wife, Valerie Edwards, should have custody over his son, Elijah, as opposed to the boy's British Columbian—and (white) Dutch-Canadian—mother, Kimberly Van de Perre. The Supreme Court of Canada barged into this custodial fray because the Supreme Court of British Columbia had *unanimously* decided to award custody over

Elijah to Edwards, given that, as a North Carolina resident, he could provide his son with, as Naomi Pabst writes, a more "authentic black experience than he could [have] in Canada." In its own 9–0 unanimous decision, however, the Supreme Court of Canada overturned the lower court, finding, for one thing, that "racial identity is but one factor that may be considered in determining personal identity; the relevancy of this factor depends on the context." Arguably, by discounting Elijah's mixed-race—or "Black"—identity as less important than other matters in determining child custody, the court was able to think in racially inflected modes even while speaking anti-racist nostrums. Even more wickedly, the Supreme Court of Canada simply reversed—like a mirror—the racialist pondering of the British Columbia court. The lower court had found that, "in a part of the world [North Carolina] where the black population is proportionately greater than it is here [British Columbia]… Elijah…would have a greater chance of achieving a sense of cultural belonging and identity."

So custody went to the African-American father and his wife. Inadvertently, perhaps, the British Columbia court, by emphasizing the child's "blackness," saw no comfortable future for the boy in "white" British Columbia. In contrast, the Supreme Court of Canada, by discounting Elijah's African-American heritage and identity, thought that it was being anti-racist when, in reality, it had also denied the child's potential *African-Canadian* identity. Pabst posits that the lower-court decision effected "on one level a deportation of a black [Canadian] subject to the United States", albeit for ostensibly anti-racist—or even, mischievously,

"Afrocentric"—reasons. However, the Supreme Court of Canada nullification of the lower-court decision was also a denial of intervener arguments favouring "forced judicial consideration of race because it is essential in deciding which parent is best able to cope with difficulties biracial children may face." In short, the provincial court wanted to "African-Americanize" Elijah Van de Perre while the Supreme Court wanted to de-racialize him. Neither jurisdiction recognized his wholeness—African-American and Dutch-Canadian, or *African-Canadian*, and "biracial" and, in fact, multicultural (Anglo-Afro-Dutch-Americo-Canadian).

The existential vitality of this case is that it reveals the continuous dilemma of African Canadians: How do we achieve visibility for "blackness" in a culture that prefers to repress it in the name of anti-racism? Hune-Brown notices that "talking about race" makes Canadians "uncomfortable": "There's a distinctly Canadian feeling that if we all act halfway decent and just ignore it, the race thing will more or less sort itself out." According to Euro-Canadian literary scholar Daniel Coleman, "The ruptures of racial and other forms of internal violence that deny the nation's aspiration to become the peaceable kingdom, make up the constitutive losses [of status] which settler-citizens are constantly reminded to forget in order to aspire to and belong within White Canadian settler activity." White Canadians have little interest in remembering past episodes of racial inequality or exploring current practices of racism. However, this peremptory, utopian denial disarms the victims of racism, granting white supremacy, by default, its blithe, backslapping triumph.

Certes, I maintain now as I did in 1997, "*race, per se,* is not everything for African Canadians. No, it is the struggle against erasure that is everything." Pabst realizes, "Some of [the] vicissitudes [of blackness and whiteness in Canada include] an active repression of black cultural contributions to the Canadian social and discursive landscape, and active anti-black discrimination, historically and in the present." The supreme "evaporation" of "colour" from the situation of Elijah Van de Perre must be read in the context of a general Canadian tendency to claim to be so resolutely "colour-blind" that the "blackness" of Black people cannot—must not—be recognized, for to do so would constitute "racism" or, ironically, "special treatment" as in affirmative action or employment-equity programs. The general desire to "wish away" racism by whitewashing it or by "wishing away" Negroes has the effect of creating a "covert blackness," the Black person or body that the white Canadian prides themselves on "not seeing," because they don't see "race." For this reason, the very concept of the "visible minority" becomes a bit of a joke, for, in most cases, the *most* "visible" minorities—dark-complected persons of colour—are usu-lly invisible in the most high-status offices and roles.[22]

Thus far, I have merely hinted at what makes African-Canadian thought *original,* but now I will be try to be more explicit. Because Canadian society is constructed as an ethnic/racial hierarchy, with the WASP monarch at the summit and African and Indigenous people at the bottom, and because, as Hune-Brown writes, "immigration laws hand-pick the wealthiest, most educated, most outward-looking Asians," Black and visible minority groups orient themselves toward elitism too. There are several implications of this finding. First, Canadian white supremacism prefers to manifest itself as a professional and courteous—even liberal—*institutional* practice rather than as openly repugnant individual behaviour. Thus, the official response to uncivil, uncouth, "redneck" racism may be genuine revulsion and astonishment while the practice of invisible racial *discrimination* continues. I emphasize "discrimination" because the act does not represent wholesale barring of Blacks or others but rather the selection of a choice few—because elites respect elites—to co-optively improve the optics of the *de facto* ruling-class.[23] (Canadian white supremacism loves to foreground select persons of colour in its "see no racism, hear no racism, speak no racism" chorus line.)

Thus, Negro elites may be offered and may accept blandishments of one sort or another, and may even be encouraged to advocate "on behalf of" unwelcome Africans, but only behind closed doors. Fung reminds us, "In Canada the gatekeepers, whether they are knowledgeable and progressive or uninformed and reactionary, are almost all white." This monochromatic stewardship *of everything and everyone* is undemocratic but suitable to the unspoken aristocracy (the pseudo-meritocracy) of Canadian society. Thus, racism is left to the ignorant to perpetrate and to elites to alleviate while the people are propagandized to accept its viral manifestations as alien and "American" happenstance. Additionally, the anti-racism advocate, as soon as they loudly express their disquiet, will find that there is a hierarchy even of grievances and that Black folks' concerns regarding policing or schooling might be of less consequence than redress for historical injustices committed against other, once powerless—but now empowered—minorities. (The success of these *ethnic*-minority-redress campaigns is almost always related to the increasing international clout of the originating nations—Japan, China, etc.—in trade and finance. While Africa remains less developed—i.e., more impoverished—it will be difficult for the African Diaspora to win reparations for the transatlantic slave trade, even though this "Crime Against Humanity" is what permitted the global economic expansion of the West between 1492 and today.)

The positive aspect of mutual, interracial-ethnocultural campaigns for redress is that they allow for beneficial alliances and/or coalitions to be forged. The danger, however, is that the specificity of Negro struggle can be lost or diluted by the attempt to champion every *other* ethnic grievance in the state (or monarchy). To make matters even more complex, different black ethnicities or nationalities can have different experiences with white racism in different parts of the country. So, in Nova Scotia, for instance, the slavery-descended Africans can be less welcome than middle-class, educated Jamaican immigrants; in Ontario, the Jamaican-Canadians can be less preferred than the "quieter" Bajan-Canadians; or, in Quebec, African-Americans can be preferred to Haitian-Canadians; etc.

These super-subtle forms of Negrophobia must be related, once again, to the hierarchical structure of Canadian society as much as they can be related to the divide- and-conquer strategies of white supremacism. Nevertheless, the variegated experience of white racism, which can be so spectral that "newcomer" Africans may not even be aware of it, adds to the difficulty of organizing Black communities and neighbourhoods around projects of anti-racist protest, especially on a national basis. Too, the effort to organize Black Canadians, even within a city, let alone a region, is challenging, for the would-be advocate must speak across sub-national, immigrant, ethnic, religious, linguistic, cultural, and class distinctions. One might feel tempted to shout, "Blacks unite / to Wrongs right," except that it would need to rhyme differently in French. Too, a prosperous mixed-race Trinidadian-Canadian who identifies as being more "Chinese" or "Indian" than "Black," who is "failing" in his or her effort to, say, become the CEO of the Royal Bank of Canada, may yet feel little inclination to support the Haitian-Québécois farm worker who is forced to eat his lunch beside a stinking outdoor toilet, and vice versa. Then again, one cannot discount the comforts and inspirations that our various cultural formations provide. Nor should we forget that only 60 percent of African-Canadians agree that they are "Black"—first—at least on census forms.

According to the 2001 Canadian Census, Canadians are either overwhelmingly Christian (77 percent) or "nothing" (16 percent), and more than 80 percent are "white," presumably of European background. Afrocentrists—especially if of Islamic persuasion—will face challenges in trying to organize "Black" communities on the basis of "race" and/ or a separate religion, for there are relatively few Blacks and few truly Black *communities* with a distinct land base and separate (not "segregated") institutions. Instead, Black

Canada is largely a theoretical concept lived within the strictures, structures, and orbit of a European-constructed and European-dominated state. Moreover, African-Canadians are considered marginal economically and inconsequential politically. Thus, the articulation of black nationalist, pan-Africanist, or even Afrocentrist agendas will strike many ears as wrong-headed. In Canada, Elizabeth II is much more "legit" than Malcolm X; it's the Queen, not Martin Luther King Jr., who counts.

Because Canadians still speak mainly English or French, and because these are the two official languages, the Anglo-Saxon/Britannic and Gallic base cultures are the dominant ethnicities too, even within a multicultural framework (that Quebec—with its distinctive legal, religious, and educational system—resists, anyway). Now that Chinese and Italian are the next most widely spoken languages in Canada ("Canada 2001"), these ethnicities should enjoy greater cultural cachet and currency too. For the black artist or intellectual, what these facts mean is obvious: our art and thought will circulate mainly within an anglophone or francophone milieu; it will not be racially insular to either "environment": rather, English whites or French whites will be able to "overhear"—accidentally or deliberately—the content of whatever "black-focused" discourse is being undertaken in either official language. If the African-Canadian writer, scholar, or activist is translated, or is bilingual, the potential out-of-group migration of their work will be even greater, thus diffusing it and, potentially, diluting its intra-group importance and/or impact. On the other hand, it would be a good idea for African-Canadian intellectuals to build linkages among Canadian Chinese, Italian, and other cultures too, in order to ensure the utmost circulation of our ideas and concerns. In Canada, Black nationalism and Pan-Africanism must be liberal, open-minded, inclusive, and catholic to succeed. Thanks to our relatively high rates of interracial coupling, anyway, we have no choice but to be ecumenical in our thought. Our Marcus Garvey is half Mao and half Garibaldi.

Given that we do not occupy, wholly, for the most part, discrete sections of cities or provinces or regions, our politics must definitely be of the rainbow-coalition variety, appealing to the deep pockets of elites and to the ballot-sheet pencils of the masses. Similarly, our art is more likely to be multicultural in discourse than it is to be monochromatic.

Bearing in mind that the Canadian Constitution empowers only the federal and provincial governments, black activists must target provinces and provincial capitals and major cities, where blacks tend to congregate, for access to arts, Afrocentric education, employment equity programs, and electoral campaigns. We need to have a series of strong provincial institutions, located in major cities and provincial capitals, before we can even dream of a national infrastructure. Moreover, Black intellectuals must infiltrate *provincial* bureaucracies if we want to make "black consciousness" a national reality or presence.

Clearly, Negro activists, artists, and intellectuals exist, in Canada, in a white elitist and white supremacist context, wherein angry denunciations of racism—even with proof provided—create little report. For this reason, our discourse must be witty, punny, ironic, satiric, and "educated" (i.e., elitist). Not only that, but many of us originate from homelands—in the West Indies and in Africa—where we have been taught to accent diction, grammar, and knowledge, resulting in a contribution to literature that is at a Nobel-level.[24] Too, as much as we may be tutored in the classical texts of the Diaspora, we also tend to favour the elite texts of Europe: the African-Canadian literary text is chock full of European allusions and intertexts, along with African Diasporic "samplings."

Our predicament remains that, though we reside in a state with racist practices, we cannot easily utilize either black nationalist or Pan-Africanist nostrums to counter these pernicious elements. Instead, we need to advocate—as almost all of us do—*black* histories in Canada, build alliances with other minorities (especially the First Nations—who have a privileged relationship to the Crown—even if the Crown seldom respects it), insist on recognition of mixed-race persons of all heritages, reorient provincial education systems to include more materials on African-heritage peoples and our civilizations, and practise a radical ecumenicalism and ferocious cosmopolitanism. We need to be both provincial "agitators" and outside "cogitators."

In the end, the special circumstance of the African-Canadian activist, artist, and intellectual is to be, automatically, a citizen of the African Diaspora, with a Canadian passport and a polyphonous consciousness, and a multicultural, multiracial set of global affiliations. Our mirror is a kaleidoscope of (blood)stained glass.

[*The CLR James Journal*, vol. 20, no. 1/2, 2014]

~

Black Canadian activists, artists, and intellectuals—in contesting a racism that demands our erasure so as to ensure the placid operation of (compulsory but savvy) white supremacism—have no choice but to act as sleuths, historians, and archivists, to dredge up disappeared communities (such as Hogan's Alley of Vancouver and Jollytown of Nova Scotia) and to retrieve muted biographies (such as those of Richard Preston or Sylvia Stark). We must become adept bibliographers and esoteric scholars to be empowered to wield irrefutable intelligence versus bureaucracies of propaganda. How else to achieve a pedagogy of demystification and complementary political empowerment? Or so the chasing essay proposes.

~

Toward a Pedagogy of
African-Canadian Literature

1.

ALTHOUGH I CANNOT disprove its disreputable but formidable rival's claims to pre-eminence, teaching might just be the "world's oldest profession." Strangely, however, many of its PhD'd practitioners, who direct thousands of minds over the course of decades-long careers, are casually placed in charge of unsuspecting classrooms without even a single course in pedagogy to their names. It is a curious employment, this role of being a professor, where one must strive to educate, but without any of the training that a kindergarten teacher is expected to have.

I am a good example of this irony: I, too, lack expertise in the area of pedagogy. When I helmed my first class as an adjunct assistant professor, at Queen's University in the spring of 1994, purporting to offer guidance in Modern English Literature, I asked a senior professor to vet my syllabus to ensure that it reasonably represented the entirety of poetry, drama, fiction, and non-fiction in American, British, and Canadian literature between 1900 and 1994. Charitably, he did so, but I still ended up with a syllabus that surprised a few of my students with its unstinting emphasis on Queer identity, feminism, anti-racism, and anti-imperialism, despite, perhaps, our assiduous efforts to avoid controversy.

Something there is in literature, in the stories we tell, that insists on provocation. Thus, teaching literature can change everything by changing minds. Given the radical potential inherent in the task, tutelage in literature is an enterprise fraught with ideological pitfalls. Undoubtedly, Socrates backed this precept, and he paid with his life for his questioning of poetics and for his dissident views on governance, although he was not a writer and he sought no political office. Plato taught that the ideal Republic should banish poets, but in the actual polity in which Plato lived, it was the teacher, Socrates, who was expelled—martyred (as Plato recounts in the *Phaedo*). Even now, in bourgeois-democratic multicultural society and liberal-progressive culture, to assess, say, Marxism, or the efficacy of terrorism, or sex education, is to welcome threats, censorship, and, occasionally, expulsion—from school or from society itself, through jailing or exile.

The teaching of racial minority literatures should not, ideally, involve such risks. Applying supposedly universalist paradigms, we can say, "They are like us and we are like them," even if the us-and-them paradigm executes a benign violence. Better yet, we can say, "Like us, they bleed; and they want the same things we want: prosperous, healthy, pain-free lives, plus peace, love, and happiness." In practice, though, as literature keeps telling us, the principles of reception and interpretation—of understanding—are not that easy. South Asian–Canadian scholar Arun Mukherjee advises that

"'Western norms' and 'Western' values" constitute a "fake universalism which is really Euro-American ethno-centrism talking about itself in the vocabulary of 'the human condition' at the same time that it denies the humanity of others." As South Asian–Canadian scholar Chelva Kanaganayakam indicates, Mukherjee insists that "the dominant discourse in North America dehistoricizes and depoliticizes everything so that non-white, non-male, working-class ways of apprehending reality seldom get a hearing." Mukherjee provides the example of "such classics as Jane Austen's *Pride and Prejudice*, where large dinners are eaten in feudal homes with not a servant in sight—as though the dinner had cooked and served itself." Mukherjee also recognizes that, when a racialized minority complains about the depiction of its exemplars in a text, their concerns are dismissed:

> Let the black parents scream about racism in *The Adventures of Huckleberry Finn*. We will continue to teach it as a classic. And we will continue to exclude texts that the blacks themselves have written. And, yes, we will talk about the spectre of censorship when we hear such talk.

The repression of a discourse of race within our—Canadian—literature and criticism (our classrooms) reflects our anxiety about our own racism: the preservation of Euro-Caucasian privilege and power.

Indeed, the Canadian alarm about race and racism (a worry inspired not because the social category and the social practice exist but because they flourish here, in The Great

White North) poses problems for the teaching of any racial minority literature. This point applies to that literature I choose to term "African-Canadian."[25] Our national imaginary luxuriates in the tales of the Underground Railroad—fugitive African-American slaves seeking shelter in truly free, truly welcoming Upper Canada—and in the beautiful baritone of the Reverend Dr. Martin Luther King Jr. sermonizing across the air of our very own CBC.[26] We tune out, however, our own practice of slavery and racial violence (see "The Charivari" in Susanna Moodie's *Roughing It in the Bush* [1852]) and the resultant slave cemeteries in Upper Canada. But we also choose to forget our own Canadian anti-black segregation, polite but firm, conducted in locales across the Dominion, casually inhibiting careers and inconveniencing thousands of African Canadians—or coloureds, or Negroes, as we were then known.

The price of our ignorance is, we teach Harper Lee's *To Kill a Mockingbird* (1960)—a patriotic, rah-rah Yankee race-relations tract—instead of *Any Known Blood* (1997) by Lawrence Hill, which shows us the Ku Klux Klan at play in Oakville, Ontario, or instead of Joy Kogawa's *Obasan* (1981), which reminds us of the unbearable fact of our dispossession and imprisonment of Japanese-Canadians during the Anti-Fascist War. Yet to teach ourselves about African-Canadian literature is to gain entrée to the real history of this country, not the feel-good nostrums of the beer commercials and the televised heritage moments, which, as is hypnotizingly obvious, studiously avoid labour strife, racial contretemps (including anti-Semitism), and Indigenous versus Crown contestation.[27]

To peer at African-Canadian literature is to come face-to-face with an analysis of confederate imperialism, voiced by the marginal blacks of African America and the migrant blacks of the Caribbean and the exiled blacks of Africa. Hear the Afro-Ontarian writer Carol Talbot: "I am a voice crying in the wilderness, on the fringe of the diaspora." To encounter African-Canadian literature is to lose one's comfortable innocence regarding the experience of race in this country. New Zealand scholar Mark Williams tells us that "race relations were...crucial to colonial New Zealand's sense of superiority" vis-à-vis Australia." Who could deny that we use the discourse of race to trumpet our moral superiority over the USA? This unreal discourse renders us incapable of hearing the dissent of African Canadians from our adulation of our untainted "European" nobility. Most troublingly, given our fervent need to nation-build, to construct a society distinct from Britain, France, and the USA, we must whitewash our history. There is nothing new here. Williams reports, "Both Australia and New Zealand since the 1970s have sought independently to fashion 'postcolonial' identities for themselves, yet in both cases the sources of new identity lie in a shared and embarrassing colonial past." African-Canadian literature poses this challenge to Canada: Can you accept responsibility for your own past injustices— Stop talking about the USA!—and seek not to perpetuate them now or perpetrate them ever again?

Such urgent, even intemperate questions, Kanaganayakam tells us, "have been asked before and those who ask them often suggest answers hoping that the issues would be put to rest, only to realize later that their views get transformed to join the repertoire of questions." In his germane article "Pedagogy and Postcolonial Literature," Kanaganayakam warns that the ideas and approaches "we use to teach postcolonial literature ... often [mean] we become accomplices in subjecting postcolonial studies to a form of colonization."

To strengthen this charge, Kanaganayakam quotes Dipesh Chakrabarty's argument that "concepts such as citizenship, the state, civil society, public sphere, human rights, equality before the law, the individual, distinctions between public and private, the idea of the subject, democracy, popular sovereignty, social justice, scientific rationality, and so on all bear the burden of European thought and history." Wise is Kanaganayakam's caution regarding our ability to teach minority, marginal, or postcolonial literature outside of supposedly European concepts. Yet we must also account for the powerful ways in which empire-disseminated ideas (usually haughtily hypocritical) were mediated by African, Asian, and Aboriginal counterarguments. For instance, the American Constitution evolved first to permit African slavery and then to forbid it.[28]

Practically every idea identified by Chakrabarty as "European" in origin was modified and indigenized via struggles between settlers and natives, masters and slaves. In brief, the Enlightenment shone on everyone. Its illumination allowed "uncivilized" Africans and "savages" to see the deep cracks within and vast bloodstains upon the marble edifice of European civilization. Moreover, all the splendour of

Rome, the majesty of Paris, the glory of London, and the magnificence of Madrid were founded on the gold looted from the Americas via the sweat and blood of African and Amerindian slaves and, later, the coerced migratory labour of South Asians and Chinese. When Jean-Jacques Rousseau wrote, in *The Social Contract* (1762), "Man is born free, but everywhere he is in chains," an African, toiling in Montreal or Mississippi or Martinique, could have answered, "No, monsieur, you are free; I am in chains." Slavery and imperialism constitute the Original Sins of modernity. Thus, Paul Gilroy posits that the migrations of black intellectuals, during slavery and afterward, and their subsequent theorizations, produce "a Counterculture of Modernity."

Both Kanaganayakam and Chakrabarty must leave room, then, for the ways in which the marginalized speak back to their "downpressors" and challenge, thereby, modern discourses of liberal humanism to produce humane behaviour, not excuse inhumanity. African diasporic discourses strive, frequently, to answer Machiavelli with Martin Luther King Jr.—if not Malcolm X. For instance, in his *Foundations of an African Ethic*, Bénézet Bujo asserts:

Communitarianism in its critique of the "unfettered self" or of "atomism" against liberalism is entirely in keeping with African ethics, which rejects the idea that being a human person and acting responsibly is merely the result of having assented to rational principles, or arguing and thinking rationally.

"For Black Africa," Bujo goes on to state, "it is not the Cartesian cogito ergo sum (I think, therefore I am) but an existential cognatus sum, ergo sumus (I am known, therefore we are) that is decisive." In other words, the colonized and enslaved Others (of Europe's imperium) retained alternative belief systems—philosophies and faiths—that checked the Occident's violence-prone and money-hungry liberalism. Europe imposed modernity via cannon and gun, but the subjugated made haste to force reform upon it. The concepts that Chakrabarty deems European were actually tested, disputed, refined, and even improved in the very realms that Europeans thought uncouth.

In teaching African-Canadian literature, then, for instance, one may note the rhetoric of liberty employed by the master class but applaud the ways in which African-Canadian enslaved and free people worked to undermine the political economy of slavery via a counter-discourse foregrounding the hypocrisy and cruelty of the masters. See African-American-cum-African–Nova Scotian writer David George, active during the late 1700s, who, in his memoir, recognizes the irony of having had a vicious master whose "name was Chapel—a very bad man to the Negroes." In the first sentence of Robin W. Winks's *The Blacks in Canada*, we encounter again the voice of the archetypal black who wittily talks back to white authority. In this case, a black youth answers an apostle (or an apologist) of white Christianity:

> "You say that by baptism I shall be like you: I am black and you are white, I must have my skin taken off then in order to be like you." Thus in 1632 did "un petit

nègre" rebuke the Jesuit missionary Paul le Jeune for claiming that all men were one when united in Christianity.

The Neanderthal practices of European modernism elicited, from its coloured victims, responsive discourses that had the effect of truly modernizing modernity. Indeed, the violence of European conquest, in this case visited upon African linguistics, met with an opposing indigeneity. The libertine aggression of slavery and colonialism was countered by the verbal inventiveness of its subjects, who, despite their disempowered status, altered the imposed European tongues, driving them toward a condition of music, i.e., black music.

Kanaganayakam notices that, because "postcolonial studies is a fallout from Empire and that English departments tend to be custodians of postcolonial literature, there are commonalities across the globe and these departments function in similar ways to inscribe certain forms of knowledge." Given the duplication of models of enquiry from English department to English department, as well as the replication of syllabi and theoretical approaches, Kanaganayakam wonders whether practitioners of postcolonial studies "may be guilty of recolonizing the field." His concern is a galvanizing one. But there may be no proper response other than to demand repeatedly that those who teach the literatures of the once-dispossessed and the twice-exiled anchor their pedagogy in historical and socio-political analysis. As Ato Quayson states, our duty is "to interrogate a social domain into view." Mukherjee admonishes teachers: "What is needed is explication, not erasure and assimilation." The texts of subalterns must be foregrounded, set in their own original contexts of political disputation and social discord, not whitewashed—reduced to blandishments—by a wishy-washy universalism. Describing so-called Commonwealth novelists, Mukherjee reminds us they have had to build "structures which...allow them to capture the spiderweb of relationships which constitute community life in the developing countries." These writers—and African-Canadian ones are no exception—tend to imbue their texts with the realism of lived experience (no matter how much "magic" they may also invoke).

Instruction in postcolonial texts, or of minority literatures, should be as uncomfortable and as discomfiting as the realities that forced them into being. Why should the study of a slave narrative make anyone feel good? When Marie-Josèphe Angélique, an enslaved woman in colonial Montreal, relates her life story, telling of how she was forcibly bred for the sake of profits for her master, and when we read of her torture and execution for arson in 1734, we ought to feel disturbed.[29] But we should read her story alongside the satirical sketches of the pro-slavery British North American (Nova Scotian) intellectual Thomas Chandler Haliburton, who bids his main mouthpiece and most famous character, Sam Slick, to utter this notorious statement: "Niggers...those thick skulled, crooked shanked, flat footed, long heeled, wooly headed gentlemen, don't seem fit for much else but slavery."

Such sentiments help us understand why African peoples had to struggle so long and with such difficulty to achieve the abolition of slavery, and to appreciate that Negrophobia and anti-black racism date from the origins of European modernity.[30] Similarly, when David George relates his experience of Virginian slavery—"the greatest grief I then had was to see them whip my mother, and to hear her, on her knees, begging for mercy"—we must connect it, almost genetically, to the Montréalaise Lorena Gale and her play *Angélique* (1999), where one reads, "Then is now. Now is then." Gale bids us to consider slavery as an earlier mode of black immigrant (woman) labour exploitation: "Unless otherwise stated, the slaves are working in every scene in which they appear, either in a modern or historical context." In one scene in the play, Angélique's master, François, "reaches around and removes Angélique's uniform, revealing period undergarments beneath her modern clothing." Such anachronistic imaginings compel us to address slavery not as a long-passed spasm of history but as a living component of contemporary labour (and race) relations. Teachers of such texts must move just as fluidly in history, navigating canal systems of "periods," toing-and-froing, as necessary, to allow for an adequate *explication de texte*.

Critics may bridle at this impolitic emphasis on the politics of a text. Aesthetics are the basis of the humanities, I agree; but so are civics. Hence, the poetics of a text should be excavated along with its politics. Kanishka Goonewardena pushes for a holistic criticism, asserting, trenchantly, for instance, that "those who do not want to talk about global capitalism should be silent about postcolonialism and diaspora."[31] Our central duty, as teachers, is to get the history right, which means utilizing several sources and approaches, from the anthropological and folkloric to analyses of the practices of political economy. Perry Anderson cautions us, sagely, that the major problem in contemporary historiography is "representation omitted rather than misrepresentation committed."

Thus, we must seek out histories that set forth narratives encompassing race, culture, gender, and class analyses. This must be one of the criteria, as Indian scholar Sumit Sarkar witnesses, "for distinguishing between less and more valid versions of the past." While Kanaganayakam holds, properly, that "writers would like their texts to be read and taught as texts rather than as position papers," their plays, poetry, novels, short stories, essays, histories, letters, songs, libretti, journalism, and scientific analyses are wholly embedded within the discourses of their moment while they also impinge on the discourses of our own.

Perhaps it is the failure to explore the resonant real-world contexts of texts that reduces their teaching to a rendering of rote interpretations that rout their upheavals. Arun Mukherjee advises, "Simply teaching Third World literary texts does not change consciousness."

2.

The entrée of African-Canadian literature into the Canadian academy will provoke and stimulate discussions of the usually unspoken. For instance, if we teach "I Fight Back," a poem by the Jamaican-Canadian Lillian Allen, we will accent the North American capitalist adventurism named in this stanza:

ITT ALCAN KAISER
Canadian Imperial Bank of Commerce
These are priviledged [*sic*] names in my County *sic*]
But I AM ILLEGAL HERE.

In classic African-Diasporic fashion, Allen emphasizes the irony of the welcomed presence of American and Canadian transnational corporations in Jamaica while her own body, black and female and Caribbean-raised (after the displacement effected by slavery), is not welcome in Canada. Beyond this reading, though, lurks yet another, a deeper analysis, one that should outline Canada's unspoken, unheralded imperialism in the Caribbean. Indeed, in the 1870s, the Anglo-Canadian nationalist and British imperialist Canada First movement called for "closer trade relations with the West Indies, with a view to ultimate political connexion" (qtd. in McNaught 157). Canada was a self-governing state in the empire, one whose anglophone leaders viewed it as a conduit of British power in North America, but some were tempted to move beyond the colonizing of the "North-West Territories" and to venture into the Caribbean. Although Canada could not establish a political dominion within the Caribbean, several of its transnational corporations—Alcan, the Bank of Nova Scotia (Scotiabank), and the Royal Bank of Canada, to name a few—did "invade" the region.

While Allen's work allows us to contemplate aggressive Canadian commercial and political policies in the Caribbean, we may inspect the writings of white Anglo-Canadian author William Stairs, a Halifax native active during the nineteenth century, for a better understanding of Canadian imperialism in Africa. Indeed, Stairs's adventures in Africa in the late-Victorian era included, according to one of his dust jackets, "condoning decapitation and mutilation."[32] If we dare to recall Canada's imperialist ventures on behalf of or in support of Great Britain (when it was, by hook and by crook, "great"), we might better appreciate why the 1993 Somalia peacekeeping and food-distribution mission ended in elite Canadian soldiers torturing two Somali youths and lynching one.

To consider black immigration to Canada, one may examine a rich assortment of texts from African-Canadian literature, including a novel by Trinidadian-Canadian Dionne Brand, *In Another Place, Not Here* (1996). Many significant passages in the novel foreground the interlocking complex of race and identity—or identification—in urban Canada. African-Canadian literature, in general, demands this unflinching confrontation with the facts of white supremacy and black resistance in Canada.

Because civic experience is multi-faceted and superficially ahistorical, the history and currency of African-Canadian cultures may serve to reveal the operations of oppressive state practices, both domestically and internationally, and foster probing of these institutions of domination. Most importantly, the examination of this literature allows readers to encounter fine and fiery texts that stimulate judgment and judgment calls. As Sartre declared—introducing the 1948 publication of *Orphée noir*:

Negritude is, in its essence, poetry. Upon this one occasion at least, the most authentic revolutionary program and the purest poetry derive from the same source.[33]

—the black revolt, against imperialism, against racism, against second-class treatment. I sound Sartre again:

> To each epoch its poetry; for each epoch the circumstances of history elect a nation, a race, a class to seize again the [revolutionary] torch, in creating situations which can express or surpass themselves only through Poetry.[34]

Perhaps that moment, that opportunity, filters through African-Canadian writers today.

My conclusion is a practical one: to invent a provisional syllabus for African-Canadian literature. To design such an instruction vehicle, I must divide the literature into a series of themes or periods or both. However, in the case of African-Canadian literature, which possesses both a long history (only since 1785) and a relatively small group of contemporary literary texts (the majority dating back to 1964), periodization enacts, in itself, a thematization.[35]

My proposed categories are not so much a product of historical dates as of chief concerns that reflect the different periods in which different groups of African Canadians arrived and settled. My tentative schema employs these silos:

1) *Slavery* (in Canada and experienced by proto-"Canadians" elsewhere);

2) Settlement (i.e., narratives situated in the historic Black Canuck communities);

3) Immigration (mainly since 1955);

4) Homelands (commentaries on originating col-

5) onies/nations) and *Diaspora* (meditations on the African Diaspora via slavery, imperialism, and economic migration);

6) Urban (city-based, pop-culture-influenced, contemporary writing);

7) and two generic categories, *Criticism* (academic writing or *belles-lettres*)

8) and *Juvenile.*

Naturally, this syllabus is only tentative, suggestive, selective, and brief. Readers possess total liberty to replace any of my catalogued texts with others of their own choosing.[36]

[*Shared Waters: Soundings in Postcolonial Literatures,* edited by Stella Borg Barthet. Brill, 2009]

∾

For African-Canadians, *pedagogy* is a synonym for—no, a palimpsest of—*anthropology, archaeology, economics, geography, history, law, philosophy, politics, psychology, sociology,* and *theology.* To teach our literature is to reorient eyes from dimly lit caverns and taverns, to liberate us from Gothic penitentiaries and shadowy premises, so that we may bask in enlightened solarity, not rot in obscurantist insularity. Because every writer is an intellectual, so are African-Canadian playwrights and historians, teachers and sociologists, scholars and judges. To read among the decalogue of plays discussed in the next essay—an anthology of works all produced in this century (though most were born in the last)—is to encounter scribes who envision Canada as a land of black souls on black ice, an environment in which babes are born dead or die young, and fertility comes to sterility.

~

Ten African-Canadian Plays to Watch (Catch)
Thus Far This Century

THIS SURVEY ARTICLE cannot be—and will not be—comprehensive. Worse, it will be impressionistic, in that I will merely list those plays, of which I am aware, that have been produced in this century, generally more than once, while also giving a cursory summary of the import and/or meaning of each piece.

I debut by proposing that, in terms of literary criticism, drama provides the best window on a culture. To critique a play is to undertake a cultural vivisection; one finds exposed the brains and guts, the nervous system and the bowels, the heart and lungs, of the community (communion) under examination (or interrogation). To come to comprehend the polyphony of accents, perspectives, and viewpoints that is African Canada, all one needs to do is look at a few of the plays. My survey will be chronological, by publication. Productions will be noted where germane. My "Decalogue" follows.

The Captive (1965)
This play, the first published by an African-Canadian playwright in English, should not be part of my survey given

that it is very much a twentieth-century, Civil Rights–era creation. Written by Trinidad native Lennox John Brown, who died in 2004, the play is included here because it was "re-produced," likely for the first time since 1965 (at the Ottawa Little Theatre, the play's publisher), at Memorial University of Newfoundland, in St. John's, in March 2018. *The Captive* is important not only because of its premiere position in African-Canadian drama in English but because of its plot and characters. Although the play is set in the mid-1960s, in Toronto, its black-male-dominated cast reflects the multicultural nature of African Canada, a multiculturalism that is disrupted by class orientations and by different attitudes toward "integration" versus Afrocentrism and/or Pan-Africanism and/or Black nationalism. Brown's West Indian and African gents are students en route to becoming bourgeois professionals; the African-American is a fiery activist; the African-Canadian is an affable railway porter—i.e., a laughable proletarian drunk. Though the four black men collude to kidnap and terrorize a white man, supposedly a member of the Ku Klux Klan, their paper-thin unity is torn apart because the African and the West Indian are both lusting after the same white woman.

Tightrope Time: Ain't Nuthin' More than Some Itty Bitty Madness between Twilight & Dawn (1986)

Walter Borden's one-man show is the signature publication of the African–Nova Scotian (Africadian) ex-teacher and ex-journalist, poet, playwright (really poet-playwright), and actor (his principal livelihood). The play, which is on the verge, as I write, of a fourth, revised edition, mirrors the Holy Bible or—maybe better—Walt Whitman's *Leaves of Grass*.[37] I make this suggestion because different editions feature different materials, and, to use the abbreviated title, *Tightrope Time* has the same evolving structure, morphing in answer to the shifts in Borden's political consciousness, social conscience, and ethical conundrums.

It began life as a magazine feature, typed up on a then avant-garde (now vintage) IBM Selectric typewriter—in Souvenir font—utilizing the so-ultra-modern interchangeable ball head. It appeared in a humble publication called *Callboard*, the house organ of the Nova Scotia Drama League (later Federation), in 1986, on pulp-novel-bad-quality paper (newsprint, more-or-less, and *not* acid-free). The production of this script, Borden's one-man-show text, was an act of cultural guerrilla warfare launched by Astrid Brunner, *Callboard*'s editor, and her ally, Norval Balch, who snapped the dozen or so photos of Borden (in character makeup and garb) for the original chameleonic and shamanic parts. Then a PhD candidate in English and later a publisher of fine books, Brunner, also an artist's model, poet, and theatre devotee, knew what she was getting (into) in publishing that original version of *Tightrope Time*. She was announcing that Black Nova Scotia (i.e., Africadia)—via a complex heritage of slavery, resistance, segregation, resistance, and possession of Black Atlantic roots in Africa and African America—had produced, in Borden, a consummate articulator of all that jazz, gospel, and down-home rhythm-'n'-blues. *Tightrope Time* is, in part, a semi-autobiography of a seminal saltwater, up-from-the-*Roots* intellectual, Beat-Greenwich-Village-via-

North-End-Halifax-Africville-Soul-Bro mash-up of Amiri Baraka and Allen Ginsberg. The play next appeared in Djanet Sears's seminal anthology, *Testifyin': Contemporary African Canadian Drama, Volume 1* (2001), and then was published by Playwrights Canada Press in 2005.

So far, only Borden himself has played the starring role(s), for this one-man show is an exploration of the psyche of an Afro-Métis, African Baptist, Africadian artist-intellectual, familiar with Harlem and Amsterdam (where the play represented Canada at the World Multicultural Drama Festival of 1987), who is also Gay and Pan-Africanist. His psyche is a kaleidoscope of types: an "Old Man," an "Old Woman," the "Minister of Justice" (who comments on injustice), the "Minister of Health and Welfare" (who diagnoses alienation), the "Minister of the Interior" (a black cultural nationalist), the "Minister of Defence" (an activist), a "Pastor," and three transgressive sexual types—a hooker, a drag queen, and a hustler, all of whom skewer bourgeois pretensions and hypocrisies. The director of this phantasmagoria of characters is "The Host," who is the mature version of a once-traumatized "Child." As of 2018, the play is slated to be published again, again with revisions, beginning with the title. Now entitled *The Epistle of Tightrope Time*, the work is now the product of a youngish-in-style but venerable elder (Borden turned 76 in 2018). Where once he leaned heavily upon African Americans—Lorraine Hansberry and James Weldon Johnson for direct quotations and material inspiration—Borden is now much more reliant on his own thought and perceptions. It may be time to consider *Tightrope Time* a classic.

dark diaspora...in dub (1991)

Jamaican-born ahdri zhina mandiela published her *dark diaspora...in dub* in 1991, in the same year that the play was first produced by b current, a black woman–centred performance troupe based in Toronto. The play is actually a series of linked lyric poems, to be spoken, sung, and danced by six women, described as "chanters." If this dramaturgy sounds familiar, it should, for it riffs off of Ntozake Shange's "choreopoem," *for colored girls who have considered suicide / when the rainbow is enuf* (1976). *dark diaspora* is itself best thought of as a "choreopoem," with its lyric contents sketching black women's herstory from Africa through the Middle Passage to the Caribbean and then to Canada. The dub aspect is best read as the utilization of outspoken and unapologetic political poetry backed with music. It is a form of recitation associated with Jamaica and Black British performers post-1948. (Think of Linton Kwesi Johnson.) However, here, in her piece, Shange is nudged from Motown and its Afro-Christian context and into a Bob Marley and Rastafarian vibe. Mandiela's piece was revived and revised by b current in October 2016; it was restaged under the title "diaspora Dub."

Harlem Duet (1997)

Djanet Sears's second play (after 1990's *Afrika Solo*) is a landmark in African-Canadian theatre history. For one thing, it made Sears the first African-Canadian playwright to win Canada's highest award for published drama, namely the Governor-General's Award for Drama in English, in 1998. It was also the first African-Canadian play to be produced at the Stratford Festival, English Canada's premiere theatre, in 2006. It has also been oft-produced, and not only in Canada but in New York City, the precise home of Harlem. As the title suggests, its principals are two: a black man, Othello, and a black woman, Billie. The characters' race is of mortal importance, for, in this imaginative prequel to Shakespeare's *Othello*, Sears explains Othello's supposedly otherwise inexplicable acceptance of Iago's lethal lies about Desdemona as being the result of a deadly curse (and/or poison) imped upon the Moor by his first—spurned and scorned—wife, Billie. The reason for Billie's slo-mo execution of Othello? Well, not only has Othello left Billie for a white woman (Mona), he's also spent all of Billie's inheritance (left by her deceased mama) to help himself unto a doctorate and into the professoriate (with a plum post in Cyprus) while denying her any financial assistance for her university tuition and, worse, denying her the possibility of childbearing: he's abandoned her just as she is on the cusp of menopause and after she's had an abortion to please him and then suffered a miscarriage due to his shrugging her off.

So the play stages a dialogue—debate—duet between "integration," which Othello favours, and "Afrocentrism" or Black nationalism, which is Billie's preference. The stakes are winner-take-all, for Othello's "Oreo" (black-complected but white-acting) behaviour condemns Billie to impending homelessness, pennilessness, and childlessness. In contrast, her crypto-fascist belief in something that looks and sounds a lot like (black) eugenics drives her crazily homicidal enough to contemplate pushing an interracial couple (black man, blonde woman) in front of a Gotham City subway train.

Yet Sears does not allow the audience to make any easy choice between the theses of Othello and Billie. If Othello is "free" to marry a white woman, what happens to the possibility that he could wed—and lift up into the middle class—a black woman *and* father visibly black children (and, alongside their mother, build up transferable wealth and IQ attainment for their offspring)? However, if one adopts Billie's perspective, in the name of race unity and Pan-Africanism/Black nationalism, one must eschew the blandishments of the *Playboy* "philosophy," which promotes colour-blind canoodling and enjoyment of bourgeois luxury as most commendable. Billie's world-view is Frantz Fanon applied to procreation, as if there were a chapter in his *Black Skin, White Masks* entitled, "The Man of Colour and the Woman of Colour," and not, as in fact there is, "The Man of Colour and the White Woman." One can also read Eldridge Cleaver's analysis of black-and-white, sex-and-class divides in America (as expounded in "The Allegory of the Black Eunuchs") profitably alongside Sears's play.

Also instrumental in this play is the utilization of multi-media to marry different eras of black activism; recorded, conflicting sound-bites (Malcolm X and Martin Luther King Jr., etc.); and music (including the presence of a live jazz combo); all to emphasize that the debate between "integration" and "nationalism" remains a perennial dilemma. The play fluctuates between eras—Civil War US, the Harlem Renaissance, and then-contemporary 1990s Harlem. Should a black person seek liberal, individualist fulfilment? Or does one have (should one have) a communal (and thus conservative/conservationist) commitment to "the race"?

Riot (1997)

Born in Canada's centennial year, 1967, and raised in the nation's capital, Andrew Moodie came of age in the English-French-bilingual, multicultural, and liberal (live-and-let-live) vibe of Pierre Elliott Trudeau's Canada. By 1995, Moodie had imbibed enough of that *Geist* to strike the nation's conscience with *Riot*, a play whose first line, "Fuck Quebec!," was like a guerrilla bomb tossed into a Victorian mansion, given that it was uttered at the very moment when 49.1 percent of Québécois were about to vote to leave Canada and set up their own country. Well, the "separatists" lost that vote (narrowly), but Moodie's *Riot* seized the moment and won the day by presenting an urban Canada—Toronto—more fractured by race and class in 1992 than by language, thus the debate about Quebec becomes part of the allegorical machinery related to injustice. If francophones are oppressed by anglophones, blacks are oppressed by whites throughout the country, including in supposedly progressive Quebec. (So explosively relevant was the play in 1995 that CBC TV dedicated a portion of its nightly newscast to broadcasting the opening scene and offering an analysis of its import.) In addition, in moves reminiscent of Lennox Brown's *The Captive*, Moodie's six-person cast explores the homophobia, sexism, and classism of many members of the sextet, though all are tenants in the same rooming house. They may all be black; they may all experience racism; but they are all black in exceedingly complex and contradictory ways and are not necessarily accepting of one another. The play ends with a queer thug grabbing his phallic gun and skedaddling to the US (reversing the Underground Railroad) while another character, more bourgeois romantic in inclination, throws himself on his back, in the grass, looks up at the stars, and waxes very schmaltzily and movingly about the sexy cool chic of, yes, P.E.T.

Although I could not find any production history for this play in this century, I will assert that *Riot* is too important to omit from this survey, even if its sole production was by Toronto's Factory Theatre in 1995, and even though Moodie has written other plays that have been produced since. Indeed, I would set *Riot* beside Sears's *Adventures* as a play that is also trying to establish links between blackness, Canada (history, geography, politics, and sociology, including criminology), and African American struggle. *Riot*'s title refers both to the 1992 Los Angeles race riot protesting the acquittal of white police for the beating of black motorist Rodney King and the sympathy riot in Toronto, versus police "brutality," that was very Canadian in that it featured a multiracial cast of looters, all chanting "Remember Rodney King" as they smashed windows and made off with VCRs and Sony Walkman–type devices. Moreover, one must note that African-Canadian plays are often welcomed with acclaim and then permitted to vanish into obscurity, given that Canada has no deathless commitment to black art and/or achievement. The exceptional African Canadian artists are those who become superstars in the United States. These "happy few" are never permitted to become ephemera. So, for this reason too, I ask you to look up Moodie's *Riot*.

Angélique (1999)

Lorena Gale's *fin de siècle* play, produced as recently as 2003 at Hart House Theatre, takes up the true, historical account of colonial Canada's best-known enslaved woman, namely Marie-Josèphe Angélique, who died gruesomely in 1734. A native of Madeira, Angélique was accused of an arson that destroyed a goodly swath of central Montreal, Nouvelle-France. She was tortured into a "confession," then hanged, her body burnt at the stake and her ashes thrown into the Saint Lawrence River. Herself a bilingual Montreal native, Gale excavates the biography of the enslaved woman and the history of slavery in colonial Canada to lay bare the patriarchal sexism that forced Angélique to bear children—capital/property—for her white master as well as for black "studs." Gale exposes the labour exploitation of Indigenous and African people as well as that of white peasants and of white women by white male aristocrats. She juxtaposes dexterously elements of eighteenth-century and twentieth-century society to make the point that the racism, sexism, and classism of *then* is still apparent *now*, though contemporary workers may be immigrants and liberalism and multiculturalism now work together to obscure the pernicious persistence of ugly oppressions. The play ends with a prophecy that, as black people multiply in Montreal, only then will there be an opportunity for them to realize real equality and true justice.

Consecrated Ground (1999)

Born in 1950 in Halifax, George Elroy Boyd was a teenager when the 150-year-old village of Africville was torn apart, piece by piece, between 1964 and 1970. Just as Marie-Josèphe Angélique is the best-known colonial Canadian enslaved person because of her alleged epic crime and her definite Gothic end, so is Africville the best-known Black Canadian settlement. Its church was desecrated by bulldozers and the community disrespected by being taxed for, but not receiving, essential services such as water and fire protection. Indeed, waste pick-up wasn't necessary in Africville because the City of Halifax located its garbage dump right on the doorsteps of residents' homes, so that the villagers had to set out rat poison instead of refuse bins.

No wonder, then, that Boyd opens his teleplay (the first version of *Consecrated Ground*) with a close-up shot of a rat and a background shot of a bulldozer: the City of Halifax had weaponized urban planning and unleashed biological warfare against Africville by setting the dump—an emporium for vermin—right beside the black community. Also in the teleplay, as in the later play, Boyd treats us to a landscape of sterility—winter ice, snow, the dump. His true hero is a heroine, the main protagonist, Clarice, or Leasey, who, as the play begins, has a baby boy asleep in a crib. But, under these Eliotic, *Waste Land* conditions, the babe is subject to frostbite and rat bite and is soon killed by the latter—and so, slain indirectly by Halifax's urban planning. Having ancestral and natal ties to Africville, Leasey is insistent that her dead son be buried in the hamlet, but her husband, Willem, who has married into the community, accepts the Haligonian propaganda that casts Africville as "a slum by the dump." He credits the media perspective that damns Africville as a symbol of segregation that must be destroyed to spur on racial integration and support a new commuter infrastructure that would see a second bridge span Halifax's harbour at what was then called "Negro Point." So, while his wife campaigns to see her infant son's body interred in the frozen ground of wintertime Africville, Willem, as household head, signs away their home and land (that is to say, Leasey's family home and ancestral land) to the City of Halifax. His decision suits liberal individualist expediency, but at the cost of sacrificing his wife's conservative agrarian and maritime communal values, including that of local burial in the people's cemetery.

Due to Willem's betrayal, Leasey, already childless, will soon be homeless, landless, and husbandless, for she tells Willem to leave when she finds out about his literal sellout of her home and her values. Though she succeeds in burying her son, Tully, in the frigid earth of the churchyard, her victory is desperately, consummately pyrrhic: the bulldozers will take her home and house just as the rats have taken her son. No longer fertile, she cannot hope for another child. Although Boyd does not clarify whether there's any chance for a rapprochement between Leasey and Willem, the tragic arc of the play achieves greater force if there is no new generation available to carry on. Published in 1999, *Consecrated Ground* earned Boyd, who died in 2020, a Governor General's Award nomination for best drama in English in 2000. Its first production was undertaken by Eastern Front Theatre in 1999, and then it was revived in this century by Obsidian Theatre in 2004. The play's concentration on a landed or grounded identity that conflicts with the floating signifier of the capitalist consumer has a thematic counterpart in

Sears's *Adventures*, just as Leasey versus Willem is a replay, ideologically, of the contest between Billie and Othello in *Harlem Duet*.

The Adventures of a Black Girl in Search of God (2002)

Djanet Sears's third play is another landmark in African-Canadian theatre, becoming the first Black Canadian play to break out of the ethnic ghetto, so to speak, and break records for attendance and ticket sales. First produced by Nightwood and Obsidian Theatres, in 2001/02, it was then picked up by the A-list-oriented Mirvish Productions and staged at Toronto's Harbourfront Centre in 2003/04. In between the premiere and the second production, the play was published. Adapting her play's title from George Bernard Shaw's 1932 collection of short stories, *The Adventures of the Black Girl in Her Search for God (and Some Lesser Tales)*, Sears seeks not to spoof Christianity (as does Shaw in his titular story) but to allegorize the African-Canadian search for roots and belonging—an oneness with Canadian geography and history.

Being a Black British-born dramatist, Sears nods to the British dissident, radical, socialist-inclined playwright Shaw, but she also riffs off of African-American antecedents such as Sam Greenlee's 1969 novel, *The Spook Who Sat by the Door*, which also features subversive blacks who become "invisible" in white society by pretending to be menial or casual labourers (cooks, cleaners, maids). Sears also seems to echo Julie Dash's 1991 film, *Daughters of the Dust*, with its mysticism-infused evocation of the Gullah culture of the South Carolina sea isles as an untainted-by-modernism (industrialism and capitalism) natural Eden. (So, Sears's play concludes with a mother eating dirt and then making love to her husband beside a creek.) The vibrant use of colour and of actors to represent elements could be a comfortable interface with Ntozake Shange's influential 1976 feminist play, *for colored girls who have considered suicide / when the rainbow is enuf: a choreopoem*. There are references, too, to Spike Lee's 2000 film, *Bamboozled*, which catalogues, in its conclusion, a massive garage sale, so to speak, of exaggerated "blackface" or minstrel-related knickknacks, dolls, figurines, toys, souvenirs, and "novelty" items. In Sears's play, all such gags and gewgaws are liberated by a nocturnal army on the prowl for Sambo lawn ornaments and the like, to reclaim these disparaging *objets* and replace their oversized, Bozo-the-Clown grins with dignified, civil smiles.[38]

Certainly, the central argument of the play is that Black Canadians—born-and-bred or come-from-away—erase the negative depictions of blackness in Canada (even if masked as genteel comedy), contest the erasure of black presence in history books and maps, and *implant* the *place* of blackness in Canada, as lived and as historical experience, so that it cannot be uprooted. This political-philosophical struggle has a class aspect, a gendered dimension, and a generational divide. Indeed, one way to digest *Adventures* is to consider it a disguised blackening-*cum*-eroticization of that Canuck uber-cultural-mainstay Lucy Maud Montgomery's *Anne of Green Gables*—to name the trifecta of book (1908), stage musical (1965), and movie-and-TV-series (1985). (There's also a theme park near Charlottetown, PEI, plus a museum.) Just as the redheaded, freckled Anne is the Pippi Longstocking of country-and-western-Romantic, Anglo-Canuck culture, so is Sears's "black girl" the symbol of harmonization and unification with the fertile earth of rural, black-settled Ontario. But what makes Sears's signification incendiary is that she is claiming Canada as a black-people's space, thus flouting two centuries of propaganda not only extolling it as "white" but even attempting to negate (while definitely repressing) Indigenous peoples.

'da Kink in my hair: Voices of Black Womyn (2005)

First produced in 2001, Trey Anthony's debut play, showcasing again the intra-group multiculturalism of African Canada, this time set in a black woman–oriented beauty salon in Toronto, was such a major success that it was—like Sears's *Adventures*—picked up by Mirvish Productions in Toronto in 2005 and turned into a box-office smash. That success led, in turn, to a one-hour Vision Television pilot and then a weekly TV series that ran for twenty-six episodes over two seasons on the Toronto-based Global Television Network in 2007 and 2008. Not only that, but the play was produced abroad, in both San Diego and London.

In the piece, Anthony utilizes the patented, polyphonic, black multicultural cast (some born or raised in Canada, others having West Indian backgrounds) that one sees in Brown, Sears, Moodie, and, arguably, Borden (given his multi-character-playing solo actor). Like Sears and Borden, Anthony also revels in an African-American interest, and it is to be found here as it is for Sears (in *Adventures*) and mandiela—in Shange's *for colored girls*. Shange's play ends: "I found god in myself / & I loved her / I loved her fiercely," and the seven-lady-spectrum, a septet, repeats the couplet, singing until they form a "tight circle." Well, if Shange's play concludes with a gesture favouring multiracial liberal feminism, Anthony's ends with a "celebration of Blackness"— of black womynism—with the female cast performing "an African dance" while chanting, "I've been wearing black all my life." One can imagine Sears's Billie shouting the same line at her ex-hubby, Othello, and so Anthony's play exudes the identical black-womyn-uplift rhetoric of *Harlem Duet*'s Billie. We also read, at the end of Anthony's play, that the "womyn" inhale and then exhale as they heal one another (of self-hatred for their black skin and "kinky" hair).

There's an obvious connection here to the first mainstream Hollywood film to attract black women filmgoers explicitly, namely Forest Whitaker's 1995 *Waiting to Exhale*, which was adapted from Terry McMillan's eponymous novel. The major difference here is that Toronto is not Harlem or South Central LA: it is not a black "ghetto" composed mainly of African Americans with a smattering of Latinos. Instead, it is multicultural and multiracial, so that the women entering into the beauty salon derive from the farthest swathes of the African Diaspora. Which is not to say that they avoid issues of sexism, sexual assault (including incest), white racism, intra-group "colourism" or "shadism" (discrimination of light-complected blacks against those of darker tint), as well as class cleavages that may be aggravated —literally—by the accent(s) that one adopts. It is to say that the conflicts can never be played as only a matter of "race" or "colour."

Shakespeare's Nigga (2013)

Joseph Jomo Pierre mirrors Djanet Sears's achievement in *Harlem Duet* by plotting a play derived from Shakespeare's imagination but updated pointedly, poignantly, or perversely, to present the proud Moor Othello and the sable villain of *Titus Andronicus*, namely Aaron, as archetypes of Malcolm X's demonology and hagiography. Thus, Shakespeare himself is an enslaver, with a loyal "house slave" (to employ X's terminology) who is in love with Judith—W.S.'s haughty, hot-blooded daughter. However, Judith despises Othello, whom she views as too much an "Oreo"—yellow-bellied, lily-livered, despite his black skin. Instead, she lusts for the plantation's bad boy, the "field slave" (*pace* X) Aaron, who's never met a white throat he hasn't wanted to cut or a book that he hasn't wanted to burn. Othello tries to tame Aaron via torture but only hardens Aaron's will to rebel. In the meantime, Judith finds that Aaron, as a "hard" black man, is a good find for her bed, and soon she is impregnated. When Othello learns that Judith has been taken by, or has given herself to, Aaron, he sets out to slay the renegade, but he is too late. Aaron has now roused all the enslaved people to revolt, claim their liberty, and torch the Big House and its library—Willy Shakespeare's favourite abode.

Yes, this plot-turn upsets The Bard of Avon, but he respects Aaron for being a black macho, a hard-ass, while Othello, in contrast, is a bit of a "limp wimp," so to speak: Aaron is the "nigga" punk; Othello is the nerdy intellectual. Meanwhile, Judith, regretting that she has fornicated and whelped a black bastard, wants to murder her newborn, but Aaron stabs her to death instead. One might want to consider this play as just a tad influenced by the 2012 "Blaxploitation" drama *Django Unchained*, directed by Quentin Tarantino, which presents Django as a John Shaft character who can kick a lot of white butt and then ride off into the dawn with his Ebony Queen of a wife. Though Pierre's play has been produced just once, by Theatre Passe Muraille and Obsidian Theatre, in February 2013, the Trinidadian-Canadian actor and playwright follows both Sears and George Boyd in having seen his play nominated for a Governor General's Award in Drama in 2013.

I hope that this review of ten African-Canadian plays staged in this century will whet appetites to seek them out, try them, digest them, and, first, to swallow them whole as "live" productions. While the playwrights are all Black Canadians, they derive from the African Diaspora—from Britain (Sears), from the Caribbean (Brown, mandiela, Anthony, Pierre), and from Canada (Borden, Boyd, Gale, Moodie). While African-American literature and culture are influences for most Canadians, Shange's danced play, *for colored girls*, is the major intertext for many, with even Shakespeare serving only as a runner-up. The particular brilliance of African-Canadian drama is that it is polyphonous, deploying voices and accents from the whole of the African Diaspora and its positions and development in Canada. Arguably, the most produced dramas are also those with the smallest casts, ranging from Borden's single-actor (but multiple-character) piece up to Sears's *Harlem Duet*, with its focus on a couple plus three side characters. (Sears's large-cast and epical-in-concept *Adventures* is the exception.) A few of the plays have crossed international boundaries, but most are produced in Canada. Moreover, most of the plays have been published by three presses: Blizzard, Sirocco, and Playwrights Canada. Furthermore, very few of these plays are chronically produced, and both Moodie's and mandiela's deserve to be only provisionally present in this 2000-on review. However, three of the ten— as publications—have received nominations for Canada's highest award for print drama, and one—Sears's *Harlem Duet*—won. Two plays—Anthony's and Sears's *Adventures*— migrated to commercial stages, and Anthony's *'da Kink* even crossed over to television. I think it is fair to say that my sampling here is representative of the excellence of African-Canadian playwriting. The fault lies not in ourselves that our plays are not produced more often.

[*Anglistik,* vol. 30, no. 1, 2019]

∾

As we have seen, most African-Canadian dramatists feature the dismemberment of communities, the disintegration of households, the sundering of lovers, and/or the survival of atomized soloists, individuals left to their own lonesome devices. One exception is those writers who sight hope in gatherings of women, from which hopeless males are excluded. In other words, African-Canadian dramas run closer to tragedy than not. But that tendency exists because the playwrights favour realism over fancy and set their scenes in a polity that would erase black presence by execution (*Angélique*), demolition (*Africville*), threat of incarceration (*The Captive*), and deportation or exile (*Riot*). For instance, even a cursory examination of the application of the death penalty (by hanging) up to its suspension in 1962 and then its abolition in 1976 will find several cases of African-Canadian men railroaded—fast-tracked—to the gallows in what were, really, judicial lynchings. Or so the next essay alleges via an examination of relevant true-crime historiography or fictionalized dramatizations.

∽

White Judges, Black Hoods: Hanging-as-Lynching in Three Canadian True-Crime Texts

MURDER, WRITES LITERARY theorist Frank Davey, is the crime "Canadians do not commit."[39] The act, he writes, is seen as "an Americanization of Canadian streets, a spread of violence from the south, a breakdown of Canadian values."[40] Davey speculates that murder is viewed as "un-Canadian" because it seems more congruent with "the American ideology of individual freedom and of free-market competitiveness" as opposed to a Canadian ideology of state-supported collective action."[41] Thus, Davey suspects, Canadians believe that murder is "committed not by Canadians but by strangers among us—by the Irish in the nineteenth century, by Italians, and currently by Jamaican and Irish gangs. In this view it is the foreign culture that creates murders and murderers, not the Canadian one." This mythology fingers America as an exporting warren of treasonous libertarians, "freedom fighters," gangsters, rebel patriots, gun-club militias, aggrieved postal workers, weekend warriors, serial killers, and mass murderers.

The obviously bloody cultural history of America, a nation that Canadians think they know intimately, serves to excuse us from scrutinizing our own responsibility for our own homicides, which must be of lesser consequence because they are motivated more by passion than by ideology. If, as Peter Conrad writes in *The Hitchcock Murders*, "Imperial America sought to consolidate its power by the Roman pomp of its architecture, and to erase the stains of history with successive coats of white paint," how much truer has been this endeavour for Canada, though we favour the gravitas of the Gothic over the grandiosity of the Romanesque in our architecture. In any event, Canadian identity is founded not only on the negative declaration "We are not American" but on the positive belief "We do no evil—and we never have."

Still, race complicates the Canadian dismissal of murder and murderers as "beyond the pale." However, we cannot know this truth unless we look beyond legal texts and accounts of Canadian murderousness and injustice to examine legal and popular culture archives in order to fathom how profoundly notions of law and order or right and wrong are embedded in black-and-white discourses. Moreover, as historian Jim Hornby points out, legal documents are often the only chronicles available of Black Canadian lives, though these accidental biographies posit them as either suspects or actual lawbreakers. Hornby comments, "Any group is misrepresented when described through the experiences of those members who are charged with criminal offences." In addition, "while blacks are underrepresented in most of the historical records…they were very probably overrepresented in criminal prosecutions, and thus in court records."

We need be careful, too, to recognize that, in popular public conceptions of race and offence, "blacks and criminality are understood to go hand in hand," or so says African-American Nobel Laureate Toni Morrison. One need be wary of the stereotyped criminalization of Africanness, blackness, or Negroness; yet one must recognize that it is in the would-be incriminating documents of transcripts and other trial matter that Negrophobia or anti-black bias and/or simple, elementary racism may find *itself* incriminated, even to the extent of the exculpation of the convicted and/or condemned citizen. In such cases, the supposed black hoodlum exchanges his stereotypical hoodie for the painfully exonerating mantle of victimhood or martyrdom. However, the removal of the "hooded" or "hoodwinked" status sometimes occurs long after the removal of the accused from among the living. What hangs in the balance, in such inquiries, is the credibility of our reading Canadian justice as colour-blind or as being invested solely in a Platonist and/or Judeo-Christian notion of *Truth*.

Concluding my 2002 article, "Raising Raced and Erased Executions in African-Canadian Literature: Or, Unearthing Angélique," I argue that African-Canadian writers "are summoned to banish the disquieting silence around racially biased incarceration and state-sanctioned murder in Canada." I go on to find that we must "examine all texts," legal and other, "to begin to determine the lives of our 'martyrs' in colonial, modern, and postmodern Canada and to begin to hear their voices speaking back to us." Although this cultural studies impulse is freshly salient given recent protests—in Canada and the United States—asserting that "Black Lives Matter," my commission behooves us all urgently: it is only by examining the historical record of trumped-up charges, perjured testimony, false evidence, all-white or all-male juries, and wrongful convictions—or, rather, of when the pseudo-royal court morphs into a putative kangaroo court—that we begin to reveal the fissures in the marble edifices and statuary that represent our laws.[42]

Three recent works that take up this commission are Debra Komar's true-crime account *The Lynching of Peter Wheeler*, Louise Delisle's play *The Days of Evan*, and David Steeves's legal-history essay, "Maniacal Murderer or Death Dealing Car: The Case of Daniel Perry Sampson, 1933–35." I choose to conjoin a non-fiction account of an actual crime and a likely fraudulent conviction, a historically inspired dramatization of a homicide and a hanging, and a groundbreaking legal essay to reveal how popular writer, creative writer, and scrupulous scholar may all sift relevant evidence to expose instances of probable racialized skullduggery.

Indeed, my textual trio addresses three cases in which the alleged perpetrators of capital homicide were all black Nova Scotia residents and, despite doubts on many accounts, were hanged. Komar scrutinizes a death penalty case on the cusp of the twentieth century. Playwright Delisle and scholar Steeves focus on hanging cases of the 1930s. Of this group, only Delisle is black, and only Steeves is male. More vitally, only Delisle avails herself of the licence of a creative writer to re-imagine socio-historical facts to dramatize her impression of the impact of racism, alcoholism, and sexism on a rural, South Shore, Nova Scotia, Africadian clan in the mid-1930s. In reviewing these texts, I seek to highlight how their authors engage the too-often invisible—in Canada—category of race (save in regards to First Nations peoples, whose racialized existence is literally *constitutional*). I hold that Canadians have always found it difficult to scrutinize race as opposed to language and class.[43] (In contrast, America has a highly developed discourse of race but an under-developed discourse of class and virtually no discourse on language except that Spanish may be voiced where corporate profitability and/or demographics warrant.)

Moreover, the "Peace, Order, and Good Government" idealistic preamble to our Constitution influences Canadians to relegate criminal episodes to the noir—or whitewash—of oblivion. Thus, there exists 1) a general Canadian tendency to culturally obliterate criminal acts and 2) an aversion to racial discourse. The exceptions to these rules are 1) the nineteenth-century Métis leader Louis Riel, who led 1869 and 1885 rebellions against the Canadian government, and 2) the Mohawk Warriors who manned and "womanned" the barricades of Oka, Quebec, in the summer of 1990, to protect a cemetery against municipally backed golf-course infringement. It should be possible to add the Air India Flight 182 bombing of June 23, 1985—Canada's greatest mass murder, in which 329 people, most of them Canadian citizens, died as the result of sabotage cold-bloodedly carried out by, probably, other Canadians. However, because these Canadians were South Asian in heritage and either immigrants or the children of immigrants, the tragedy has been racialized or extra-territorialized as *theirs*, not *ours*. Canadians, says Davey, tend "to define the killer or killers as alien to everyday experience, and perhaps even as alien to English-Canadian experience," an interest that increases when the criminal—or victim—is non-white or non-

Canadian. In *True Crime, True North*, a study of the Anglo-Canadian true-crime pulp mags of the mid-twentieth-century, Carolyn Strange and Tina Loo find that most of the stories "chronicled the police chase, skipped quickly through the trial and moved toward its inevitable outcome: the guilty verdict, which restored social harmony and reset moral values." Strange and Loo agree with Davey that race provided a way to both stigmatize offenders and eliminate them from ballyhooed white Anglo-Saxon norms of citizenship:

> Racial profiling wasn't a dirty term in the 1940s pulps; in every story race provided a shorthand explanation for certain sorts of people's purported propensity to commit certain types of crimes. Anglo-Canadians and Northern Europeans were cool-headed...(unless addled by drink or maddened by temptresses); Southern and Eastern Europeans and francophones were brutish and lusty; Americans were greedy and sharp; and Native peoples were prone to be passionate and uncivilized.... Cases involving Asian or black victims or perpetrators were rarities. Pulp writers pandered to English Canadians' anti-Native prejudices and fears of European "foreigners," but they simultaneously reassured readers that law and order Canadian-style was there, ready to right any and every wrong.

Indeed, racialized murderers were understood to represent inferior cultures that were either "inordinately passionate or beyond the pale of civilization." Canuck crime writing relied on "racial explanations for criminality."

Given the foregoing assertions, the interventions of Komar, Steeves, and Delisle are most welcome in furthering our understanding of the ways in which Canada has historically demonized, excluded, and/or judicially oppressed or—in effect—*murdered* those considered racially inadmissible to the Canadian polity or resistant to assimilation or unredeemable. In examining the work of Komar, Delisle, and Steeves, I will move from popular true-crime to creative writing and end with a brief assessment of a work of undoubted scholarship.

The Lynching of Peter Wheeler is Debra Komar's second study of a historical crime. Komar posits that Wheeler, convicted of and executed for the 1896 rape and murder of fourteen-year-old Annie Kempton in Bear River, Nova Scotia, was the innocent victim of popular prejudice, police persecution, and yellow-press racism. Kempton was a white working-class country maiden, practically an orphan due to her parents' need to live and work elsewhere. For his part, Wheeler was a swarthy sailor, "peripatetic," says Komar, and understandably so, being a mariner since the age of eight, in 1877, but one who found himself ready to settle in 1884— "for the foreseeable future"—in Bear River, and willing to do domestic as well as forest work to earn his keep. From the age of fifteen until his arrest at twenty-seven, Wheeler lived in the home of the spinster Tillie Comeau, whose surname and Bear River domicile imply an Acadian heritage. Komar relates local gossip that paired the twain as clandestine lovers, but she fails to recognize that Wheeler, born in the French-Creole parleying, British African, Indian Ocean isle

95

colony of Mauritius, might have been a handy interlocutor, as well as boarder, for the presumably francophone Comeau. (Later, we learn that Wheeler "reads Latin as well as English and talks French fluently." However, this possibility is not the only racially inflected insight that Komar overlooks, and such omissions hinder her basic thesis that racism wove Wheeler's noose.)

A globe-trotting forensic anthropologist and now an Annapolis Royal, Nova Scotia–based author, Komar reconstructs well the facts: Kempton was found kneeling, face down, in a sticky, bloody puddle, her underclothes disarrayed, her throat slashed, her head bashed. Wheeler, who found Kempton's body, was shortly fingered as the prime—and then sole—suspect, for the then-incriminating reasons that he was "coloured," a sailor come-from-away, and may have engaged in chit-chat with the victim or bantered about her with pub pals. Indeed, regional newspapers quickly fingered "railway employees" and "Italians" as suspicious characters and likely killers, so the foreign and the off-colour were immediate suspects. Though the "Italian railway workers" were soon released, the idea that the malefactor had to be a non-WASP non-Canuck now coloured the public mind. This was a tragic omen for Wheeler, mainly because he was an alien who had lived near the Kemptons (as Tillie Comeau's boarder) for a dozen years and had been the first to raise the alarm regarding the murder.

Komar declares Wheeler a "feasible" suspect, partly for the reasons stated, plus his proximity to the victim and his claim to have merely stumbled upon Kempton's corpse. Still,

Komar's pondering of Wheeler's suspect status skirts racial determinism. We read that Wheeler possessed "a world-class analytical brain," but this intellect crowned an "unfortunate eggplant-shaped physique" or, rather, "short stout stature," which earned him the "endless mocking" of "burlier," if less brainy, shipmates. No evidence is cited to confirm that Wheeler took a lot of ribbing from his saltwater fraternity, but no matter: "What he lacked in mettle…, he made up for in bonhomie." Komar fails to note the discrepancy between Wheeler's supposed unpopularity and the fact that he put regularly to sea to earn extra money and thus was readily able to work as a seafarer. Komar also states that Wheeler was "rough-hewn, but courteous and polite if not terribly refined." Bluntly, she says, he lacked "social graces": "He was not a gentleman…, but he was every bit a man, despite his diminutive size and odd shape." One sign of his intelligence was his "caustic wit"; one sign of his capacity for alleged viciousness was his enjoyment of "saucy exchanges."

The effect of these details, which Komar seems to have gleaned from a newspaper "confession" (though she does not pinpoint the source of her revelations), is to construct Wheeler as a "foreign" threat, not so much because of his different anatomy (he is male, if not a Nordic he-man or an aristocrat) but because of his intellect. Whatever exoticization or Orientalization was undertaken by the provincial press in 1896 seems to be reiterated, with terrifying innocence—if subtlety—by Komar. Given that, in her terms, Wheeler is a smart (or sly) vegetable-shaped person with a penis and an inferiority complex, it becomes imaginable—"feasible"—that he could have raped and murdered Kempton. However, one must wonder why, after twelve years of living near her on the same road, he would have chosen suddenly to attack her—and not Tillie Comeau, with whom he lived, or some other woman somewhat farther along the coast. Grimly, Komar's own reconstruction of Wheeler casts him as a monster in physique and nasty in speech. Komar also harps on Wheeler's sailor employ, his travels for seven years as a shipmate, his "solitary and untethered life," his supposed lack of any "special lady laying claim to his heart," and his "vagabond ways." These aspects of Wheeler's life should be not odd but sensible: he was a mariner, thus, literally, a "drifter." But, after seven years of the Seven Seas, as a youth aged only fifteen, he put into Bear River, deciding, in effect, to be a landlubber and casual day labourer, while still seafaring, at intervals, but mainly dwelling in Comeau's abode.

Still, Komar terms Wheeler as "rootless," thus Orient-alizing him as Semitic, that is, if we recall the Stalinist slur for a Jewish intellectual, a "rootless cosmopolitan." To recap Komar's own cataloguing of Wheeler, he was an off-shore, off-colour sailor who falsely claimed Australian nativity but was often deemed, by the local press, to seem "a Spaniard or Portuguese…and of a mulatto color," or, rather, to seem kin to swarthy Europeans,[44] often considered sub-"Caucasian" in the Nordic-European-dominated racial hierarchies of the day, and he is "untethered," or, let's say, a cast-off. Thus, Komar casts Wheeler as a kind of déclassé Othello, who, like Shakespeare's Moorish naval general, has finally decided to settle down, with liking or love for a white woman, and whose jealous passion for her must mandate her death.[45]

Wheeler becomes, palpably, a pulp-magazine villain. Intriguingly, Komar, sighting the deliberate darkening of one newspaper depiction of Wheeler, likens it to the "one century later" blackening of African-American murder suspect O. J. Simpson's face on a *Time* magazine cover. We should recall here that one of the framing narratives of the Simpson trial of 1994/95 was that he was Othello-esque, driven by fantastic, sexual jealousy to murder his ex-wife.[46]

Komar is correct that Wheeler's pseudo-landed-immigrant status helped to fit him for the noose. However, another way to appreciate this finding is that Canadians of colour are never accepted as being, well, Canadian, and having a right to be—to exist—in the country. Scares over Jamaican "gangs" or Chinese students "taking over" Canadian university campuses are all means of suggesting who has a right to belong to the national imaginary, who does not, and who thus may be classed as a predatory interloper.[47] The occasional notorious murderer or prostitution-ring operator, if a person of colour, serves always handily to configure the crime as un-Canadian and the criminal as an alien.

Komar ratchets up her de facto racialization of Wheeler, stating, "He also maintained a firm grasp of his true place in the world, exhibiting none of the usual immigrant striving." This sentence also serves to Orientalize Wheeler, but with doubled negatives: first, he demonstrates the stereotypical apathy and fatalism for which some "othered" ethnics are critiqued, for allegedly allowing despair and lethargy to vitiate ("manly") rugged individualism and the (Protestant) work ethic. Secondly, Wheeler is unlike other "othered" ethnics who seek supposedly to dominate discrete sectors of the economy and the class structure, to either displace or to join WASP elites by "striving" to amass wealth and garner concomitant political clout. Yet, even while Komar castigates Wheeler for not, alas, fitting in successfully in Bear River, she ignores her own contrary evidence that 1) he never failed to be hired as a sailor and 2) he had something akin to domestic tranquillity in Bear River, even perhaps enjoying a nostalgic recollection of his Mauritian home by trading light-hearted banter in French with Tillie Comeau and in English with Anne Kempton.

Komar does submit, however, that a kind of local, civil Ku Klux Klan (in judicial black robes, police uniforms, and press badges) conducted the trial-by-media and conviction-by-racism that resulted in Wheeler's hanging— or legal lynching—in Digby, Nova Scotia, in September 1896. Komar's study does convince us that a Halifax detective, Nicholas Power, abetted by the press, led the drive to hang Wheeler, which he achieved by criminalizing the part-time sailor and obfuscating the timeline of Kempton's murder. States Komar, Power "was never one to favour those born in warmer climes, particularly swarthy ne'er-do-wells that took up with the pale-skinned belles of the north." Again, Power's prosecutorial zeal suits a tabloid construction of criminals as coloured and/or perverse. Power seems to answer to the psychological motivation of white Western racists and imperialists that Martiniquan-Algerian scholar Frantz Fanon provides: "When European civilization came into contact with the black world, with those savage peoples, everyone agreed: Those Negroes were the principle of evil." In addition, because "the civilized white man retains an irrational longing for unusual eras of sexual license, of orgiastic scenes, of unpunished rapes, of unrepressed incest," says Fanon, "the Negro is taken as a terrifying penis." Granted this perspective, Power was motivated to set a noose about Wheeler's neck as a device to warn other men of colour to keep their distance from white women and to stay in their place as vassals of white (economic, political, and armed) supremacy.

Though Komar cites racism as a primary reason for Wheeler's execution, her analysis remains superficial. She registers that "in 1896 Canada was unfathomably, unrecognizably racist" and that "clashes verging on race wars were inevitable." She does not contextualize this finding and so ignores the Riel Rebellions in Manitoba (1869) and the North-West Territories (present-day Saskatchewan, 1885) as constituting, in part, "race wars." Closer to home, Komar ignores the 1880 race riot in Bridgetown, Nova Scotia, that put a white man in the grave and a black man on death row.[48] The Bridgetown history is particularly germane to the Wheeler case, for the riot was touched off by white males upset by interracial dating while popular cries—headed up by Power—for Wheeler's death were compelled in part by the fancy that a "Coloured" man had "outraged" a white woman.

Though she is certain that racism triggered Wheeler's hanging, Komar is, strangely, uncertain about Wheeler's race. He was, she says, "a dark-skinned man of ambiguous ancestry and indeterminate parentage." She asserts, though, that Wheeler was "dark-skinned, woolly-haired, and foreign-born." Yet, knowing that Wheeler was a native Mauritian, Komar could have researched the Creoles—or Métis—of that nation, the result of unions primarily between Africans and French but also sometimes between English and Indian and/or Chinese.[49] Mauritius flies a "rainbow flag" for this precise reason. Though Wheeler's parents married in England, they were likely Mauritian Creoles, an identity that Komar never explores. I do speculate that Wheeler's noted, unaccented English was due to his Mauritian boyhood and schooling. He was also adept in French.

Komar tells us that "Wheeler was a marked man, a dark cloud on the region's snowy white landscape," but Komar is herself oblivious to the racial demographics of the area. She describes the region as "insular" and the residents as "homogeneous."[50] Yet Bear River was (and is) home to Mi'kmaq; plus there were notable Africadian communities in Lequille and Delaps Cove (both near Annapolis Royal), Bridgetown (Inglewood Road), and in Jordantown and Acaciaville (both near Digby). In fact, the only other person to meet suspicion, briefly, for Kempton's death was Joseph Pictou, a Mi'kmaw man from, indeed, "a small reserve just outside of Bear River." Komar omits the patriated Acadian communities adjacent to Bear River and ranging down the southwest, Fundy-side coast of Nova Scotia, from Digby to Yarmouth, the so-called District of Clare. Yet no Nova Scotian could have thought the province whites-only or even WASP-only in 1896. All anyone had to do to know otherwise was read Thomas Chandler Haliburton's *Clockmaker* sketches— often lampooning blacks but also recording the presence of francophones in his protagonist's Annapolis Valley and Cobequid Valley travels. Moreover, anyone taking a train to Yarmouth or to Digby or to Halifax would have traversed

Mi'kmaw settlements and Negro communities. Their presence was not new. This point leads me to urge that the debate over race, specifically of the status of blacks (Africadians) in Nova Scotia, has continued virtually unabated since enslavement in the 1760s and official emancipation in 1834. The occasional show trial of supposed black villainy serves to underline—or reanimate—in public discourse two complementary ideas: 1) blacks are innate criminals; 2) they belong in jail or on slave plantations; thus, they cannot circulate as free Canadian citizens, not without suspicion, not without surveillance, not without meeting conditions.[51]

In the end, Komar's study hints that Detective Power deserves disgrace; Wheeler deserves a posthumous pardon; and the Government of Mauritius deserves an apology from the Government of Canada. Her investigation of the police and media manipulations of the Wheeler case establishes that Peter Wheeler was "lynched," not hanged. (She notes that one newspaper described the people of Bear River as "Southern negro-lynchers.") However, the full context of the politico-legal chicanery to which Wheeler fell victim is lost due to Komar's insufficient grappling with race as the *bête noire* of her study.

The eldest of a family of seven children, born and raised in Shelburne, Louise Delisle graduated from high school, became a nurse, and then became devoted to theatre, eventually founding the Black Pioneers Acting Troupe, the group for which she crafts her plays. Her passion is Shelburne County Africadian history, and so a notorious hanging of a local black man in 1937 is of interest, and so we have her play, *The Days of Evan*, which appears in her collection, *Back Talk: Plays of Black Experience*.

Given her subtitle emphasizing the lived experience of South Shore Africadians, one may presume rightly that the Africadian Delisle will take an explicitly Afrocentric view of the injustice that she dramatizes. Moreover, as a creative writer, she need not respect any demands of realism or objectivity in addressing the hanging that is her concern. Her first adjustment, then, is to title the play, *The Days of Evan*, thus displacing the play's true subject, the execution for murder of Everett Farmer, early on the morning of December 14, 1937, in Shelburne, Nova Scotia, for having shot his brother, Zachariah, to death, in cold blood, on August 1, 1937. Delisle is convinced that the justice system was out to lynch Farmer for having slain his half-brother Zachariah (who becomes "Mack" in the play), although Farmer claimed he acted in self-defence and to protect his family.

I do not know what original research, if any, was undertaken by Delisle in preparing her play. However, journalist Dean Jobb covers the Farmer case in his 1988 *Shades of Justice: Seven Nova Scotia Murder Cases*, and he favours poverty, rather than racism, as the inspiration for Farmer's conviction and execution. Jobb finds that Farmer could not afford a lawyer; the court-appointed lawyer had little time to prepare a defence, there was no money to support an appeal, and no one bothered to pen a letter to the Department of Justice Remission Service to request commutation of Farmer's death sentence. Jobb acknowledges that the trial jury was "all-white," not due, perhaps, to segregation but because "the requirement that jurors own land disqualified many [blacks] from jury duty." Jobb registers that one writer, Alan Hustak, claims that "race was a factor in the conviction," but Jobb also urges that Hustak's account of the case is "marred by a number of factual errors" or "several factual errors." Jobb agrees that the Farmer case was a test of "how the justice system dealt with a penniless black man facing the gallows," but he does not find that it failed due to racism: "Lack of money undoubtedly prevented Everett from mounting an effective defence, but the charge of racial discrimination is impossible to prove or disprove."

I suspect that Delisle, through penning *The Days of Evan*, seeks to overturn Jobb's downplaying of racism as a chief motive for Everett Farmer's execution. In a sense, she reads between the lines of Jobb's account to stress the role of race in Farmer's case, and does so for a homely reason: she is a lifelong resident of Shelburne and, as an Africadian, may sense the racial subtleties of the town far better than does Jobb, whose chronicle is invested in official accounts and archival records. I will speculate that Delisle relies on oral history and community gossip about the facts of Everett Farmer's—or Evan's—guilt. Naturally, Delisle's choice to employ drama to explore the Farmer case signals a perfect reliance on oral testimony, for that is what we will hear from the stage. In sum, Delisle's *The Days of Evan* is her backtalk to Jobb's reliance on white establishment officials—lawyers, judges, journalists, politicians, and their records and documents and oral histories—to decide how vital a role, if any, Negrophobia may have played in taking a black man's life.[52]

Revealingly, then, Jobb's account of the Farmer case recounts interviews with a Shelburne businessman who, as a young reporter, had covered the Farmer trial (and whose own father was the sheriff who held Farmer in custody); a lawyer; and the niece of Farmer's attorney who had gone on to become the first Nova Scotian Acadian elected to the House of Commons. While Jobb does utilize spoken insights and anecdotes from white officials and professionals, he does not seem to have sounded any Africadian Shelburne citizens' opinions of the case. Delisle's play challenges this omission. Her Africadian heroine, Susan, says succinctly, but comprehensively, of the Nova Scotia (or Dominion of Canada) justice system, "Their justice is just wrong."[53]

While Shakespeare's *Othello* is evoked in the image of the supposed dastard Peter Wheeler attempting to rape Anne Kempton and cut her throat, Delisle, perhaps due to feeling haunted by the Farmer case, allows the ghost of another Shakespeare play, *Hamlet*, to help animate her own. Recall that *Hamlet* commences with the apparition of the dead King Hamlet summoning his son, Prince Hamlet, to avenge his murder. Act 1, scene 2 of Delisle's play opens with the "Ghost of Evan" visiting his wife, Susan, on the night following his execution. Just as King Hamlet's ghost prods Marcellus to state, "Something is rotten in the state of Denmark," so does the "Ghost of Evan" allow Delisle to posit that a like rotten-ness afflicts the province of Nova Scotia, if not the Dominion of Canada. The backstory of Shakespeare's *Hamlet* is that Claudius has slain his brother, King Hamlet, usurped the throne, and is now bedding Hamlet's Queen, Gertrude, who is now his. King Hamlet's ghost directs Prince Hamlet to correct matters *now*.

In Delisle's play, the "Ghost of Evan" represents a man

slain by the state—the Dominion of Canada—due to improper application of the death penalty when he, Evan, was merely thwarting the intent of his brother, Zachariah, to murder him and his children and rape his wife. As Komar's treatment of Wheeler reproduces him as a downscale Othello, so does Delisle's revision of Farmer reproduce him as an even unluckier type of Shakespeare's ghostly royal. Indeed, if the Bard's King Hamlet is a ghost because he could not arrest his brother's insidious and murderous plot against him, Evan is a ghost, in contrast, because he did prevent—violently—his brother from seizing his wife and endangering his household, which includes eight children. Furthermore, if *Hamlet* is a play that is partly about the failure to take timely action to prevent catastrophes (so Prince Hamlet's hesitation to promptly stab King Claudius to death engenders arguably the destruction of his royal bloodline as well as the immediate ruling-class of Denmark), Delisle's play, again in instructive contrast, shows that taking immediate action can also engender grave results.[54]

Whereas *Hamlet* opens with the prince of Denmark garbed in funereal black, Delisle's act 1, scene 1 opens with Susan "dressed in black." Arguably, too, Delisle replaces Jobb's Hamletian hesitation to call a spade a spade (pun intended) with an insistence on the primacy of race.

Jobb recounts the story that Everett Farmer visits the Shelburne police chief, next the Shelburne County Mountie, who then picks up the coroner, and then all four drive to Farmer's "decrepit two-storey frame house." The detail is vital: Everett has just journeyed from his shantytown locale into middle-class stolidity, as a black man under suspicion, if not arrest, and now these establishment figures are in his home, save that it is, says Jobb, "decrepit." Delisle replays this scene to accent the racial peril into which her Everett— or Evan—has just placed himself. First, his decision to report his killing of Mack (Zachariah) is hotly contested by his wife, Susan, who is busy trying to scrub up the blood from the slaying. Evan tells her that he will go "to talk to the sheriff." She replies, "He'll never believe you. You know that." However, Evan does go to see the sheriff, but, by doing so, he becomes basically a dead man walking.[55] Delisle has her sheriff address Evan in terms echoing Southerners' stereotypical derision of African Americans. Her version of the Shelburne police chief (pretty much now a Dixie type) calls her Evan "boy," severally, accuses him of being into "the shine" (moonshine), and labels all Shelburne black males "niggers."

In Jobb's rendition of this meeting, the police chief is pure probity, along with the RCMP officer, who reads Farmer his rights. In contrast, Delisle transplants South Shore Nova Scotia to the US South, so her whites mimic old-line Confederates. (By doing so, Delisle insists that readers and spectators remember that, because mainland Nova Scotia was settled by New England and Southern slaveholders, first as Planters and then as Loyalists, their historical anti-black attitudes, persisting in the province, link it to Dixie.) For his part, Jobb positions the police and the coroner at the killing scene as careful examiners of evidence, finding Zachariah "seated upright in a chair, with his legs crossed; there were no signs of a struggle.... The head was drooped forward, revealing a gaping bullet wound to the right side of the neck." Importantly, Zachariah's eyes were "closed," and "an unlighted self-rolled cigarette [lay] in the dead man's lap."

These notes would be interpreted, in the Farmer case, to suggest that Everett had shot his brother while he was asleep, thus removing self-defence as a defence and rendering him plausibly guilty of capital murder. Reproducing this incident in her play, Delisle has the sheriff declare that he cannot see "any signs of a fight" between the brothers, while the coroner, Dr. Muller, says, "This man was shot sitting down…. Look at his legs, they are crossed…. And his eyes are closed like he's asleep. I would have to call this murder." Dr. Muller also claims, "Seems to me that somebody tried to cover up a murder, by cleaning up the blood." Seeing the death scene cast in a light that could get her husband hanged, Susan intervenes: "I crossed [Mack's] legs so he wouldn't fall off the chair, Sheriff. I closed Mack's eyes to make him decent…. I cleaned [Mack's blood] up, I couldn't leave that mess. I got eight children in the house."

Susan's statements are to no avail. The sheriff handcuffs Evan, and as he leads him away, "whispers" to the suspect, "Your black ass is goin' to hang." Dr. Muller chimes in, "Talking about killing two birds with one stone. We'll get rid of both these niggers." Delisle hereby talks back to Jobb's depiction of official decency with a scene that turns the lawman and the coroner into KKK conspirators whose investigation of the crime scene is merely a process to slant evidence in order to ensure that Evan enters the hoosegow and meets the noose. No wonder, then, that Delisle's act 3, scene 1 opens with four anonymous white men—representing the power structure of police, law, medicine, and journalism—conspiring to not "let this nigger get away with this"; for, if "they can murder their own, they will murder us"; thus, "we have to hang this nigger"; "No such thing as a fair trial here today."

Moreover, this lingo is closer to that of Klansmen than it is to the "federal fisheries inspector"; "a merchant, a barber, a boat builder, and a spar maker"; plus "two fishermen, two labourers, a painter, a farmer, and a driver," who comprised the actual Everett Farmer jury. Again, Jobb presents the trial of Farmer as a matter-of-fact affair hindered only by a lack of preparation time for his attorney. In Delisle's presentation of Evan's trial, the judge asserts that Evan has already confessed to murder, he calls Susan "girl," and he denies that the Crown's comments are "prejudicial" because "the truth is never prejudicial." Ultimately, Delisle has an elder black woman tell the court, "If it wasn't for you high and mighty white folks, the poor man [Evan] wouldn't be sittin' here." In Delisle's play, because the verdict is a foregone conclusion, there is no charge from the judge to the jury about how and what they should deliberate. But Jobb sees only one potential omission in the actual Farmer trial, and that was the alleged failure of the judge to inform the jurors that they could recommend mercy.

Jobb does provide some social context for Farmer's trial, revealing thereby some sensitivity to the influence of the popular racism of the day. First, the coroner's inquest was "packed with spectators," and the pursuant trial so overshadowed the county fair that "a special detail of RCMP officers" was required to help control the crowds. Second, the verdict prompted two local Christian ministers to complain that whites were neglecting "to provide moral and religious training for the people of the race to which the convicted man belongs." Moreover, white Christians were setting a bad example for coloured ones, for "cases of venereal disease and illegitimate births in Shelburne were on the rise." Third, some journalists felt squeamish about the all-white jury, and so one testified, anonymously, that "the judge, lawyers, and court officials treated [Farmer] with the same courtesy and consideration that they would have accorded a man of wealth and position."

Read together, the public's intense interest in the potential hanging of a poor black man, the white clergy's exploitation of the "crime" to try to shame white Christians into behaving less immorally and with less prejudice, and sensitivity to the fact that an all-white jury could pervert the decorous nature of Canadian justice, all suggest that no one in 1937 Shelburne viewed the case with anything like race-neutrality. It is likely that the tacitly racialized public response to the Farmer case is precisely what prompted Delisle to propose that Shelburne, in 1937, is as much the site of a deadly racist conspiracy of whites as were, notoriously, many Dixie cities in the Civil Rights Movement era. I believe that Delisle obtains this re-reading of the Farmer case by employing her own life experience of Shelburne, as a black woman, as well as the folk wisdom conveyed through Africadian speech, to pry open the racial subtext denied by professional—but superficial—objectivity (as in Jobb's reportage). Thus, she closes her play on a note of anti-black racism.

Evan's widow, Susan, hears a "voice from outside" shout, "We will kill you all before this is over! Do you hear that, niggers?" However, the "voice" is threatened by Evan's female survivors and flees. Then, as Evan is hanged, the spiritual "Swing Low, Sweet Chariot" is heard, thus asking the audience to make a connection between black enslavement long ago in the American South and black oppression in contemporary Canada. Thus, *The Days of Evan* verifies John Scaggs's insight that "all crime fiction is trans-historical." I will add that it is also transnational and cross-cultural.

I am unfair to conclude my canvass of my subject texts with David Steeves's excellent, prize-winning article, "Maniacal Murderer or Death Dealing Car: The Case of Daniel Perry Sampson, 1933–35," which appears in *The African Canadian Legal Odyssey: Historical Essays*, edited by Barrington Walker and published by the Osgoode Society for Canadian Legal History. I am, after all, juxtaposing with Komar's popular true-crime writing and Delisle's fiction-staging play a work that is indubitably scholarly, i.e., grounded in exacting research. In the comparison, Komar and Delisle could suffer, save that Delisle does have the safety of fiction backing her effort, while Komar is able to reach a general audience that Steeves, almost certainly, cannot and will not. Assuredly, Steeves merits the benefit of a few cursory observations about his exemplary study.

My red-letter point is that Steeves, a New Brunswick–born, Dalhousie-educated, Toronto-based lawyer, seldom loses sight of the racial context of the legal drama that began on a July night in 1933. In the case history, the bodies of two boys, brothers Edward and Bramwell Heffernan, were found near each other alongside railway tracks. The boys had been out the evening of July 19 picking blueberries, and there was some thought that they had met a passing train in a disastrous accident. An "inconclusive coroner's inquest" was soon followed by months of "fruitless investigation" by police. Eventually, one white officer, befriending a mentally deficient Africadian Great War veteran over several weeks, was able to ask him to "x" a confession and then lead RCMP officers to the murder weapon, a rusted knife with blood-like stains, which could not be conclusively identified as being human, let alone as belonging to either of the deceased brothers.

As in the case of Peter Wheeler, Sampson became a suspect simply by having been a "coloured" man who was seen "in the area where the boys were last observed." Just as Wheeler was suspicious by virtue of being a swarthy foreigner, so did Sampson's darkling apparition—in the vicinity of the Heffernan brothers—render him a suspect. Yet Sampson had good reason to be in that "neck of the woods" on that night: he lived there.[56]

So, unable to solve the case and lacking any credible suspects, Corporal Walsh of the Halifax RCMP began to visit Sampson at his home, shared with his mother, between October 20 and December 13, 1933. On one such occasion, Sampson was taken to the RCMP headquarters, where a white woman who had seen a Coloured man walking in the opposite direction from where the Heffernan boys' remains were later found was asked if she could pick out this Negro from a line-up. Steeves does not tell us that all the other men in the line-up were white, but he does tell us that they were all uniformed and plainclothes officers. Given that the RCMP did not accept a black officer until

1969,[57] Sampson must have stood in a line-up in which he was visibly the only black. Parsons was able to choose the single Negro from among the whites with ease. Eventually, after more questioning from more officers and a visit to the murder scene, all of which took place without any notes being taken, Sampson was asked to "x" a confession, based on what he had supposedly told the police, but employing a vocabulary far above his limited intelligence. Notably, Sampson was "unable to either read or write."[58]

Tried for the deaths of the Heffernans, Sampson faced—as did Wheeler earlier and Everett Farmer later—an "all-white judiciary." This was no accident, nor was the all-white jury a case of bad luck. Therefore, Jobb's assertion in the Farmer case that his all-white jury was a happenstance is not so straightforward as it sounds. Steeves's research on jury selection in Halifax proves that Nova Scotia's government scrupled— specifically in Halifax—to set jury selection in such a way, regarding income and property holding, that almost no blacks and few white working-class persons would ever be considered as jurors.

Thus, despite scrupulous cross-examination of Crown witnesses and a recommendation for mercy from the jury, Sampson was convicted of murdering the Heffernans and sentenced to death. However, his attorney, Ormond Regan, appealed the conviction successfully, partly because Sampson's x-signed confession to the RCMP had been lost and partly because of the Crown's prejudicial comments regarding Sampson's decision not to testify. A new trial was ordered.

Steeves shows that, upon empanelling the new jury, Regan challenged several would-be jurors on their racial attitudes, inquiring whether they "might be prejudiced in respect of colour," thereby exposing and introducing into the second trial the fact of "widespread intolerance towards [Haligonian] African Nova Scotians." Regan was able, in fact, to show that "at least half of the jurymen called to the stand to give evidence respecting their own competency admitted frankly that they were prejudiced against the prisoner and hence incapable of rendering a true and fair verdict." Surely, not all of those who admitted prejudice were acting on racial bias, but realistically some must have been, and it is presumable that some of those who actually got to sit the second Sampson trial were biased racially against the prisoner. Regan's tactic was, I believe, to set the stage for a second appeal of a second conviction by proving that Sampson could not possibly have received a fair trial given the tainted jury pool. I assert this possibility due to the sage evidence Steeves provides.

Yet jury bias was rendered almost inevitable given that, as Steeves's research pronounces, the province of Nova Scotia amended its Juries Act in 1890 so that potential Halifax-area jurors were drawn from ten polling districts in the "predominantly white areas of the downtown core and residential South End." Significantly, too, potential jurors had to have a net worth of at least $4,000 for grand jury service and $800 for admission to a petit jury panel. Such relative wealth was far beyond the reach of most Haligonian Africadians, and none of them lived in the designated jury-pool catchment area, anyway.

Moreover, during Sampson's second trial, a letter was received by Sampson's attorney that threatened the organization of a lynch mob to dispatch Sampson unless he was hanged by November 21, 1934. Steeves reads this incident as indicative of "a long-standing animus against African Nova Scotians and others within Halifax's ethnic minority community." It also serves to indicate that some white citizens considered the justice system merely an extension—under civil guise—of the anti-black attitudes prevalent in the common weal.

Not surprisingly, Sampson was soon again found guilty and again sentenced to death. However, Regan, his attorney, organized appeals that failed—but not until there was a hearing at the Supreme Court of Canada on the question of jury bias as a ground for exclusion. Although Regan prepared the appeal, he was not able to argue it himself because of "Sampson's continued financial difficulties." Notably, Sampson's penury did not prevent his lawyer from having a final appeal heard before the Supreme Court of Canada. This fact is a striking contrast to the failure of Everett Farmer's lawyer to even send a letter begging a commutation of his client's sentence. It also suggests that Jobb's finding that poverty, not racism, doomed Farmer to the gallows must be nuanced substantially.

I end my study here, but I posit that Steeves's examination of the Sampson case establishes that it is impossible for us to understand the operation of racism within judicial discourse without taking into account the presence of racism within the larger society. Likewise, the narratives of Komar and Jobb of their respective interests—the cases of Wheeler and Farmer—accumulate authority only when racism is accorded due analysis by the authors. When it is not, as Delisle seems to feel is the case regarding Farmer, she feels free to exhume the racial subtext by applying folk memory and lived experience as well as riveting oral testimony to reconfigure a legal hanging as a conspiracy of lynchers. Indeed, she recognizes the ethnic and racial and gender dynamics in play, in setting up the execution that transpires in *The Days of Evan*, that Komar sometimes gets right in her treatment of Wheeler but that Jobb chooses to pooh-pooh in his coverage of Farmer's doom.

Steeves's research reveals that Nova Scotian justice was never colour-blind or "innocent" when it came to consideration of the rights of black suspects to judicial fairness—and that there was actual legislative connivance to deprive black suspects of a right to a jury of their peers. His scholarship insists on the fact of racialist and classist conspiracy, while Delisle points to the same in the imagined trial of Evan. Komar also finds that a complex of yellow journalism, WASP intolerance, and police machinations ended up frog-marching Wheeler to the gallows. Read together, however, these works charge that blacks are often considered foreigners, or interlopers, and are likely to be incarcerated and/or executed because of a general suspicion that they have no business being here (in Canada), first of all, and, secondly, no business being free.

I wager that a careful sifting of our archives regarding race-inflected trials will establish the haunting possibility that police procedural misconduct and judicial malfeasance regarding black suspects is a subtle nullification or repealing of British Slavery Abolition and/or American Emancipation. In other words, our fathoming of the law library will find undoubtedly that the bland term *race relations* is a euphemism for an endless civil war between empowered white supremacists and their racial and ethnic subjects.[59]

[*Canadian Law Library Review*, vol. 41, no. 2, 2016]

∿

The legal problem for African-Canadians is our existence as perpetual aliens who must not be allowed freedom of mobility—to walk, to drive, to live—wherever we wish. Rather, we must be halted, interrogated, harassed, surveillanced while shopping or entering a residence, arrested and incarcerated, or strip-searched on a public street corner, clubbed or shot or tasered to death or found—hanged by sneaker laces—in a cell. Such is the fate of individuals—sometimes couples, sometimes families. But whole communities—such as Jolly-town and Africville—can also be vapourized by highway crews, or, elsewhere, graveyards can be desecrated (see Price-ville, Ontario). Thus was white-faced Halifax satisfied to see Africville—on its sesquicentennial—rendered rubble and its citizens forcibly "relocated." Soon, however, novelists arose to rewrite Africville just as Longfellow rewrote Acadie, to turn it into a test case of their own suspicions that democracy is only a palimpsest for apartheid. Such is the finding of the pursuant essay.

∿

Reading the Africville Novel

IT IS A TELLING CANADIAN irony that the most famous
Black community in the country is one that no longer
exists as a discrete set of homes and infrastructure, or even
as a postal address. The perpetual, if now spectral, existence
of Africville, a village adjunct of Halifax from its origins
during the War of 1812 to its demise (due to the economics
of urban renewal and the politics of racial integration) in
the 1960s, underlines the phantasm that is race discourse
in Canada.

The bulldozing of the hundred homes of the 400 Africville residents (and the 1967 destruction of their Seaview
United Baptist Church), undertaken between 1964 and 1970,
enacts however the prime policy regarding black history
and culture in Canada, which is, arguably, to raze it, to
erase it. Thus, in her study, *Razing Africville: A Geography
of Racism*, Jennifer J. Nelson asserts that the obliteration
of the seaside North End Halifax community is "a story
of white domination, a story of the making of a slum, and
of the operation of technologies of oppression over time."
Nelson views Africville's levelling as "a deliberate moment
within a larger colonial project of spatial management,"
wherein "certain (black) bodies are consistently produced as

marginal within various facets of dominant white culture," and wherein Africville becomes a mirage or "image in the white imagination."

From this perspective, the recuperation of the flattening of Africville is not so much a narrative of shame and blame as it is one of shock that a distinctly Black village could ever have flourished on the northern coast of the city of Halifax. Certainly, politicians, professors, and media pundits have pontificated, over four decades now, over whether the officially termed "Africville Relocation"[60] (i.e., the demolition of their households and removal of Africvillers to downtown Halifax) was the right thing to have done, or whether it was "done right." But few commentators—apart from former residents and descendants—have insisted that Africville had a right to exist and that a right exists still to seek its reconstitution. In other words, the standard response to the Africville Relocation is regret and apology for the smashing of homes and of kinship networks rather than to assert the inviolate viability of a Black community thriving on the coastal, semi-rural fringes of a white-dominated and casually segregated city. To canvass a few of the literary treatments of Africville and the Relocation program is to realize that the different memorializations of Africville also project the place of race in the Canadian social imaginary. Yet it also seems the case that, to put race in its "place," authors end up putting it "no place," thus reproducing the perfect social constructions that commanded the destruction of Africville as an "anti-racist" measure that was also, in the end, "anti-Black." The literary imagination of Africville is no innocent endeavour but rather a quarrel over

Lebensraum—I use the Nazi term conscientiously—that is to say, over whether an identifiably, verifiably *Black* community may exist in Canada, not on the basis of segregation but on the basis of choice.

Before I examine some creative literature, I need to recall basic history. The community of Africville coalesced on the south shores of Bedford Basin, in response to the 1749 founding of Halifax (as a strategic North Atlantic British naval base); the importation of enslaved people into Nova Scotia and the expulsion of Acadians in 1755; the arrival of New England (and Southern) planters and the people they enslaved to Nova Scotia in 1760; the 1783 arrival of 3,500 African-Americans, mainly free; the 1792 exodus of 1,200 blacks from Nova Scotia and New Brunswick to Sierra Leone; the gradual decline of legal slavery in the Maritime colonies of British North America, even before Imperial abolition in 1834; and the arrival of 2,200 "Black Refugees" from the War of 1812 to Nova Scotia, between 1812 and 1815.[61]

To impede, if not prevent, the constitution of a farmer class among the black colonists and formerly enslaved settlers, their land allotments were either parsimonious or were set upon swamps, marshes, and/or rock, some distance apart from white-dominated villages and towns. The black settlers' segregated and second-rate land allotments were too hardscrabble to sustain cultivation, and so they were forced to seek labour or domestic work in the adjacent white towns and villages.[62] In some cases, they abandoned remote communities to migrate to the environs of Halifax, where their employment opportunities were greater.[63] Thus, by the close of the War of 1812, an *ex nihilo* black community, consisting of migrants, "squatters," and a few landowners with deeds, began to develop on Bedford Basin, separate from white citizenry, to be sure, but within walking distance of downtown Halifax.[64] Says Nelson, "The new residents fished, began keeping livestock, and explored opportunities for waged labour in the nearby city."

By 1849, a black community known as "Campbell Road Settlement" had come into existence at the northern terminus of that eponymous road. We may say so with certainty, for, in his 1895 *A Brief History of the Coloured Baptists of Nova Scotia*, Peter E. McKerrow reports, "The Campbell Road church was organized about 1849." McKerrow also advises, "A few hundred yards from the church [are] the placid waters of Bedford Basin, beneath whose surface Fathers Burton, Preston, Thomas, Bailey, Carvery, Dixon and Boone"—a roll call of pastors—"[have] buried in the likeness of Christ many willing converts in the ordinance of baptism." By 1895, then, the Campbell Road Settlement church—later known as Seaview United Baptist Church—had been served by half a dozen pastors whose waterside baptisms were already notable community events. McKerrow's history also reports that, as of 1895, the Campbell Road settlement—soon to be renamed, anonymously but popularly, "Africville"[65]— has "a fine day school [of] which nearly all the children of schoolable age [take] advantage.... A community of intelligent young people, much is expected of them." Thanks to McKerrow's history, we know that, by the end of Queen Victoria's reign, Campbell Road—or Africville—boasted a church, a school, and parochial traditions such as water baptism. Indeed, the church faced the water, so we must credit that, along with fishing, boating and swimming were also communal pursuits.

Nevertheless, McKerrow includes this tantalizing sentence in his commentary on the Campbell Road Settlement, or Africville: "This little Zion of late has been the subject of much comment, being in such close proximity to the city" of Halifax. Perhaps, then, as early as the turn of the last century, the Campbell Road blacks had already begun to hear talk of their planned removal or doubtlessly the natter of white displeasure over their location. For one thing, although Africville residents had built houses and institutions, "their" land was also being bisected and crisscrossed by the roads, rails, and cables of sophisticated urban capitalism as well as being tainted and polluted by the adjacent placement of factories, slaughterhouses, an infectious disease hospital, the city prison, and, by the 1960s, the city dump.

Even though Africville's setting was bucolic, it was also easy for photographers and editorialists to play up its "slum" status by focusing on the presence of the garbage deposits. In her review of journalistic, folk, sociological, and political accounts of Campbell Road/Africville, Nelson finds, "While simply home for the black community, for whites, Africville signified many things—a slum, a repository for the waste of society, a site of danger and degeneracy, a social problem, an object of pity and attempted rescue, and…a mirror in which the white community saw its superiority reflected." It is no exaggeration to say that Africville was branded, early in the twentieth-century, as a site of crime, contagion, corruption, and canker.

By 1911, then, a *Maclean's* magazine writer named it "the abode of little more than innocent shiftlessness, but such places are adapted to the breeding of vice and crime." For McKerrow, Campbell Road is "little Zion"; for *Maclean's*, it is little Babylon. Sociologists Donald H. Clairmont and Dennis William Magill quote a "prominent white businessman" to the effect that "[Africville] wasn't regarded as part of the city of Halifax...and [the city] didn't regard, I suppose, the people as people, certainly not as citizens." Then again, Africville came to serve Haligonians, claim Clairmont and Magill, as a "deviance service centre," that is, as "a place to go for bootleg booze and fun."

Due to constructions of Africville as a site of dirt, deviance, and disease, or, simply put, as a "dump," the former residents seek to dispute such dismissive and disparaging portraiture. Literary scholar Herb Wyile recognizes, "The fate of Africville has dramatized the marginality and political vulnerability of Black people in [Atlantic Canada] and galvanized them to a greater level of social, political, and artistic self-assertion." Clairmont and Magill also register that, by the 1990s, conceptions of Africville had morphed from the "stigmatized" to the "celebrated." They credit "the people themselves" for insisting on a reevaluation of Africville as "a community to be proud of, a fine community..., and even an heroic community since its people struggled against so much racism and neglect."

Clairmont and Magill see the artistic and cultural rehabilitation of Africville as stemming from the "crass" attempts by the City of Halifax to remove the last, elderly resident: trying to induce him to yield his land by brandishing a sack of cash in his face. While I trust that former Africville residents were outraged by city hall's treatment of the last Africville resident (and, thus, by extension, of themselves), it must be noted that the first artistic reconstruction of Africville came from the pen of an African-American musician, composer, poet, and anthologist, Frederick Ward (1937– 2017),[66] who had been bound for Europe when a dock-workers' strike stranded him in Halifax in 1970. Shortly after disembarking, Ward began associating with ex-Africville residents and, most importantly, rewriting their specific lingo and cadences for himself. The result of this work was his first novel, *Riverlisp*, published in 1974, which is a masterpiece, but which is also a meditation on African-American culture from the standpoint of a Baha'i who is in "exile." Thus, *Riverlisp* is not set in Africville but in "Ambrose City," which resembles more fully an American city—or the black "ghetto" in a big city—than it mirrors either Halifax or Africville.

Riverlisp is subtitled *Black Memories*, and that phrase marks the novel's autobiographical and biographical purpose. The fiction seems a palimpsest of Ward's memories of his Kansas City, Missouri, childhood,[67] or, rather, a conjoining of his recollected experiences with his transcription and transformation of the memories and voices of Africville "displaced persons."

Ward's novel begins with commentary from Ambrose City—ex-Riverlisp—residents. Their insights seem to echo the experiences of Africville relocatees. Ward's Marcy, one reads, "[would] break down and cry cause Riverlisp, it were home. The onliest home she done left, it be four times now, and come'd back to." This description— utilizing Ward's characteristic agrammatical emphasis on orality, or the *sound* of Black English—also echoes the oft-stated yearning for home that is a staple trope of Africville relocatees. Likewise, when Ward allows another character, Mr. Jim Miles, to map the contours of Riverlisp, his report again chases ex-Africville residents' descriptions of their lost home: "Nobody claim th woods and swamp hind em. I means, we all just goes there and uses em to hunt rabbit, take care of our wants, or whatever. We aint on welfare here." (Here I will ask the reader to appreciate that Ward's prose is Joycean in its calibre and chivalric in its efforts to capture the nuances, accents, and colourful intonations of African-American, and African-Canadian, speech.) Replace "hunt rabbit" with "catch fish" and one has a factual description of Africville life.

Moreover, in a documentary film about the Africville Relocation, a former resident, Daisy Carvery, angrily addresses a meeting, defending the bulldozed community as one where no one had to accept welfare.[68] The parallels between Africville and Riverlisp are even clearer when Jim Miles recalls, "Last year come'd and th city, Ambrose City, started surveying and then we come'd like th Indians dispose...something. Dispossess'd? Yer, that's right." The signal difference between Riverlisp and Africville is that, in the fictitious instance, Jim Miles is "thankful them government hadnt tore the church down." Nevertheless, both the imaginary community, Riverlisp, and the actual place, Africville, share problems regarding sewage treatment and other services that fictitious Ambrose City and the real Halifax are supremely arrogant in refusing: "The stream did come'd river as it simi-circled the town and on to empty. It run'd thru many backyards and was fed into by great drainage pipes that jutted out of the earth and seemed to spew out a dark yellowish brown vomit." In short, like Africville, Riverlisp is a quasi-segregated rural extension of its host city: "Our church is standing in the beautiful grove at the farthus end of that [dirt] road. And many others lives out near the hills and swamp."

Despite the correspondences between Halifax/Ambrose City and Africville/Riverlisp, Ward is not interested in reiterating the travails of Africville, not even as fiction. Instead, Ward renders a Northern version of a black community of the American South or Midwest so that he can test theological ideas related to his Baha'i faith. So, yes, Ambrose City is oppressive toward the people of Riverlisp; however, these Protestant Christians themselves oppress persons of other faiths, such as Judaism, which the tale of Micah Koch makes clear in terrible tragicomedy. A Bible salesman who flogs his wares by asserting that "FUTURE DISCOVERIES" of divine revelations will be made available for those who buy subscriptions to receive "the bibles of the different religions of the New Testament," Micah falls in love with the awesomely black and beautiful Purella Munificance. The two are soon lovers, for they "see'd the Lord in each other's face and being." Yet other Riverlisp residents react to the interracial relationship with ad hominem gossip: "Some out of fear some were jealous and others just vicious." This teasing divides and devastates the lovers: Purella becomes an emotional wreck, weeping in the street, while Micah just seems to drift and lose weight. In the end, desperate for reconnection with Purella and the black community, Micah is urged to convert to the community's only superficially tolerant Christianity. Although the Baha'i message that "all th Messengers [religious prophets] is one spirit and loves us cause we is one" is intoned, this spiritual liberalism—a version of integration—is delivered with the requirement that Micah abandon Judaism for Christianity. However, even with such a sacrifice, he will not be reunited with Purella, just better positioned to vend more bibles. The immediate soulful union of Purella and Micah is dissolved via sexual or racial jealousy.

There are also violent incidents in fictitious Riverlisp that are exotic to the historical Africville. The fatal shooting of "Miss Jessup's Boy" for allegedly—and stereotypically—trying to steal a chicken ("He's a nigger, ain't he?") is a tale more reminiscent of casual Southern atrocity than of Northern disregard. Furthermore, the passage seems to allude to a prose sketch—namely "Blood-Burning Moon"—in Jean Toomer's 1923 African-American classic, Cane, than it is a recitation of chronicled Bluenoser, racialized social violence. Ward's words, "Dust obscured everything—made the sun—dirty," answer Toomer's refrain, "Red nigger moon. Sinner! / Blood-burning moon. Sinner!" But Ward's surest echo of Toomer is the racial harm that he depicts, a shooting death that is rendered obliquely, less viscerally, than is the case for the lynching that Toomer pictures.

Similarly, Ward's poem "Claireesa," treating a woman "dancin leapin in th / streets like a wild / somethin," seems to mirror Toomer's portrait of "Karintha" in Cane: "Karintha, at twelve, was a wild flash"; "her sudden darting past you was a bit of vivid color, like a black bird that flashes in light." Like Toomer's Karintha, Ward's Claireesa is a kind of daemon—or Jimi Hendrix–style "Voodoo Chile": bewitching, seductive, and perilous to love.

Evidently, Ward uses *Riverlisp* to canvass significant African-American intertexts. His desire to recollect African-American voices and cadences inspires Ward more than any desire to document Africville. His novel also serves Ward as a pulpit from which he can preach, or "rap," about his Baha'i beliefs, a faith that most assuredly has more African-American adherents than it does Africadian[69] disciples. In the novel, then, a character states, "My friend, Dolphus, done tol me of your meetings and talks on love and oneness of human beings and of Baha'u'llah," and explicit Baha'i belief is also voiced: "All peoples mix with the spirit—that's oneness."

Beyond the opening pages of *Riverlisp*, Africville vanishes as Ward shifts his attentions to ringing changes upon African-American intertexts (and accents) or testifies to the spiritual transfiguration catalyzed by the Baha'i faith. While the City of Halifax bulldozed Africville into rubble and rubbish and recollection, Ward relocates it into religion and literature. Nevertheless, when Ward introduces us to the Negro enclave of Ambrose City, and relates the memories of Marcy and Jim Miles, he is producing, simultaneously, one of the first literary survivals—or revivals—of Africville, if filtered through the exotic sensibility of an African-American expatriate. Ward's later novels—*Nobody Called Me Mine* (1977) and *A Room Full of Balloons* (1981)—are even more superficially connected to Africville, despite the dust-jacket assertion of the last novel that claims that Ward has given us "the songs, stories, jokes, and other poems of the citizens of Africville." Instead, Ward's childhood home of Kansas City, Missouri, is his principal focus. Although his fiction is actually distant from Africville, Ward has published poetry that righteously opposes the Relocation. These poems appear in his 1983 collection, *The Curing Berry*.

It was not until 2006 that Africville received full-fledged novel treatment; in both instances, the authors happen to be white. *Last Days in Africville*, by Nova Scotian children's book author Dorothy Perkyns, is aimed at a juvenile readership. Stephen Kimber's *Reparations* is, however, an adult-oriented novel by a professor of journalism at the University of King's College, in Halifax.

In his first novel, Kimber explores the political corruption and civic racism of 1960s to 1970s Halifax and Nova Scotia via the libel-proof safeguard of a *roman à clef*, naming names, as it were, by coining fictitious ones. Yet his veil of fiction is thin enough for local readers to identify the probable model for at least one of its protagonists, namely Uhuru Melesse—né Raymond Carter—a black lawyer who defends a black bureaucrat[70] who has been surreptitiously funnelling government moneys to Africville "exiles," thus affording them unofficial "reparations" for the Relocation. *Uhuru* is Swahili for *freedom*, and *Melesse*[71] could accord with *malice*; thus, the black lawyer represents both freedom and enmity. These sensibilities mirror those of Africville's ex-citizens, but the character of the black lawyer summons up the real-life, Halifax-based but internationally noted activist and attorney Burnley "Rocky" Jones (1941–2013), who was a significant leftist radical voice for Africadians *et al.*

Kimber's plot depends on the Africville-raised Uhuru contending with a seemingly white judge, the significantly named Ward Justice, who was a childhood friend. Both of these characters embody and recall the events of the 1960s and 1970s and what Kimber has termed Nova Scotia's "attitude of casual corruption," the perquisite of the well-connected well-to-do. In his review in the *Chronicle Herald*, Robert Martin describes Kimber's Halifax as featuring the "boil" of racism and "the cancer of corruption":

> Politicians use a local brothel as a social club and order police cars as unpaid taxis when they're too drunk to drive. Lawyers who run the back rooms of politics use their offices as storehouses for cases of vote-buying booze and solve problems with envelopes—sometimes even suitcases—full of cash. The media cut deals to kill stories. The cops are thugs.

For Martin, *Reparations* presents the "citizens of the black ghetto"—Africville—as having been "losers in a race war as white politicians…razed their community in the 1960s." He's not wrong. Although the Relocation program utilized the Judeo-Christian rhetoric of integration and a liberal-welfare model of state-intervention to ameliorate substandard housing, illiteracy, unemployment, and other social blights, the unfolding process was likely hostage to "sleazy politics." Equally problematic was, says Nelson, a "paternalistic approach...characterized by broken promises, bureaucratic disorganization, and lack of long-term planning."[72]

By authoring the novel as he has, pitting flawed black lawyer against "fake" white judge and "Freedom" versus "Justice," Kimber emphasizes a legal trope and courthouse drama, evaporating the destructive violence of the bulldozers into the political chicanery of a forty-year-gone past. There are lurid twists: not only is Justice revealed to be partially "black," he is also guilty of a hushed-up vehicular homicide, in which he, as a white driver, "flattened" a black kid's chest "like a pancake"; worse, the victim is the toddler son of his black mistress, Rosa, who has also been Melesse's lover. Moreover, the little boy had been Melesse's child. This novel also seems to relish the smells of piss and puke, the struggles over control of the wealth of the East Coast fisheries, as well as the cozy deals among the public, interlocking networks of lawyers, journalists, politicians, and entrepreneurs, and the *private* arrangements that they pursue with bootleggers, bordellos, and cops. Nevertheless, the novel's very title—*Reparations*—announces its embeddedness in the courtliness of law as opposed to the raw fact of white-manned and white-commanded bulldozers demolishing the dwellings of a century-and-more-old Africadian settlement.

If, as Nelson asserts, the Africville forced relocation fulfilled "a program of white displacement of black people" and was "the logical continuation of race domination," Kimber's decision to deploy lawyers as his adversaries has the effect of curtailing and containing the demolition of Africville: lawyers debate the causes of, and responsibility for, a death, but the corpse remains a corpse. This point is literally true, in the case of Melesse's son, but it is also true in the dispatch of Africville itself—despite a jury's exoneration of the "reparations"-paying civil-servant "fraud" Howe.

If Ward's *Riverlisp* revisits classic African-American texts, so does Kimber's *Reparations* echo white-liberal "redemptive" anti-racist novels. Alan Paton's 1948 *Cry, the Beloved Country*, an anti-apartheid fiction, reifies the Negrophobic violence of South Africa into a Judeo-Christian discourse of love and charity and an Abe Lincoln notion of justice as malice-toward-none.[73] In Kimber's climax, Justice confesses that he killed Melesse's son, and Melesse looks at him, at first with rage but then with the realization that Justice is now only "a broken old man sitting on a park bench," and then decides that "it was too late for hate. Too late for guilt, too." This moment recalls the meetings between Paton's white-liberal hero, James Jarvis, and Reverend Stephen Kumalo, the "Native" African preacher whose son has slain Jarvis's son. (Here, the parallels between Kimber's narrative and that of Paton are screamingly obvious; one might also consider Kimber's use of "Uhuru" as his hero's "African" moniker to represent a nod to Paton's work.) Ngwarsungu Chiwengo tells us that, by novel's end, "It is love and spiritual growth that empowers Jarvis to transcend his anger and to create a profound relationship with Kumalo and to eventually transform his community."

If Kimber reverses Paton (a black man forgives a white man for murdering his son), his novel also replays the courtroom spectacle of Harper Lee's 1960 *To Kill a Mockingbird*. In Kimber's case, the attorney hero is black, but also more of an opportunistic, photogenic, careerist, and breast-obsessed anti-hero than he is role-model material. Nevertheless, the *past* is the place of racism, even if exacerbated by the boozed-up, slush-funded, hush-hush wheeling-dealing of the plush and cash-flush local white plutocracy. Just as Ward compasses Africville to reconsider his Kansas City past, so does *Reparations* relocate Africville as a "Paton"-place or "Lee"-way[74] of freedom once lost and justice once denied. It is also as a site of would-be Christian kindness bedevilled by lust for (black) women and greed for profit and position. Racism itself—barring the noxious examples of a few cops—is less a problem than are poverty, alcoholism, lying, adultery, and other less sexy but more lucrative forms of, well, "cheating." In any event, by elevating the execrable once-upon-a-time action of bulldozers into a decorous present-day discourse of academic legalese, *Reparations* executes a de facto exoneration of "the way things were" because that's "just how it was." The "tragedy" of Africville is terrible, but there is always a book to be written and money to be made while the networks of corruption that colluded in its desecration remain, in reality, unperturbed.

Another novel to treat Africville is *Big Town: A Novel of Africville*, published in 2011 by Stephens Gerard Malone, also a white Nova Scotian but one with a predilection for Gothic tones and melodramatic plots. *Big Town*, Malone's fourth novel, too easily turns black and white into a harlequin, or minstrel, cast. Indeed, his novel seems to want to import William Faulkner to Nova Scotia, to give us local-colour yokels who are off-colour yahoos, nincompoops, and ne'er-do-wells. Malone's narrative focuses on the efforts of a cognitively challenged white youth, Early Okander, to befriend an Africville schoolboy, Toby Daye, and a white Catholic schoolgirl, Chub, while enduring the atrocious depravity of Early's papa, D Jay (whose moniker really ought to belong to a rapper), and the greasy social-climbing of Chub's parents.

These three amigos, so to speak, might remind one of *The Mod Squad*, a US television detective drama that ran from 1968 to 1973. The show featured a black, a blonde, and a Bohemian, all "hippies" turned undercover cops. However, Malone's trio—a black, a blonde, and a bumpkin—are seriously dysfunctional. Early (whose surname suggests the "Okie" of the Great Depression) is raped by every adult white male or black female who relishes the crime; Toby loathes his black skin so much that he attempts—fatally—to bleach himself white; Chub's dad philanders to forget his dying wife, while his daughter is confused about her own gender identity. Unlike Early and Toby, Chub has access to cash. Yet, surprisingly, just like penniless, trailer-trash Early, Chub lives next door to Africville, which some characters scruple to malign as a "slum." Given the trials the protagonists undergo, it is understandable that the novel must end dismally, with Toby dead, Africville dying, Chub gone, and Early assaulted—perhaps fatally.

Malone's strength is his attention to local lingo. (*Cocksucker* is to Halifax what *motherfucker* is to Harlem.) However, Malone's interest in rewriting other texts (for instance,

Mazo de la Roche's *Centenary of Jalna*) renders Africville a palimpsest of John Steinbeck's fugitive Okie camps or, as in Kimber, a more liberal version of *To Kill a Mockingbird*'s Macomb, Alabama. Moreover, Malone's tomboy, Chub, seems modelled on Lee's tomboy, Scout. *Big Town* might even be described as William Faulkner plus fellatio. Its cast of sluts, rednecks, blackguards, oafs, and addled Negroes renders Africville a kind of *Tobacco Road* by the sea. (I reference Erskine Caldwell's 1932 novel.)

Malone sets his novel in the early-to-mid-1960s, just as the demolition of Africville is commencing. So, even as Africville houses vanish, one by one, Malone studies the friendship of the misfits and the later sundering of their bonds. Thus, by the end of *Big Town*, one knows little about Africville, but we are assured of the *possibility* of racial fraternity, just as we note that some folks—white and black—are deviant to the point of being outright evil.

The most recent example of the Africville novel is Jeffrey Colvin's debut, *Africville*, published in 2020. Colvin happens to be, like Ward, African American, and, also like Ward, he presents us with an Africville (which his US publisher retitled "Africaville") that is more fanciful than fact-based, so that the book's title is fairly superficial—or superfluous. Here, Africville is known as Woods Bluff, and influential community members are Jamaican (two facets of Colvin's imagining that do not align with the historical hamlet at all). Strategically, Colvin warns us—but not until his afterword— that he has fictionalized "many of the characters, place names, and incidents from the village of Africville." His story, he tells us, serves as a mere "companion" to the plethora of more or less realistic narratives.

So what is Colvin's *Africville*—in terms of place, people, and plot? Where does he deign to visit? Well, this place is—like the historic Africville—a seaside district of the city of Halifax, though considered a warren apart, so that residents pay taxes but never receive public utilities, neither water nor sewer. The citizens should feel beleaguered, and they do.

As Colvin's tale opens, the Halifax Explosion of December 6, 1917, has just occurred, and Woods Bluff babes are stricken by a malady that's curable by neither spell nor medicine. Exceptionally, however, the girl who will become the progenitrix of our saga, Kath Ella Sebolt, survives the killing fever thanks to the black magic of folk-crafted dolls and, some fifteen years on, becomes the love interest of Omar Platt.

Early in the novel, we meet characters who live in Woods Bluff—not yet Africville (in Colvin's conception)—and who possess surnames utterly alien to the historical hamlet, which may have more to do with signalling a creative writing MFA's appreciation for W. G. Sebald (or so I speculate). In any event, consistent with the determined pattern, Kath Ella's best friend, Kiendra Penncampbell, also bears a surname that likely never graced an Africville tombstone.

Yet tombstones rather than chapter divisions should mark this novel. As Kath Ella quits herself of her virginity and only later of her naïveté, best friend Kiendra dies. Next, soon after sweating all over a delighted Kath Ella, Omar dies. Avoiding a troublesome future as an unwed mother, Kath

Ella removes to Montreal, marries a Québécois, Timothee Peletier (a deliberately errant spelling for "Pelletier"), and gives birth to Omar's son, Etienne.

Fast-forward a decade or so, and Etienne is a schoolboy at a Quebec boarding school, when he learns that his mother, one Kath Ella, has died. Suddenly a young man, Etienne removes to Alabama and finds that he passes nattily for white. Married, with his own son, he wishes to reach out to Timothee's parents, but he arrives back in Canada only after his grandmother Claire has died, "several hours earlier." With his father already dead some years before, Etienne himself soon expires, in 1984. His son, Warner, now takes centre stage, so that the last third of the novel narrates his search for roots and belonging, a quest that brings him to Canada and to Africville—or, rather, its spectral afterlife: the photo albums and recollections of the Relocation survivors, now pepper-shakered across the city.

It's his great-aunt Luela who tells Warner of his "Almost Gone"—deceased relatives who live on in memory until the deaths of the last people who knew them well. Mainly interested in his father and patrilineal grandmother and grandfather, Warner looks up the 1968 news stories detailing the demolition. In this sidereal account, Africville is itself one of the "Almost Gone," but survivors recall and journalists report:

By the end of the following week, however, three houses had been abandoned in New Jamaica. The following Tuesday Luela was awakened at three in the morning by a rumble so loud she thought a battalion of military tanks was invading the bluff. The next morning, eight bulldozers sat in the yard of one of the abandoned houses. Four had huge hydraulic arms and gaping metal jaws that seemed capable of chewing up anything in their way.

It may seem churlish to point out that there was no such neighbourhood as "New Jamaica" in the real Africville; however, it is notable that Colvin's strongest writing in the novel is his recapitulation of the hamlet's razing:

> The evening Luela returned home to find her house desecrated, she was unable to leave the porch for several minutes....She entered the house hearing noises—the memory of her father George whistling in the back room, of Shirley washing Kath's hair on the back porch. Having let go of her desire to have a child, Luela felt this house—the Sebolt home—was her legacy.

But, despite her efforts—and those of other Woods Bluff people—the homes are knocked down, one by one, the church splintered to smithereens, the Sebolt cemetery itself slated for removal. Warner excavates a history of alienation and dispossession. But not to worry.

In the wake of Lawrence Hill's 2007 novel, *The Book of Negroes*, and David Bradley's *The Chaneysville Incident*, from 1981, Colvin is likely correct to close his gift-to-morticians novel (Warner's baby dies as we reach the conclusion, and a new matriarch, Zera, is seen studying a casket for herself) with a "happy" ending that sees nothing vital change. Some family remains will get buried in the precincts of a vanished community, with or without official permission. This conclusion seems to enact an unsatisfying blend of Toni Morrison's *Song of Solomon*, from 1977, and George Boyd's 1999 Africville play, *Consecrated Ground*.

Lookit! Jeffrey Colvin can write. And he will dazzle future reviewers, I'm sure. But he might have taken a page from one of his own characters and sounded his relationship with himself and his own roots before presuming blithely that he could do so for a recherché but imaginary Africville and its residents, who are almost always discards—cast-offs—before they even have a chance to be blueprints.

[*Cultural Challenges of Migration in Canada / Les défis de la migration au Canada*, edited by Klaus-Dieter Ertler and Patrick Imbert. Peter Lang, 2013; *Literary Review of Canada*. 28.1 (January-February 2020)]

∼

Only later do the eulogists, the epic poets, and the tragedians arrive to remember the dismembered and recollect the *disjecta membra*, to retrieve the archive of the discarded: Africville after Africville after Africville. Even so, the romanciers and balladeers, drafting their nostalgic encomia, are inking words on snow, evanescent and ephemeral, for they are merely capturing phantoms and peopling ghost towns. Yet never will Canada yield ground to the memoirists and the historians of race; no, not unless every Canadian place name is exchanged for a Dixie one. For the Canadian imagination is still reverentially, resolutely imperial (if at a social-class remove from the monarch—a distance as vast, really, as that between the throne and a canoe), so that London is reconfigured as Ottawa, Paris is Manhattanized as Montreal, and the moors reappear as tundra. So what we countenance is the disaster of our tacit divorce from Europe, our stranding amid an American continent of bellicose bons vivants, where law and order is lynch mobs and gum-chewing gun-toters. We read disaster as our apocalyptic fate at being an impotent appendage of empires, so that Halifax can vanish under a wartime mushroom cloud—just like Hiroshima. This idea motivates the next essay.

∾

Halifax, Hiroshima, and the
Romance of Disaster

IN 1967, JUST BEFORE Christmas, all anticipation of gifts and
sweets was driven from my seven-year-old mind by public
memorials of a ferocious explosion that had laid waste my
pseudo-natal city a half-century before, on December 6,
1917. When I viewed photographs of the devastation, witnessed commentaries on radio and television, and studied
commemorative newspapers of this local disaster, I was
frightened out of my wits. I could not sleep easily anymore,
for I worried that, were a new blast to occur, the glass in my
bedroom window would rend me in my bed. But I was also
thrilled: Halifax was *special* in a wickedly eccentric fashion.
It had experienced a world-class disaster, a human-made
explosion second only to the atomic obscenity of those
in Hiroshima and Nagasaki, which I now heard about for
the first time, thanks to the comparisons with the Halifax
Explosion, occasioned by the collision of the Norwegian
vessel *Imo* and the French munitions ship *Mont Blanc* in
Halifax Harbour.

Two months later, my mother took me, now age
eight, to the brand new Halifax North End Memorial

Library, whose name kept alive the horror of that Great War morning, when scenes more typical of the Somme and Ypres were visited upon my city. Thanks to my very first library card, I began to haunt the Memorial Library, and I was drawn, again and again, to a display case that housed relics of the blast. One of these items was a book whose title I never forgot: *A Romance of the Halifax Disaster* (1918), authored by Frank McKelvey Bell. Later that same year, 1968, I saw a documentary on the atomic bombing of Hiroshima that employed, incongruously, the beautiful if schmaltzy melody of "L'amour est bleu" (Love Is Blue), composed by André Popp with lyrics by Pierre Cour and popularized by Paul Mauriat as a 1967 smash-hit instrumental. (Every time I hear that diabolically dulcet tune, I remember Hiroshima's destruction.)

Between the ages of fourteen and fifteen, for a year-long middle school science project, I designed my own low-yield atomic bomb, complete with scale drawings, to be detonated, naturally, in Halifax. Though my precocious, righteously apocalyptic Christianity and private sci-fi syllabus informed my project, I also undertook it because I suspected that Haligonians are comfortable with catastrophe. In my science writing, I fantasized that, in a Third World War nuclear exchange, Halifax would be a target for either Soviet missiles or a spy's dirty bomb. (I even invented a term for the special blast effects of nuclear weapons: *hurriquake*, a fusion of *hurricane* and *earthquake*.) My project demanded that I superimpose upon Halifax's 1917 ruins the 1945 dust of Hiroshima, that I contemplate the romances of the Haligonian disaster in tandem with those of Hiroshima's holocaust. Thus, I learned that disaster is catastrophic and catalytic, earth-shattering and erotic. But I also sensed that it is such emotion-impacted events that shape a writer, that cause their consciousness and philosophy to gell—or shift. That is the conceit of this essay, that we may productively contrast Bell and John Hersey and Hugh MacLennan, for disaster appeals to romance, a love story that palliates the horror of catastrophe while pornographically exploiting its carnage.

While this essay bears affinities with literary trauma theory, it is not affianced to such. It is more interested in capital-R Romance, with how disaster births the grand digressions (or distractions) of new couplings, new affairs, that represent both reconstitutions of selves and societies as well as the dispatch of what used to be. If Northrop Frye is right that "the apocalypse is the way the world looks after the ego has disappeared," so does disaster reveal Eden's desolation, fearsome to behold, while also suggesting, implicitly, that surviving Adams and Eves start afresh— this time with piety. Always, before the new heaven and the new earth can be born, Babylon must crumble and Sodom and Gomorrah be incinerated. Thus, while trauma may silence some (the "traumatized"), it may excite, inspire, and invigorate others, particularly artists and intellectuals. I hold with the agonizingly insightful critic John Fraser that "violence"—and disaster means damage and hurt—"is usually the cutting edge of ideas and ideologies." In his sanguinely brilliant *Violence in the Arts*, published in 1974, Fraser posits intellectual engagement as an antidote to trauma, accidie, or paralysis:

What counts above all is the clarity, integrity, and validity of one's thought, the completeness of one's commitment to one's own ideas, and a clear-sighted understanding of the ways in which, in the short or the long run, those ideas connect with the physical world, the world in which violences occur. And to the extent that thinking, especially the thinking of those in positions of power, ceases to have those virtues, to that extent we are increasingly going to have the kinds of violence that fail to achieve their ends or that achieve ignoble ones.

To sum up, Fraser advises, "In general, violence or the possibility of violence is a great sharpener of judgment." Bearing Fraser's precepts in mind, it may be pertinent to consider disaster as a progenitor of innovation rather than as a dead zone of nostalgia, a rut of repetition, or an abyss of memory. Indeed, it was the horror of Crimea that gave us modern nursing in the models of Mary Seacole and Florence Nightingale; it was the killing fields of the Great War that spurred on modernism; and it was the bombing of Hiroshima and Nagasaki, plus the original and sustained threat of cosmocide—the nuclear annihilation of all life on earth—that gave rise to postmodernism.

In *Bomb Culture*, his classic 1968 work on the inception of our era, Jeff Nuttall distinguishes between the victory over Hitler and the victory over militarist Japan: "The world of the European Victory was a brown, smelly, fallible,…an old-fashioned, earthy, stable place,…where good was good and bad was bad." In contrast, "the world of the Japanese victory was a world in which an evil had been precipitated whose scope was immeasurable." Nuttall continues: "The first victory was a victory confirming our merits and security. The second victory destroyed them irrevocably." For him, the A-bomb detonations that urged on the surrender of the Japanese Empire erased black-and-white morality and made the future "a void." The only coherent reply to this constant looming aporia is to partake in "a game of chance, some absurd pattern of behavior."

Yet that's old news: war always alters combatants—materially and philosophically. Certainly, neither Ezra Pound's "Hugh Selwyn Mauberley" nor T. S. Eliot's "The Waste Land" could have served to modernize English verse were it not for the truth that Tennyson cannot contemplate the mass carnage of total war. J. M. Cohen describes Great War soldier-poets Robert Graves and Wilfred Owen as Apocalyptics, and the conflict they critique as a Spenglerian doom that had befallen Western culture.

Though we may justly deem the Halifax Explosion a minor event[75] in contrast to the mass slaughter of French and Belgian battlefields, for the writers who attempted to chronicle its impact, it was an entrée into *history*, and not merely as chronicle but as prophecy. Walter Benn Michaels points out that "a history that is learned can be learned by anyone (and can belong to anyone who learns it); a history that is remembered can only be remembered by those who first experienced it and it must belong to them." It is the claim to a "recollected" history that permits the presentation of coherent identity—no matter how mythical its constitution.

So what sort of identities do the blast narratives of Halifax and Hiroshima articulate, and what sort of history do they memorialize or consecrate? The latter question merits address, for trauma can easily be a staple of tourism, here in Atlantic Canada, where disasters have been plentiful, from the Acadian Deportation in 1755 to the extinction of the Beothuk of Newfoundland, from the sinking of the *Titanic* on April 15, 1912, to the crash of Swissair Flight 111 off the coast of Nova Scotia on September 2, 1998. Tourism promoters have erected a visitors' centre that serves to "interpret" the Acadian exile, trumpeted the coastal graves of *Titanic* victims, installed a memorial at the Swissair crash site—near the already naturally fatal, though picturesque, Peggy's Cove—and even memorialized Halifax's bulldozed Africadian village of Africville as a seaside park.[76] Happily, but also problematically, our homegrown treatments of the Halifax Explosion, while penned to please a market, are also critical comments on our history as well as would-be prophecies of future endeavours, i.e., they constitute de facto policy options.

Lieutenant-Colonel Frank McKelvey Bell authored *A Romance of the Halifax Disaster* in 1918 and saw it published while immediate relief of the homeless and wounded was still being effected. So his narrative is partly situated in a hospital, where nurses, doctors, soldiers, do-gooders, and the stricken interact. In this setting, patients heal or die; gallant youths, having taken to arms, been wounded, and are now convalescing, fall chivalrously into ladies' arms. Bell's emphasis is cold-blooded sentiment: there's the melodrama of broken hearts plus the tragedy of a dead child; then there's the springing up of love, as tends to perennially occur, just as the worst realities of the explosion and the attendant winter are diminishing. In brief, one may safely jettison much of the romance as claptrap and cliché, while rare photographs of the battered North End display surreal ruins that repel any authorial description.

Bell's squib is most important for what its "explosive" subject allows him to say. His previous book, *The First Canadians in France: The Chronicle of a Military Hospital in the War Zone*, published in 1917, was itself a novelization of "the heroism and self-sacrifice of the non-commissioned officers and men of the Army Medical Corps—the boys who, in the dull monotony of hospital life, denied the exhilaration and stimulus of the firing line, are, alas, too often forgotten." Admitting that "the pill of fact herein is but thinly coated with the sugar of fiction," McKelvey prays the reader will extract "a picture, however indefinite, of military hospital life in France." Having already determined the Canadian field hospital overseas situates a kind of domestic bravery amid war's horrors, McKelvey is well-positioned, in the subsequent novel, to think through the implications of the Halifax Explosion from the precincts of a damaged, but still operative, garrison hospital.

Bell begins with romance. In midsummer 1914, upon the moonlit "rippling waters of the St. Lawrence," Vera Warrington, age nineteen, "leaned back upon the pile of cushions," recumbent in a canoe, and looked up at her companion, Tom Welsford, age twenty-two. At this moment, she appears a harem lady typical of Omar Khayyam–style Orientalism: "Her golden-brown hair, lit up by the moonbeams, framed her fair face in an ethereal halo." But appearances are deceiving. When Tom proposes marriage, Vera reacts in a manner more befitting the *au courant* ideal of the New Woman (or even the incipient flapper) than that of the swooning Victorian maiden: "I care for you more than for any other man in the whole, wide world, but I honestly cannot say whether I love you." Though Tom tries to press his suit, Vera "checks" him with her hand: she has already refused his request to forbid any other man's proposal until his return from the war: "I have read of such tragedies in life where men and women were chained by a promise which never was fulfilled."

This statement alerts us that romantic tragedy may inflict as much personal pain as any real-world disaster. The narrator instructs us, "Tom hadn't yet learned that girls, with all their seeming frivolity and light-heartedness, are really years older in the wisdom of love than men of the same age." With this passage, Bell impresses upon the reader his view that women are wiser than most men know. Later, with Tom apparently still afar, Vera is again presented in a half-erotic but also half-assertive fashion: she sits "in the drawing-room of her mother's home"; "a stray rebellious curl" rests upon one cheek; "the moist, red lips, clear cut, full and sensuous [are] slightly parted, displaying to view teeth small and of pearly whiteness"; her chest rises and falls "quickly, as if vainly smothering some pent-up emotion."

Her problem is that her mother, who, having strayed here from a Jane Austen novel, has arranged a marriage, to transpire the next day, on December 6, 1917, so as to remedy the family's "fallen fortunes." Vera is to wed William Lawson, "the son of a wealthy lumber merchant, himself reasonably affluent." Shortly, the narrator describes Mrs. Warrington's shock at her daughter's vociferous reluctance to accept the decent, dull bourgeois. The foreshadowing is so blackly inked as to seem black comedy: "Had the house suddenly collapsed she could not have looked more horrified." Dissatisfied with this tongue-in-cheek nod to the looming explosion, the narrator also advises, "Ah idle dreams! How often fate tumbles our airy castles about our ears and leaves us standing in the ruins." Still, in protest of her nigh nuptials, the ever more feminist Vera hoists "an imaginary wine glass to her lips," declares, "Here's to wedded me—the apotheosis of fools," drains it "mockingly," then throws "the visionary goblet into the [fireplace] grate" and exits the room.

One is tempted to read George Bernard Shaw's bor-dello madame Mrs. Warren into Bell's Mrs. Warrington, who, like the former, is only too aware that destitution awaits the woman who marries poorly—that is to say, who takes a lower-class husband or who lets drudgery waste her looks or who foregoes lucrative pleasure: "Poverty is a cruel master." Luckily for Vera, at the exact moment that she bids her newfound love for Tom Welsford good-bye, the explosion blasts the wedding plans to smithereens.

The narrator underlines this cheery happenstance: "Amid all the direful evidences of the catastrophe there was to Vera one bright spot—her wedding would be postponed." Better yet, as she volunteers to assist the wounded, Vera finds herself at the bedside of "a man whose white face and shallow breathing told all too surely that the end was near": this gent turns out to be the mortally stricken fiancé, William, now "limp"[77] and soon dead. As a nurse in this scene, Vera recalls the image of Longfellow's exiled Acadienne heroine, Evangeline, who, acting as a Sister of Mercy in plague-stricken Philadelphia, comes upon her long-separated betrothed, Gabriel Lajeunesse, fevered and dying: "Vainly he strove to rise; and Evangeline, kneeling beside him, / Kissed his dying lips, and laid his head on her bosom." That William dies without such a kiss from Vera is the difference between Victorianism and modernism. Arguably, in crafting Vera, Bell presents, quite self-consciously, a heroine who blends the virginity and virtue of Evangeline with the outspoken practicality of Mrs. Warren's own conscientious, if entrepreneurial, daughter, Vivie.[78]

The subtle feminism of a Great War Canadian officer is made explicit—didactic—in several paragraphs headed by the declaration that "a few rays of sunshine stream through the thunder clouds of [war's] disaster." Thanks to "this great war," "fixed traditions" are now "smashed," thereby "revealing truths which had long lain hidden under the cobwebs of ignorance":

> For tens of centuries man had pictured woman as a lovely, but inferior being whose glory was merely the reflection of his own superior light....
>
> And then came the war, and as she rose to her full height..., the new thought was forced upon him that part of his belief was wrong. The egotistic and selfish God which he had worshipped tottered and fell crashing to pieces at his feet....
>
> In the brighter light of a steadfast faith she towered above him, a new idol, a new ideal, the

woman who could work as well as play, who could fight as well as love, who could be silent under sorrow and cheerful in the face of tragedy....

Standing shoulder to shoulder with him, he was forced to concede her rights and as the scarred and battered world rolls onward a greater sympathy, a closer understanding and a deeper respect will bind man and woman together until the end of time.

Bell is clear: the disaster of war has served to emancipate women (somewhat), giving them the right to vote in Canada; similarly, the explosion has freed Vera from incipient imprisonment in a loveless marriage. Not only that, her duties as a nurse reunite her with a battlefront-injured, now convalescent Tom, who, upon first sight—after their three-and-a-half years apart—holds her hands and kisses her on the lips "out of keeping with all the conventions." Intriguingly, while the narrative begins with Vera supine, on pillows, in a canoe, now it is Tom who must half-raise himself from his hospital bed pillow to effect the unselfconscious—or *modern*—kiss that so befits Vera, the very model of the New Woman (who is Lucy Maud Montgomery in one incarnation and Emma Goldman in another). Tom now declares, "That [kiss] was worth the whole disaster," an utterance affirming that the war has revealed the actual equality of women while the explosion has removed a bourgeois obstacle to his union with Vera, a match that she agrees to readily, without seeking maternal approval. Witnessing the reconstituted lovers, a "little nurse" observes that their story is "quite a little romance—a Romance of the Disaster." Bell could not be more explicit: two catastrophes—war abroad, the Halifax Explosion at home—prove the folly of previous sexism and repression of women. Now, heterosexual romance may flourish on a *modern* basis of mutual respect.

It should be surprising to us that Lieutenant-Colonel Bell advances such advanced views in 1918, even if, all too casually, he makes his arguments over the charred and eyeless and broken corpses of North End Halifax and the cadavers in front-line posts. One may speculate, though, that Bell, who has previously trumpeted the "heroism and self-sacrifice" of male medics in France, and who now praises the Great War–borne woman as "heroic and fearless," views (female) nurses and (male) soldiers as equals. It is for this reason that he sets the action of his novel in a veritable Halifax hospital and writes glowingly of "The Old Colony," a United States ship transformed into "a marvellous floating hospital." We also read, "Soon the Khaki of the United States surgeons appeared upon the streets and in the hospitals. American nurses by the hundred worked ceaselessly with their Canadian cousins." Here again military doctors and nurses, male and female, Yankee and Canuck, are unified and equalized by repair of the "collateral damage" of the Great War and its local explosion. Ultimately, too, a soldier and a nurse agree to wed, nixing the arranged match of a merchant and a more-or-less maternally prostituted "lady."

Although Bell is progressive on gender and, arguably, on class (recognizing an equality between the "killing" and "caring" professions), he parrots standard ethnic prejudices. In the initial wake of the explosion, Tom explains, "Probably the Germans have blown up the magazines at the fort"; later, a surgeon blames the blast on "those cursed Germans.... Only hell and Germany could stand for this!" While such oaths and imprecations are apt propaganda, far more interesting is the narrative's initial explanation for the Great War and why it matters to Canada and, inordinately, to Tom. He informs an incredulous Vera, "Germany wants Canada." To overcome her doubt, he "lectures" (as she says), "Unlike Britain, Germany is a young nation—it is only in recent years, too late, that she has realized the necessity for colonization."

In other words, unlike other Western European–based empires and the United States, Germany must still expand itself through imperialism. Helpfully, if only implicitly, Tom points out that the US Monroe Doctrine, promulgated in 1823, which forbids further European colonization of the Americas on pain of war, would prevent Germany from marauding south of the forty-ninth parallel.[79] Since Asia and Africa already belong to Britain "or to Britain's friends," the "greedy German eye" has fixed on Canada's "vast forests," "limitless farms," "wonderful fisheries," "untold mineral wealth and our unrivalled harbors." In short, "Canada for them would make the cradle for a mighty Empire." Tom's (or Bell's) logic is suspect here: if the US would not welcome new European colonization in the Americas in general, it is unlikely that it would ignore a German conquest and occupation of Canada. Nevertheless, what is striking here is the recognition of Canada's position as a potential (or actual) "Empire." Too, given his properly positive depictions of American assistance to stricken Halifax in the wake of the explosion, Bell seems to argue, implicitly, for a global Anglo-Saxon Union, linking Britain, Canada, and the United States.

By putting American troops on Haligonian streets, the explosion serves to enable the development of a new Anglo-American alliance.

One other effect of the explosion is, sadly but instructively, to merge the home front and the trenches of Europe in a communion of war's misery. Early in the narrative, Tom, just returned to Halifax due to injury, enthuses, "Here, thousands of miles from the front, one can get a real rest—one is able to breathe God's good air, untainted by the vile stench of the battlefield; and to sleep without the dread of rats and vermin running over one." A few minutes later, the explosion ensues. The result is a scene, as a photograph caption states, "Like a field in war-torn Flanders." Later, the narrator—Bell—apostrophizes, "Oh, ye mothers and fathers of devastated Belgium, of war-battered France, of trampled Serbia and deserted Romania! In the days that followed [the explosion] the mourning citizens of Halifax, all too clearly, saw across the intervening miles...into the abysmal sorrows of your desolate hearts.... At last the tears and prayers of Canada could intermingle with your own." If Haligonians and Canadians were too insouciant before, too flippant about war horrors played out in practical invisibility on a distant continent, the explosion brings home the grisly waste, the unmitigated, pitiless mortality, of the struggle.

For Bell, then, the romance of the disaster is that the catastrophe modernizes gender relations and prophesizes a British-Canadian-American alliance as well as a new internationalism (at least connecting Europeans) that will soon support, in part, the striking up of the League of Nations, in 1919. Certainly, Bell's narrative resists mere documentation of the horror of the blast. Rather, it serves as a private aphrodisiac and as a public prophecy of English-speaking harmony and pan-European cooperation. The single sign of potential trouble for this scenario is the likely inadvertent ornamental use of a fasces on several pages. Although it is an ancient symbol of authority, and appears in Bell's book several years before Benito Mussolini seized power in Italy, in 1922, and associated the fasces with fascism, its affixture here is accidentally prophetic of the European ideological differences that would trigger the next world war.

American writer John Hersey follows Bell in being, in his own context, the primary scribe of a momentous calamity. Hersey's *Hiroshima*, published in 1946, is the first major literary treatment in English of the atomic bombing of the Japanese city. A work of non-fiction, based on interviews and personal research, Hersey's reportage[80] is easily superior to Bell's plodding and formulaic narrative. Moreover, while Bell relies on photographs to convey the carnage he sees in Halifax, Hersey employs victims' voices and memories to set down, vividly, the mortal—but *not* moral—ramifications of the nuclear attack on Japan. Where Bell is baldly didactic— or directly propagandistic—Hersey is not: his just-the-facts journalistic style, along with his cinematic depiction of his select six survivors, renders his text a triumph of realism— or human-interest docu-drama.

Thus, unlike Bell, Hersey dispenses with politics. He offers no rationales for the utilization of the uranium bomb; he assumes no sides; instead, he eyes the damage inflicted, the numbers killed or wounded, the weird or surreal sights, and the freakish survival of his chosen witnesses. Importantly, none of his sextet belongs to the Japanese military (itself guilty of indescribable atrocities), and one is not even Japanese but rather a German Catholic priest. If Bell desires or promotes new international alliances in his romance, Hersey's work is an elegy for Hiroshima and a de facto cry for a moratorium on the further development, testing, or detonation of nuclear weapons. Hersey wagers that, if we accept Hiroshima's victims as being like "our"—American or Western—selves, we will know that we should eliminate nuclear weapons or, at the very least, nuclear war. So *Hiroshima* works to recast the bombs' victims as human, thus casting aside the (understandably) vicious wartime caricatures of the Japanese as subhuman and inhumane.

Hersey's 1944 novel, *A Bell for Adano*, sets a precedent for the imperialist-*cum*-humanitarian values that inform *Hiroshima*. The foreword alerts the reader that the story's setting, Adano, Sicily, Italy, represents "in miniature what America can and cannot do in Europe." The premise here is, America is "lucky" to be "the international country." Thus, it can and must do good overseas, partly because it boasts citizens who are of the same cultural heritage as any foreign nation that comes under its sway: "No other country has such a fund of men who speak the languages of the lands we must invade, who understand the ways and have listened to their parents sing the folk songs and have tasted the wine of the land on the palates of their memories." Hersey's American exceptionalism ignores the similarly polyglot and multicultural constituency of Canada, but it is a forthright statement of superpower realpolitik:

America is on its way into Europe.... Just as truly as Europe once invaded us, with wave after wave of immigrants, now we are invading Europe, with wave after wave of sons of immigrants.

Until there is a seeming stability in Europe, our armies and our after-armies will have to stay in Europe. Each American who stays may very well be extremely dependent on [a European-American], not only for language, but for wisdom and justice and the other things we think we have to offer Europeans.

Hersey's latter clause hints at an essential humility: America will need to conquer Europe, but European-Americans can help to temper triumphalist tendencies by translating to other Americans a respect for European civilization even as the original Occidental continent is modified by American notions of democracy, commerce, and law. Hersey suggests here that "can-do" should learn from "the classics," even while it goes about modernizing their cultural cradles. Closing the foreword, Hersey insists that the culturally hyphenated American is "our future in the world." Yes: no "plan, no hope, no treaty—none of these things can guarantee anything" of global peace, democracy, and prosperity. Only cosmopolitan Americans can guarantee such success, and so God has already damned US isolationists.

The lesson that Hersey carries forward into *Hiroshima* is that conflict is reduced when different peoples share values and different nationals share cultures. For this reason, *Hiroshima* offers humanity "under pressure," but still resolutely human. Yet Christian conversion and a Western-cultured persona are prerequisites for rendering human the "Japs" of wartime cartoon propaganda.

Hersey's six blast victim-survivors, then, all demonstrate affinities for Christ, Europe, or the US. Dr. Masakazu Fujii, "prosperous, hedonistic"—like, say, a Hollywood plastic surgeon—is "pleased to pass the evenings drinking whiskey with friends…. Before the war, he had affected brands imported from Scotland and America; now he was perfectly satisfied with the best Japanese brand, Suntory." His profile reads like that of a member of the *Esquire*[81] demographic: professional, urbane, bespectacled, and silver-haired (he's fifty). Just days after the blast, the doctor shares talk, whiskey, and cigarettes with a Jesuit and their host. Post-occupation, he lavishes whiskey on Americans with whom he practises his English. Another MD, Dr. Terufumi Sasaki, "the Red Cross Hospital surgeon," is twenty-five, trained in China, and an idealist. Connected to the Red Cross, he is evidently partly Westernized. Certainly, he writes all his medical records in German. The Reverend Mister Tanimoto has "studied theology at Emory College, in Atlanta, Georgia," graduating in 1940, speaks "excellent English," dresses "in American clothes," and had corresponded with many American friends up to the outbreak of war. So American are his tastes, so exotic his religion, that the police suspect he is a spy. Indeed, a well-heeled and "influential acquaintance," also an "anti-Christian," has begun to denounce the Protestant minister as untrustworthy.

Yet Tanimoto is not only a Japanese man of the Judeo-Christian God; he is also the careful treasurer of his penurious church—a T. S. Eliot–style banker. Nicely, he has revenge when he reads, "loudly from a Japanese-language pocket Bible," a psalm over the prostrate form of his wealthy but dying foe. Hatsuyo Nakamura, a "tailor's widow" and mother of three living by needle and thread, but on a shoestring, has lost her husband in the Imperial Japanese capture of Singapore in 1942. She has no Western accoutrements but is presented as merely a mother doing her best to feed and clothe her children. She is devoted to her late husband's Sankoku sewing machine as her means to earn her livelihood as a seamstress. Toshiko Sasaki, a factory clerk, about twenty, is also bereft—at first—of any Occidental allegiance. However, when the blast strikes, Hersey notes, with commendable irony, "There, in the tin factory, in the first moment of the atomic age, a human being was crushed by books." In brief, a Japanese woman employed in a Western economic invention—the factory— is injured by another Western invention—the Gutenberg book—as a result of the detonation of a device that, as Hersey tells us, "no country except the United States...could possibly have developed." Crippled, on crutches, and abandoned by her fiancé, Sasaki converts to Catholicism and finds solace in reading Guy de Maupassant.

The last member I consider of Hersey's sextet, Father Wilhelm Kleinsorge, "a German priest of the Society of Jesus," is the sole non-Japanese. Significant is his identity as a national of a country hostile to the Allies but allied to the Empire of Japan: he is the "enemy"; he is "us."[82] Thirty-eight, he has been suffering from diarrhea and is "reading his *Stimmen der Zeit*" (Voices of the Times), a Jesuit publication, when the bomb explodes. Regaining consciousness, he hears

"Murata-*san*, the housekeeper,...crying over and over, '*Shu Jesusu, awaremi tamai!* Our Lord Jesus, have pity on us!'"

Hersey's portraiture gives us two doctors and two clergymen and two once-marriageable women, one of whom is a hard-pressed, striving mother and the other a convert to Christianity and French literature. Summing up his depiction of "the lives of these six people who were among the luckiest in Hiroshima," Hersey finds that they share "a curious kind of elated community spirit, something like that of the Londoners after their blitz—a pride in the way they and their fellow-survivors had stood up to a dreadful ordeal." Here again all six are read as Western and thus not reprehensible, just unlucky to have been forced to live "a dozen lives and see more death than [they] ever thought [they]would see."

It is not a Japanese war-material worker who is injured by the American bomb; it is Sasaki, who is also frankly rendered as a human being. When Tanimoto tries to rescue "slimy living bodies," he must "keep consciously repeating to himself, 'These are human beings.'" Hersey asks us to recognize the indelible humanity of his subjects. Indeed, given their occupations, they are practically modern types of the pilgrims in Chaucer's *Canterbury Tales*. Too, as Catholicism constructs and unifies the world of Chaucer's subjects, so does suffering-unto-redemption (of sorts) link Hersey's sextet to Christendom or, rather, Western civilization. They are like plucky Londoners; they are human; most of them pray to Christ; some drink; some smoke.

Though Hersey enters no debate "about the moral issue of the atomic bomb," one detects disapproval in the note that Hiroshima's victims "were the objects of the first great experiment in the use of atomic power." It also seems distasteful that America sunk "its industrial know-how" and "two billion gold dollars" into the "gamble" of constructing the bomb. Uncle Sam seems here a sadistic Midas or a well-financed Dr. Frankenstein. Hersey also allows that "many citizens of Hiroshima...continue to feel a hatred for Americans which nothing could possibly erase," and Dr. Sasaki opines that the atom-bomb wielders deserve to hang as war criminals.

But the real argument against the atomic bomb and nuclear war appears implicitly in Hersey's depiction of suffering. True: Bell also narrates the destruction of Halifax, but that calamity, a result of manmade fuels and armaments, is accidental, an almost natural disaster. He need not dwell on suffering in his romance. But the bombing of Hiroshima is an act of war: a small-h holocaust conducted on a sunny morning. Thus the bulk of Hersey's narrative is taken up with descriptions of literally defaced people; charred forms; madonnas with dead babies; an Edenic garden become a fiery Hell; a city left a plain of wreckage; and limbless, skinless, and eyeless beings—wraiths for whom death is welcome.

The former war correspondent's images are searing and almost medieval: "A man and his cart on the bridge..., almost under the center of the explosion, were cast down in an embossed shadow which made it clear that the man was about to whip his horse." Industrialized, unfeeling, remote-controlled mass murder makes, in contrast, such a primitive act—whipping a horse—disgracefully human. (It is surely more humane than the sight of "sick, burned horses, hanging their heads, [standing] on a Hiroshima bridge.")

Moreover, Hersey's gallery of horrifically injured people, dying horribly, anticipates the apocalyptic novels of Nevil Shute (*On the Beach*, 1957), Eugene Burdick and Harvey Wheeler (*Fail-Safe*, 1962), and Robert Merle (*Malevil*, 1972), but the insider-style New Journalism (which stresses story, not reporting) looks forward to such epochal testaments as John Howard Griffin's *Black like Me* (1961), a Bible of the American Civil Rights Movement. (Yes, just as Hersey establishes that Hiroshima is London under the *Luftwaffe*, so does Griffin's first-person account of what it is *likely* like to live as a "Negro" demonstrate the inherent oneness of human experience.) A straight liberal-Christian-humanist line links *Hiroshima* and *Black like Me*.

Nevertheless, if Hersey views the erasure of Hiroshima as an obscenity, it is also the precondition both for obliterating Japanese militarist imperialism and for re-humanizing the Japanese in the wake of their vilification (via propaganda). If "light from the east" refers to spiritual enlightenment wrought by Confucianism, or Buddhism, or even Eastern Christianity, the "light from the west" is "A Noiseless Flash" that vaporizes Imperial Japan and opens it to incorporation as an Asian extension of Hawaii and Hollywood. One image spells this out: a B-29 bomber drones over Hiroshima as "the dull, dispirited voice of Hirohito, the Emperor Tenno, [speaks] for the first time in history over the radio": he loses his divinity and becomes a constitutional monarch, thanks to US military superiority. In tandem with this event, the Chinese-born American Hersey, by writing *Hiroshima*, acts as an intermediary between the American conqueror and the Asian classical civilization, positing Christianity, literature, and consumerism as their most pacific meeting points. Moreover, Hersey shows, the bombing of Hiroshima is dreadful, but its victims, being like ourselves, could easily *be* ourselves, and this lesson should dissuade us from further belligerent experiment with atomic incineration.

Like Bell, whom he follows, and Hersey, whom he precedes, Hugh MacLennan is optimistic, at least regarding the future of Canada, in his first novel, *Barometer Rising*, whose plot takes the Halifax Explosion of December 6, 1917, as its ground zero. Published in 1941, the novel cannot respond to the as-yet-to-occur devastation of Hiroshima, but it can respond to the raging war in Europe, where the Axis powers are ascendant.

Nevertheless, it is the domestic front of the First World War that serves as setting. One recalls that Bell ends his romance with a paean to women's emancipation. In *Barometer Rising*, which spans the week of December 2 to 10, 1917, MacLennan's heroine, Penelope Wain, is, again—shades of Vera Warrington—the New Woman: she is a ship designer so good that Whitehall—or the Admiralty, source of the power of the as-yet-awesome British Empire—accepts her design for a submarine-chaser. A science-minded bachelorette, Penny is no blushing maid: once, she recalls "that unbelievable night in Montreal when nothing had existed but sounds in the darkness and the sense that each of them had been born for that moment." Yet the war has separated her from her erstwhile lover, Neil Macrae—just as, in Bell's more decorous narrative of a generation previous to MacLennan's, the war separates Tom from Vera: Neil and Penelope had agreed to put off marriage after their one intimate night in Montreal. In Bell, Tom and Vera part after their canoe outing in Quebec, an idyll that is sex-charged but chaste, as opposed to the citified and sultry one-night-stand that MacLennan narrates. Bell closes his narrative with racy kisses between Tom and Vera; MacLennan lets the rejoined Penny and Neil make love at first sight. In further advance upon Bell, MacLennan allows Penny to be an unwed mother, who has given up her—and the unknowing Neil's—daughter for adoption. Like Bell's Tom, who notes, in Halifax, "one is able to breathe God's good air, untainted by the vile stench of the battlefield," Neil returns to a Halifax whose "air…smells so damned clean."

But he cannot go straight to claim his Penelope. Like Homer's Odysseus, he must wander a bit, if only about peninsular Halifax, for his ex–commanding officer—the businessman father, Geoffrey, of his once-and-future love, Penny, has falsely accused him of front-line cowardice *and* declared him dead. If Neil is unable to verify his innocence, he will face a likely mortal court-martial. For his part, the elder Wain could be Jay Gatsby's pal. He's descended from an Enlightenment-age English sergeant and a Napoleonic-era merchant, whose capital accumulated in "an exporting and importing business with the West Indies, exchanging dried apples and fish, for rum, tobacco, and molasses."[83] Now the paterfamilias, Geoffrey views the war as "the greatest power-bonanza in the history of mankind," an opportunity for the rich and arrogant to become ever more omnipotent and opulent. He anticipates "a new age…of power and vulgarity without limitation, in which the prizes would not be won by the qualified but by the cunning and the unscrupulous." His greed is kin to his lust—for a mistress whose fisherman roots he despises and whose body he abuses, goading "it into the convulsions of a pleasure she could hardly control." To him, the soldier is machine-gun fodder; the worker, manure; the lover, a toy.

While MacLennan's Penny is an advance upon Bell's Vera, his Geoffrey is bluntly evil in comparison with Bell's well-meaning, unselfconsciously affluent William Lawson: Geoffrey Wain is a thoroughly unlikeable, eminently killable man, but also ungodly is the class-divided city that feeds and fattens him. MacLennan bids Neil think, "Halifax was drifting through the war in smug and profitable self-satisfaction." The explosion is necessary to erase this status quo, wherein a "complacent individual" like Wain is able to pirate the surplus created by "manual workers," who must dwell in "wooden houses crowded [upon] each other like packing-boxes" while he lives in the leafy, moneyed South End. But it is also necessary to clear the air of the lies that prevent Penny and Neil from being able to easily envision a life together.

MacLennan describes the explosion as a result of the *Mont Blanc* opening up, in effect giving birth—to destruction and mass death, but also precipitating, in due course, "a revolution in the nature of things." The explosion is, in this sense, the recent Bolshevik Revolution domesticated, eradicating class distinction and the vain fantasies of tycoons.

Thus, the prudish Aunt Maria, an aid volunteer, now welcomes "strange men who come to the door" as if "she was madam of a whorehouse." The plaster bust of a former prime minister, Wilfrid Laurier, has "a spike of glass six inches long protruding from its mouth and the effect [is] obscenely bizarre," suggesting, of course, the taboo sexual act of fellatio. The explosion has "knocked hell out of Halifax" and/or it has blown "the hinges off hell." The city looks like one "caught in the fulcrum of a battle." If "the catastrophe [has] been respectful to the middle-classes," or to the South End in general, for Penelope, "Halifax, and with it the rigid, automatic life of her family's hierarchy, [has] been blown wide apart."

Another character, once Penny's rejected suitor, views the explosion as having been "merely a release for [Neil's] violent natural energy." More significantly, Geoffrey Wain, "the descendant of military colonists who had remained essentially a colonist himself, never really believing that anything above the second rate could exist in Canada, [and who] had merely taken it for granted that [the English] mattered and Canadians didn't," is "capriciously extinguished." His end satisfies Neil, who deplores "the old men who were content to let [Canada] continue second-rate indefinitely, looting its wealth while they talked about its infinite opportunities."

But the explosion has yet a wider meaning than ridding Neil and Penny of the single human barrier to their accord. Once, it is termed a "cosmic" catastrophe. Like Bell before him, MacLennan positions Halifax's suffering as mirroring that of Europe: "It was a devastation more appalling than anything [one] had witnessed in France"; "This was not a vision transported from France or Serbia or some country that was never immune to such things, but an actual occurrence in Halifax." But Bell views the explosion as tying Canada closer to Britain and America, while the Great War itself is expected to result in European harmony. Writing while World War II rages, MacLennan knows differently. Indeed, along with the Great War—and the implicit reference to the Bolshevik Revolution—the explosion, he suggests, marks "not a decline and fall" of European imperial governance but "one bloody smash." This European wreckage, echoed in Halifax, will emancipate Canadians from a provincialism in which they never "aspire" to more than "a position in the butler's pantry of the British Empire": "And maybe when the wars and revolutions were ended, Canada would begin to live; maybe instead of being pulled eastward by Britain she would herself pull Britain clear of decay and give her a new birth."

Ideally, "Canada must remain as she is [neither English nor American], until the day she becomes the keystone to hold the world together." At the conclusion of the narrative, Neil thinks, "if there were enough Canadians like himself, half-American and half-English, then the day was inevitable when the halves would join and his country would become the central arch which united a new order." True: this thinking is reminiscent of Bell's thought that Canada could be the "cradle" of a new empire. However, it is likely spurred on by MacLennan's apparent indebtedness to the conservative thinking of Edward Gibbon in his *The Decline and Fall of the Roman Empire* and the racialist thinking of Oswald Spengler in *Der Untergang des Abendlandes*—or *The Decline of the West*. Hence, we read, in Gibbon, of "barbarians" dissolving the Roman Empire piecemeal—and of a similar fate awaiting "these big cities, these places like Boston." Or we read, in Spengler, that "the tiny states of Europe had shaped the past" but that Canada represents "unborn mightiness, this question-mark, this future."

Yes, Canada ought to be able to rise where Britain is declining. In this sense, the explosion is an apocalyptic version of D. W. Griffith's pro-Confederacy film, *Birth of a Nation*, which president Woodrow Wilson reputedly cast as "history written in lightning": when the *Mont Blanc*—an ambassador of European strife—"opened up" in Halifax harbour, it actually served to give birth to the Canadian people, now no longer provincial but, like Penny and Neil Macrae, marrying "the urbane and technical heritage of both Europe and the eastern United States." Thus, *Barometer Rising* is, in the end, a comedy—as is Bell's romance. MacLennan simply updates Bell.

Barometer Rising is MacLennan's first novel, and *Voices in Time*, published four decades later, in 1980, is his last. The Halifax Explosion commences his career, but in a sense, Hiroshima ends it. That is to say, if the first novel ends with a measure of hope—that Canada will emerge from European wars with enough confidence to stride the world stage—the last novel envisions a catastrophic end to civilization-as-we-know-it due to "clean bombs," which have a destructive power less than that of the nuclears but nevertheless tremendous. Set in the year 2030, *Voices in Time* is a post-apocalyptic novel, like Shute's *On the Beach*, which may take inspiration from Hersey's graphic descriptions of the human-exterminating effects of radiation poisoning.

The Halifax blast creates new socio-political and cultural possibilities, but the atomic bombing of Hiroshima, in contrast, makes doomsday scenarios credible. MacLennan moves from the relative comedy of the first narrative ("This explosion in Halifax was catastrophic but not tragic") to the conditional despair of the second. In the first novel, there is talk of barbarians at the gates of East Coast America and Canada; in the latter, the end has come: "The deliberate murder of truth led to the murder of a people. In our case it led to the self-murder of a civilization." Post-explosion, the world is made new; post–nuclear war, the world is finished.

Bearing in mind that Hersey presents Father Kleinsorge reading the German Jesuit publication, *Voices of the Times*, as the atom bomb explodes, and given that MacLennan's *Voices in Time* is structured around a quartet of characters with long memories—particularly of Nazi Germany and its cancerous growth and grisly demise— perhaps *Hiroshima* is as much an influence for MacLennan as is Hiroshima. However, while Hersey nods to Christ and commerce as positive ways to reconstruct vanquished Japan, MacLennan's novel foresees a general post-nuclear dystopia.

In conclusion, the Halifax Explosion permits Bell to imagine the incipient emancipation of women, the arrival of an international Anglo-Saxon alliance to manage world affairs, and the concomitant construction of a New European Order. For MacLennan, writing a generation after Bell, the explosion—now projected forward into the 1940s and the Second World War—symbolizes the end of robber-baron capitalism, the already realized sexual freedom of women (and men), and the birth of a new Canada, one that draws perceptive strength from both its English and American heritages. In *Hiroshima*, Hersey depicts, adroitly, the horror of the atomic bombing, especially the long-term mortality effected by radiation poisoning, thus accomplishing, in one book, both the inauguration of New Journalism and new life for the post-apocalyptic novel. In addition, he reads the city's destruction as mandating a cosmopolitan world, whose success can be enabled by appropriately bi-cultural Americans (such as himself) as well as by the universalizing aids of commerce and Christianity. All three books are ultimately romantic comedies, then, suggesting that trauma is not traumatic for those who choose to make art of horror.

[*Shaping an Agenda for Atlantic Canada*, edited by John G. Reid and Donald J. Savoie. Fernwood Press, 2011]

∾

Innovation, invention, experimentation, and entrepreneurial risk-taking emerge out of the stress of devastation. Perhaps the arrival of every newfangled industry, every insurgent avant-garde, is foreseen—and overseen—by espionage, the spy being the ogler of the incipient, the seer of subterfuge, and the surveiller of the alarming formation or invigorating blueprint. For every disaster, there is an accountant; for every dream, there is a spy. Possibly, Ian Fleming modelled his famous fictitious spy on a Canadian, whose encounters with Canada are always adventures with the wild, survivals of the unexpected, and refreshing of the bond—ahem—between the UK and the US. Or so indicates the following essay.

∾

Ian Fleming's Canadian Cities

WE HAVE MUCH to learn from spy novelists who, in the interests of verisimilitude and plausibility of plot, address the splintering and/or gelling of empires with a healthy dollop of realpolitik. Thanks to his career in espionage, Ian Fleming eyes Canada as a site of multicultural cities, set amid invigorating (if stereotypical) wilderness, but also as a helpful go-between for the declining British Empire and the rising American one. True: cowboy-and-Indian romanticism purples his perspective. Yet Fleming's basic realism challenges the standard view of Canada as a clutch of confederated European-founded colonies, now semi-Americanized, that exists in a state of existential angst regarding its mixed heritages, its quasi-genocidal history toward Indigenous peoples, and its pseudo-colonial relationships to the US and the UK. Fleming's enmeshment in British Imperial geo-politics— even as the British Raj was ending—furnished him with a sounder understanding of the place of Canada in a still-imperialist world-system than is the case for too many theorists who believe that globalization has nullified empires and neutered nation-states.

I distrust all postcolonialist theory that pretends that Karl Marx, Frantz Fanon, Vladimir Lenin, Mao Zedong,

Malcolm X, and the Canadian Red Tory philosopher George Grant are now passé just because credit cards and cellphones serve billions—just like McDonald's. To be provocative, I repeat their collective finding that capitalism tends toward imperialism, that "liberalization" of societies and economies challenges local cultures in their attempts to conserve traditions, and that wars are inevitable as each power-set grapples for advantage. I do not credit that these données have been superseded or that occult paeans regarding "hybridity" and "the end of history" prove the collapse of class struggle or, for that matter, of imperial ambitions: not when the Arab Spring of 2011 saw oppressed masses try to overthrow tyrannous, tacitly Western-backed elites, and not when the People's Republic of China has, as of September 2012, launched an aircraft carrier, a symbol of maritime command that goes all the way back to the galleys of the Roman Empire, which hindered Hannibal by cutting him off from his African and Spanish bases. Mao preaches, "Classes struggle, some classes triumph, others are eliminated." Maybe. But I think it truer to say, "Empires struggle, some triumph, others are eliminated."

I do not want to sound reductive, but I do want to advise, despite all good-hearted postcolonial critique to the contrary, that Great Powers—to resurrect a timeless phrase—will try to arrange resources and structures of trade and diplomacy to the benefit of their elites (with some trickle-down consumerism and teary-eyed patriotism for the masses). Moreover, if their "vital interests"—to revisit another classic phrase—seem threatened, they will terrorize, capture, and kill their "enemy" and also seize or destroy assets and infrastructure, and will issue apologia or propaganda (with aplomb) as their violent objectives are realized.

In his 1965 lament for what he saw as the demise of a British, "traditional" (English) Canada, Grant warns that the American Empire—the highest expression of "the age of progress," the summit of liberalism and the belief in human will and technology—could still preside over or represent "the pursuit of expansion as an end in itself."[84] One may object that this perception is now common sense that does not bear reiteration. Yet these points often seem absent from surveys of the global scene predicated upon the notion that empires have either evaporated or now possess merely benign configurations and passive soft-power manifestations.

Fleming believed the opposite and explores this truth in his fiction, which is often crude, Tarzanesque, pro-Anglo-imperialist fantasy. Yet it is also a conscientious attempt to think entertainingly about the exigencies of Big Powers and bit players in a bipolar Cold War world in which decadent empires were imploding. Societies and power-sets still trade with, influence, and, sometimes, attack one another, and conduct their affairs to extract maximum benefits from commerce at minimal risk of war or invasion, and nigh-imperial alliances and state-combinations are one way of attempting to curb international violence. Indeed, my current radio news reports (November 2012) tell of corruption in China, financial disaster in Greece, unrest in Egypt, and war in Gaza and Israel and Syria, with the Great Powers talking peace and prosperity[85] but jockeying for their own relative supremacy.

Our world is not, in the end, theoretical. It is a messy, bloody globe, where espionage is one of the true-and-tried means of either trying to forestall war or ensuring that one's own side wins. In his fiction, Fleming knows this actually existing state of affairs, and that is why, I urge, his broad, geopolitical depiction of Canada's cities—of their "glocal" relevance—deserves our hearing.

In his witty, jocular, and cheery discussion of "the James Bond epic," British writer and journalist Sinclair McKay discusses the 2008 film *Quantum of Solace* and comments, of its dénouement involving a Canadian agent, "One hears so little of Canadian spies; how nice for them to get a second or two in the sunshine." The statement is veddy British, for it is simultaneously a recognition and a dismissal. Yet McKay's point is honest, if wry, and one is shaken—if not stirred— to recognize that, of the official James Bond films issued since 1962, no Canadian city features in a single one. The Canadian absence from this "big-budget Bayeux tapestry that encapsulates everything from fashion to geopolitics" is readily explicable:[86] among the scriptwriters for this half-century of films, only one, Paul Haggis, is Canadian, a truth that may elucidate the aforementioned nod to the Canadian Security Intelligence Service at the close of *Quantum of Solace*—as well as the fluttering of a Canadian flag outside a Bahamas hotel in 2006's *Casino Royale*.

Canadiana materializes in a few other Bond films (in *Goldfinger*, Pussy Galore tells Bond they are passing Newfoundland, at 35,000 feet, en route for Baltimore; in *Live and Let Die*, the connection for "Canada" appears beside that for the "United Kingdom" on a United Nations translation console). Still, the generic invisibility of the nation and its cities in the series is odd, for Bond's creator, Ian Fleming (1908–64), likely took espionage training in Canada during the Second World War, and he may have modelled his secret agent, in part, on William Stephenson, a Canadian master spy who was born in 1896 and died in 1989. Stephenson's alias was INTREPID.[87] For this reason, McKay's quip about the obscurity of Canadian spies should be read as a backhanded compliment regarding their effectiveness at being quiet but deadly—adept at gathering information and assassinating foes, but anonymously and stealthily.[88]

Strikingly, though, Fleming's foundational short story, "Quantum of Solace," published in 1960, counts a Canadian, albeit obliquely. Its plot takes up the romance of a couple, "The Harvey Millers," "a pleasant rather dull Canadian millionaire who had got into Natural Gas early on and stayed with it, and his pretty chatterbox of a wife," who is English. The governor of the Bahamas relays their story to a bored Bond, who is startled to learn that the superficially bland Mrs. Miller is an ex-divorcée. Formerly a stewardess, divorced by the husband she had cuckolded, she has won redemption via hotel employ in Nassau, the position through which she has secured her new hubby, the big-bucks Canuck.

This revelation leads Bond to philosophize, "Suddenly the violent dramatics of his own life seemed very hollow," akin to "the stuff of an adventure-strip in a cheap newspaper. He had sat next to a dull woman at a dull dinner party and a chance remark had opened for him the book of real violence—of the Comédie Humaine where human passions are raw and real, where Fate plays a more authentic game than any Secret Service conspiracy devised by Governments." Strangely, in this parlour story about the philandering spouse of a low-level clerk of Empire, Fleming suggests that the blowing up of a marriage, so to speak, unleashes more real passion than, say, the blowing up of a boat—and "Quantum of Solace" the story opens with Bond bombing two.

But "Quantum of Solace" is not the only Fleming adventure fiction to cite Canadians. In the 1959 *Goldfinger*, it is in his guise as a broker for "an English holding in a Canadian Natural Gas property" that Bond encounters the deadly Auric Goldfinger. Moreover, Goldfinger's wealth includes "five million pounds' worth [of gold] or so he holds there [in the Bahamas] in the vaults of the Royal Bank of Canada." Too, to provide a cover story for his mission to ascertain (and then undermine) the crook's operations, Bond decides to tell Goldfinger that he's "thinking of emigrating to Canada." At the novel's climax, one reads that Bond's "imagination hunted round the plane wondering what he could conceivably do to force an emergency landing at Gander or somewhere else in Nova Scotia." Additionally, the plane is on course to put down "north of" Goose Bay, Labrador, and Goldfinger plans to reassemble his cronies "at Montreal." Following his final fisticuffs with Goldfinger, Bond—with the miraculously ex-lesbian Pussy Galore at his side—ditches an aircraft in Canadian waters and then listens "dreamily to an early morning radio programme."

Nevertheless, sensible is surprise at the apparition of Canada, Canadians, and Canadian sites in Fleming's wham-bam-thank-ya-ma'am fiction. Yet Fleming's World War II stint as Commander Fleming, an ex-journalist seconded to the Director of Naval Intelligence, put him in contact with William Stephenson—or INTREPID—and, thus, made Fleming privy to the Canadian's wartime spy activities on behalf of the Allies.[89] (Ben Macintyre reports that Fleming once stated, "Everything I write has a precedent in truth," and his job—dreaming up "espionage plans with convincing scenarios"—got him, as he said, "right to the heart of things."[90])

For instance, one of Stephenson's clandestine efforts—of which Fleming knew—was to visit Sweden, purportedly on business, but truly to derail Swedish iron ore from becoming German steel. Canadian author and journalist William Stevenson also quotes Fleming's account of Stephenson's notion, in October 1939, that "the Norwegian heavy-water plant would have to be destroyed by 'schoolboy adventurers'" to prevent Nazi Germany from inventing an atomic bomb. Stevenson the author maintains that Stephenson the spy, "this forty-three-year-old Canadian industrialist," planned to wreck, in the winter of 1939, the port infrastructure of Oxelösund, Sweden. Stevenson asserts that Fleming's master spy is based on the Canadian's intrepid exploits.[91]

Then again, if Bond's world, as McKay assesses, exudes "the vital taste of authenticity," it may be due, in part, to Fleming's knowledge of Stephenson's actual derring-do. Strikingly, Stevenson's summation of INTREPID as having "the courage of a man of imagination who can visualize the bloody and painful consequences of his own actions" accords with Fleming's conception of his iconic secret agent: a "harsh, cold" man, but "easily tipped over into sentiment."

Yet Bond can also consider the "consequences" of disloyalty and dishonesty. In the 1953 *Casino Royale*, Fleming's protagonist recalls the receipt of his "Double O"—licence to kill—as having been "not difficult...if you're prepared to kill people." Bond reflects, of his two kills: "Probably quite decent people...who just got caught up in the gale of the world."[92]

This fictitious rendition of the birth of 007, so to speak, tallies with William Stevenson's account of Bill Stephenson's readiness to kill—for King[93] and country, i.e., for British prime minister Winston Churchill and for the American president, namely Franklin Delano Roosevelt. However, it is Fleming who provides the reports, based in one instance on gossip from none other than then-US Federal Bureau of Investigation Director J. Edgar Hoover, about one Stephenson-conducted assassination: "Little Bill tracked down [a] traitor after seeing the decoded recoveries from a Nazi transmitter in New York. The signals told U-boats where to intercept British ships with the most militarily valuable cargoes." So Little Bill ventures in New York and liquidates the traitorous sailor. Fleming tells Stevenson, "There was overwhelming evidence against the seaman. Killing him quickly perhaps saved hundreds of sailors' lives and precious supplies."

Fleming also observed a break-in at the Japanese consulate in New York that Little Bill committed to microfilm enemy codes. Fleming declared his witness of this feat as "the spectacle of the greatest of secret agents at work." At the conclusion of *A Man Called Intrepid: The Secret War*, Stevenson asserts Fleming's approval of Little Bill as having been a master spy constantly risking death.[94] The chronicler Stevenson also relates that, "after Fleming died, a

1973 book, John Pearson's *007-James Bond: The Authorized Biography*…claimed Commander Bond really did exist and was turned into fiction to deceive his enemies." This real Bond "was said to occupy a private suite [in a Bermuda hotel] belonging to William Stephenson, his chief." (This book was really a novel—a spoof biography.)

The parallels between Fleming's secret agent and the verifiable Canadian spy are palpable. The biographer Stevenson portrays his subject as a bookworm and boxing champ. Although the Bond of the action flicks is rarely seen with a book, the Bond of the novels leafs through a select set of belles lettres. In *Live and Let Die* (1954), Bond dips into British travel writer Patrick Leigh Fermor's *The Traveller's Tree*; in *From Russia with Love* (1956), he checks out thriller novelist Eric Ambler's *The Mask of Dimitrios*; in *Dr. No* (1958), he picks up the *Handbook of the West Indies*,[95] and there is also a nod to the Fourth Earl of Chesterfield's eighteenth-century *Letters to His Son*. In *Goldfinger*, the spy keeps his Walther PPK gun in a hollowed-out book titled *The Bible Designed to Be Read as Literature*—a truly novel use of Bible criticism. In the same work, Bond recognizes literary pornography when he sees it, eyeing, in a hotel room, "a yellow-backed copy of *The Hidden Sight of Love*, Palladium Publications, Paris."[96] In *On Her Majesty's Secret Service* (1963), Bond informs his chief, M, that he enjoys Rex Stout's novels about "a fat American detective," namely Nero Wolfe.[97] *You Only Live Twice* opens with a haiku epigraph "After Basho," which Bond himself composes while engaging in a discussion of haiku and tanka poetry during a visit to "the oldest whorehouse in Japan."[98] In "The Living Daylights" (1966), the assassin relaxes with "a German thriller" titled *Verderbt, Verdammt, Verraten*. Stephenson, the Canadian spy, is said to pen poetry—Stevenson prints a sample—and to enjoy reading it, including a fragment of William Wordsworth regarding "the happy Warrior," who "does not stoop, nor lie in wait / For wealth, or honors, or for worldly state." The sentiment echoes the Bond family motto, "The World Is Not Enough."[99]

If Bond is resourceful, crafty, witty, and insouciant, INTREPID is just as dashing, wily, exuberant, and creative.[100] As a German-held prisoner in World War I, he escaped by working his employ in the kitchen to fashion "wire cutters, a crude knife, and a simple compass." If Fleming was "fascinated by gadgets," INTREPID believed that "science would bring order and peace," and he discovered "a new alloy for…high-speed turbine blades." That Bond is an adept assassin with a knack for laying waste his enemies' lairs may stem from Fleming's study at so-called Camp X, forty miles northeast of Toronto, where, alleges INTREPID, Fleming proved "exceptionally good at underwater demolition."[101]

Another connection between Stevenson's Stephenson and Fleming's Bond is the germane—to espionage—matter of intercontinental flight. For INTREPID, during World War II, one fast route between Washington and London was first to cross into Canada, then wing to England from Montreal via Labrador and Scotland. In the Bond novels, the spy flies, in *Diamonds Are Forever* (1956), toward "the southern shores of Nova Scotia."[102] In *Goldfinger*, unable to reach Goose Bay and undertaking an emergency ditching of an aircraft, Bond communicates with the "strong signal of Gander Control." In the short story "For Your Eyes Only" (1960), Bond takes "the Friday Comet to Montreal." However, he "did not care for it. It flew too high and too fast and there were too many passengers." For him, the flight is "too quick. The stewards had to serve everything almost at the double, and then [he] had a bare two hours snooze before the hundred-mile-long descent from forty thousand feet." In *Thunderball* (1961), a missing aircraft proves difficult to track because it vanishes amid "the northern traffic from Montreal, and Gander down to Bermuda and the Bahamas and South America. So these DEW operators just put it down as a BOAC or Trans-Canada plane." In *You Only Live Twice*, Bond's flight path to Japan takes him over "the Arctic Ocean, the Beaufort Sea." Notably, even as an aviation backdrop, Canada serves as the in-between space for joint US and UK espionage operations.

Author Stevenson guesses that Fleming snatched his *Goldfinger* plot from Churchill's wartime need for always-negotiable gold and Stephenson's intrigue to supply it by fleecing Vichy-controlled Martinique. In addition, the recollection of Bond's first two kills in *Casino Royale* (the novel) may be indebted to Stephenson's New York skulduggery (as recounted above). Moreover, a part of the plot for *From Russia with Love*—the plan to steal a Soviet cipher machine, The Spektor—echoes the successful British apprehension of a similar German device, Enigma, a project to which INTREPID was pivotal. Too, Stephenson predicts that, "for the balance of the twentieth century, the world would be changed by this bizarre relationship between the physicist and the guerrilla," the "sophisticated" (knowledge and exploitation of nuclear weapons) and the "primitive" (irregular, ragtag armies). That prophecy provides the premise for more than one Bond adventure.

Fine: one can establish links between Commander Fleming, INTREPID, and Commander Bond. Yet the argument that Little Bill is a chief model for Fleming's secret agent is supported by the presence of Canadian cities in the Bond tales and their importance to intrigue.

Notably, Stevenson opens the story of Bill Stephenson's life when his hero is five, and his native city, Winnipeg, is draped in black to honour the perished empress—Victoria. On this same day, January 22, 1901, that Stephenson is mourning the loss of the Queen—and of his own father in a Boer War battle, Winston Churchill, formerly on the lecture circuit in the US, crosses the border to Canada and reaches Winnipeg, where he learns of Victoria's death (3). Stephenson's purpose in juxtaposing the young Churchill and the boy INTREPID in a funereal Winnipeg is not just to parallel two vastly different lives. It also establishes, in embryo as it were, Canada's position in the biography—to act as a stealthy extension of Britain into North America, yes, and also as a metaphorical bridge between the monarchical Anglo-Saxons and their republican cousins. George W. Brown witnesses, "Confederation was achieved, not in opposition to British policy but with the aid of British policy and through a combination of forces running strongly on both sides of the Atlantic," so that, in the end, "Canada gained a western empire—the vast domain of the

Hudson's Bay Company—because she was herself part of an empire." Certainly, this role is reprised throughout the narrative.[103] Fleming stresses the same political dynamic in his fiction.

Stevenson accents this Canada-as-in-between-state idea. For him, the country is "part of the Western Hemisphere but also a confidant of Britain." When US president Franklin Delano Roosevelt first hints, in 1938, that the US might enter a looming new European war in defence of Europe and Britain, he indicates this policy in a Kingston, Ontario, speech. When, during the war, Stephenson needs to found a training base for American spies, he chooses "the Canadian wilderness." This location permits "hyphenated Americans" of European background to be able to receive secret training while preserving America's official posture of neutrality. The establishment of Camp X on "the Toronto-Kingston highway along the north shore of Lake Ontario" is a godsend for US and UK cooperation. Stevenson tells us that the site was about "300 miles northwest of Manhattan," a phrase that vapourizes the US–Canada border. He also states that the secret camp's location was selected "because it could be reached easily by FBI agents [and other allied spies]." It was also guarded from approach "on the south by forty miles of lake water and on the north by a dense, deep strip of bushland." For extra security, there were British commandos, "skilled in the use of the hatpin, the thin copper wire, and other homely, silent, lethal weapons."

Camp X—Canada—is a site of secret Anglo-Saxon and American cooperation. It becomes "a new 'school for danger' in the Canadian wilderness, where saboteurs could prepare for a suicide mission." Furthermore, in nearby Toronto, INTREPID organized a "small unit" of expert forgers. These Hogtown forgers were reputed for their skill and quality, which is a testament to the multicultural gathering of these refugee intellectuals and artists from every corner of Nazi-occupied Europe.[104] Also, near Toronto, "at Little Norway," perhaps at Camp X, Norwegian spies and parachutists got their schooling. In the end, Stephenson opines that Canada provided the UK and the US "a singular service, being part of both worlds." Arguably, that is who INTREPID was—a spy in service to the "Special Relationship," able to dine with Winston Churchill and then treat with Roosevelt.[105] So Canada tends to be a ghost or stealth partner to US and UK neo-imperial gambits. Fleming's Bond fleshes out this "Special Relationship." His prime sidekick in his capers is Felix Leiter, a CIA operative; however, he is also, via his chief, M, only one remove from the British prime minister.

Like Stephenson, Fleming treats Canada, in the Bond sex-potboilers, as a sign for the archetypal, go-to, go-between state. Hence, in *Live and Let Die*, Fleming has Bond go in London "straight down to Commander Damon, Head of Station A, an alert Canadian who controlled the link with the Central Intelligence Agency, America's Secret Service." In *Thunderball*, the references seem more negative. A minor villain, a captain, is "a big, sullen, rawboned man who had been cashiered from the Canadian Navy for drunkenness and insubordination."[106] Likewise, when the master fiend, Blofeld, is on the run, he needs "to locate the passport factory that operates in every big seaport and purchase a Canadian seaman's passport for 2,000 dollars."[107] In *From Russia with*

Love, Canada is a British dumping ground for "a certain category of foreign [political] prisoner." In fact, Tatiana Romanova, a female spy tricked by a criminal gang into luring Bond into the trap of a sex scandal, expects to receive, from the unsuspecting British, as a reward for helping Bond steal The Spektor, "the offer of a new life in Canada."[108]

Similarly, in *The Spy Who Loved Me* (1962), a Soviet defector, Boris, after being flown to England, "is settled in Canada, in Toronto." Bond explains that the British offer defectors "the choice of Canada, Australia, New Zealand, or Africa." In the story "For Your Eyes Only," Bond visits the headquarters of the Royal Canadian Mounted Police. Fleming's narrator sniffs, "Like most Canadian public buildings, the Department of Justice is a massive block of grey masonry built to look stodgily important and to withstand the long and hard winters." For Fleming, then, the Gothic architecture of Ottawa's state buildings is only justifiable thanks to the hoary notion—or season—of winter. While waiting to meet a contact, Bond reads "a recruiting pamphlet which made the Mounties sound like a mixture between a dude ranch, Dick Tracy and Rose Marie"[109] Eventually, Bond must snag a "Canadian hunting license under false pretences" so he can pretend to stray by accident into upstate New York to conduct an assassination. His cover will be that he's "an Englishman on a hunting trip in Canada who's lost his way and got across the border by mistake." To prepare his mission, Bond buys camping supplies in Ottawa and outside Montreal, including "a large aluminium flask...filled with three-quarters Bourbon and a quarter coffee." (He then colours himself with a walnut stain so that he looks like "a red Indian with blue-grey eyes."[110] Once again, Fleming offers cliché: Canada is so wilderness-connected that James Bond can turn into Grey Owl.[111]

I wager there is a touch of German "American West" fantasy novelist Karl May (1842–1912) in Fleming's own imagination of Canada. In *Dr. No*, the author refers to the "Klondyke," and in *Casino Royale*, Le Chiffre, set to torture Bond most horribly, warns, "the game of Red Indians is over."[112] For Fleming, Canadians are inoffensive, campfire-building "Germans" who are loyal to the British monarchy but able to interpret America to Europe and Europe to America. Fleming is another Brit—or European—out-doorsman-romanticist, clearly. Although the Canuck INTREPID is a major model for Fleming's Bond, Canadian cities are, for Fleming, preposterous outposts of Gothic stolidness to the point of resembling Disneyland kitsch. Notably, the Québécoise heroine and narrator of *The Spy Who Loved Me*—Vivienne Michel, herself a kind of lumberjack-jacketed Barbie doll of Duplessis-era Quebec—describes the Ville de Québec's dominant land-mark, the Château Frontenac, as "a large toy edifice out of Disneyland." But they are also a site of multicultural expertise for espionage, or crime, and house polyglot polymaths at both. In *The Spy Who Loved Me*, Toronto is depicted as "a tough town" of ex–Gestapo agents, Soviet-infiltrated gangs, and machine-gun duels.

In the Bond stories, then, just as in Stevenson's bio-graphy of Stephenson, Canada is an essential helpmate to both the UK and the US. The purpose of these local Canadian moments in a globetrotting spy's itinerary is to speak to the continuation of British imperialism in a subtle Canadian guise, or, rather, to point to a quiet Canadian imperialism that finesses British interests in a Cold War era of insurgent American hegemony. Ultimately, Fleming presents Canada as a sophisticated locale of internationalists with "American" accents, nicely subservient to Britain yet blandly subversive, able to say sorry while blowing up or gunning down the enemy. Would only postcolonialists be as savvy in their analyses![113]

Literature and the Glocal City: Reshaping the English Canadian Imaginary, edited by Ana Maria Fraile-Marcos. Routledge, 2014.

~

How can anyone forget that Canada is the spawn of empire? Our former monarch was the daughter of the former Emperor of India. So Fleming was not—is not—wrong to narrate Canada's stealthy persistence as an enabler of the Brits and an explicator of the Yanks, one to the other. Moreover, the nation is apt to march shoulder to shoulder, in lockstep, to do the espionage or military bidding of one and/or the other, always to serve their interests (which are supposedly also *ours*). Nice camouflage for both the UK and the US is Canada's Peaceable Kingdom image as a site of internationalist bonhomie and multicultural humanitarianism, that is to say, a nation of peacekeepers (never warmongers). Yet, when Canadians go to war—or Canada does its duty for one empire or another— soldiers may conduct or condone massacres, rapacious assaults, and the laying waste of streets or greenery. Worse, the horror of a distant battlefield may come to Canada with refugees and displaced persons, so that violence is domesticated. These ideas are analyzed in the following essay.

～

Writing the Pax Canadiana:
Terror Abroad, Torture at Home

For Norman Kester[114]

I am a Canadian patriot. I applaud my brave compatriots for their sacrifices in liberating Europe, primarily Italy and Holland, for preserving Britain (via their gallantry on the open Atlantic versus German U-boats), and for their stalwart, suicidal defence of Hong Kong against irresistible Japanese aggression during the Anti-Fascist War. I also delight in my nation's gutsy decision not to join its behemoth trading partner and that leviathan superpower, the United States of America, in a brutal, lawless, cowardly invasion, in 2003, of the dictator-bossed—but largely defenceless—Iraq. I offer the foregoing sentiments in advance defence of this essay, in which I will remind us that Canada—gloried as it is for its peacekeeping and peace-making interventions, at Suez and in Vietnam, Cyprus, Bosnia, and elsewhere—has not been deemed by its own scribes a pure apostle of humanitarianism.

Assuredly, Canada's Nordic phobias around race and its patriarchal, hierarchical authoritarianism, as well as its military subservience to, first, the British Empire and, now, the de facto US empire, have led its soldiers into disgusting actions abroad while allowing its police and courts to perpetuate oppression at home. Because this essay is occasioned by ceremonies saluting Canada's splendid liberation of Holland in 1945, I will examine Elly Danica's 1988 *Don't: A Woman's Word*, which discusses the incestuous abuse she endured in her Dutch immigrant family, but I will begin by scrutinizing Canadian literature treating episodes of Canadian terrorism in Africa. I seek to explore the ways in which Canadian writers—William Stairs, Claire Harris, and Danica—have revealed the deadly racism and sexism that underlie notions of an imperial *Pax Canadiana*, both within the Dominion and overseas. Though Canada has been billed as "The Peaceable Kingdom," although its Constitution enjoins its federal government to legislate for "Peace, Order, and good Government,"[115] and although its people pride themselves on their peacekeeping missions,[116] the nation can also ignore and thus endorse heinous overseas war crimes (as well as homespun settler-committed atrocities versus Indigenous peoples).

Reading that notorious masterpiece, *The Cantos*, penned by that supremely disreputable poet, the Yank crank-fascist Ezra Pound, a Canadian encounters a disconcerting passage in "Canto LXXIII." Here, Pound elegizes a young woman, now a "spirito," "una ragazza, / una ragazza stuprata / Po' prima da lor canagliana," or, in translation by William Cookson from his *A Guide to the Cantos of Ezra Pound*, "a young girl / a young girl / raped not long before by their filthy pack." To avenge her despoliation, to exact revenge for an assault on Rimini, the anonymous Italian heroine has led twenty

Canadian troops to their deaths in a minefield, where she is also "martyred." "All'inferno 'l nemico"—"To hell with the enemy"—Pound exults, and, briefly, one is bade to consider Canadian solders—liberators—as Huns and Vandals. Yet Canto LXXIII is rank propaganda, and Pound thus extra repugnant. Yet is it impossible that Canadian troops have never ever committed heinous acts, such as anything like the fictitious "Rape of Rimini"?

In this light, most disturbing is the classic Great War novel, published in 1930, *Generals Die in Bed*, penned by the American-born Canadian ex-serviceman Charles Yale Harrison, which pictures Canadian soldiers sacking Amiens, France, in 1917. Harrison's depiction of "our boys" as ecstatic looters outraged veterans who believed Canucks never committed outrages. But Harrison's homely realism, his grisly verisimilitude, forces one to ponder the veracity of the fiction. Then again, war is ugly, and even cherubic gallants and valiant generals may surrender, now and then, to sadism. Thus, Harrison narrates the cold-blooded butchering of a captured German sniper by his intended Canadian victims.

Then again, one must register that Canadian military plotting has envisioned treating the enemy to wholesale devastation and wanton horrors. In the 1920s, a Canadian colonel, James Sutherland "Buster" Brown, outlined, in his Defence Plan Number One, a strike-first strategic attack on the Great Republic, calling for "rapidly mobilized, mixed forces to penetrate as deeply as possible into the United States in order to effect a destructive retreat so as to forestall a US invasion long enough for the British to come to the rescue."[117] Like Harrison, Brown had to conceive of a Royal

Canadian Army savvy—savage—enough to obliterate adversaries and shed no tear in doing so.

But there were earlier narratives of Canadian aggression in the service of empire. William Stairs, a Haligonian Nova Scotian who joined British explorer Henry M. Stanley on his final trans-African expedition from 1887 to 1890, kept diaries that record his own and other Europeans' relentlessly ghoulish assaults on Africans. Published in 1998 as *African Exploits: The Diaries of William Stairs, 1887-1892*, Stairs's writings read like pages out of Joseph Conrad.[118] Stairs symbolizes, maintains his editor Roy MacLaren, innocence corrupted. His diaries relate "the gradual transformation of Stairs from an open, light-hearted, easy-going subaltern into someone who would condone or even himself join in acts of great brutality". Yet Stairs's Marlowesque metamorphosis is foreshadowed in his cheerful acceptance of what British Victorian poet Rudyard Kipling dubbed, in an eponymously titled poem, "The White Man's Burden."[119] MacLaren acknowledges the then-typical Anglo-Canadian devotion to British imperialist adventures:

> Young Canadians such as Stairs increasingly regarded their homeland as one part of a growing empire where they could join in the now global search for "gold, God or glory." Stairs would have known instinctively what Stephen Leacock meant when he proclaimed, "I am an imperialist because I will not be a colonial." The whole wide empire was for Stairs and his fellows part of their natural birthright, just as Canada itself was.

French political scientist André Siegfried, in his 1907 *The Race Question in Canada*, insists that the gung-ho *fin de siècle* imperialism of English Canada and the other Briton-dominated colonies attained its apex during Queen Victoria's Diamond Jubilee celebrations of 1897:

> The spectacle presented by the Empire at this moment was calculated to turn the heads of everybody, and the official panegyrists celebrated it grandiloquently. The sun never set on the British possessions. Everywhere had the Anglo-Saxon race become supreme, and established a Pax Britannica as grandiose as that of Rome. It seemed as though we were present at the birth of a new order of things, destined to surpass in splendour the Roman Empire itself.

Stairs journeyed to Africa with precisely these sentiments warming his bosom. However, upon encountering Africans cool to notions of white supremacy and hostile to foreign control, his enthusiasm waned. His response to African recalcitrance in the Belgian Congo and elsewhere was violence that neared genocide and did not stop at enslavement and (probable) rape.

Early in his diaries, in April 1887, Stairs allows that "nothing I have ever seen so completely demoralizes a [white] man as driving negro carriers. One's temper is up all the time, kind feelings are knocked on the head and I should think in time a man would become a perfect brute if he did nothing else but this." In June 1887, Stairs remarks that "a white man with a Winchester would create immense slaughter among the

194

natives as here he would be quite safe from spears and could single out and pot [shoot dead] any skulking nigger behind a tree or bush." Contemplating a village that he and his men will soon plunder, in September 1887, Stairs philosophizes on the contrast between the pacific lives of his prospective victims and the carnage and chaos he will soon unleash:

> It was most interesting, lying in the bush and watching the natives quietly at their day's work; some women were pounding the bark of trees preparatory to making the coarse native cloth..., others were making banana flour by pounding up dried bananas, men we could see building huts, boys and girls running about, singing, crying, others playing on a small instrument common all over Africa. All was as it was every day until our discharge of bullets, when the usual uproar and screaming of women took place....

That final ellipsis, original to Stairs, introduces a silence that politely muffles the screams just evoked. In August 1888, Stairs reports this Kurtzian deed: "This morning I cut off the heads of the two [Wasangora] men [we shot last night] and placed them on poles one at each exit from the bush into the plantation."[120] January 1889 sees Stairs noting, "This time I have over 130 men, a lot of slaves, boys, girls, the whole forming a regular second edition of the Tower of Babel." His military practice in Africa is summed up in this February 1889 entry: "Every male native capable of using the bow is shot, this of course we must do.[121] All the children and women are taken as slaves by our men to do work in the camps." Free to lust after African women, Stairs does so, with increasing frankness:

> It was very amusing watching the young women dancing with the men, and the particular wiggle they give very "fetching."

> At Majamboni's I thought the women and girls the prettiest and most really formed of any I had yet seen in Africa. Here the women wear dressed skins for covering, as well as the small spray of grass before and behind, freshly put on every morning.

On his second expedition to Africa, Stairs reflects, "At first, black women are shy and don't dare approach a white man. But, little by little, they get bolder and finally grow familiar." In December 1891, Stairs relishes the looks of one woman, "really quite beautiful, with regular pretty features, and certainly the most beautiful woman I have yet seen west of Lake Tanganyika." His general comportment remains just as revolting as it was on his first expedition. According to one of his correspondents, Stairs put the head of a foe in an "*old kerosene tin.*" MacLaren reports that Stairs, "on two expeditions…killed many men whose sole offence was that they resisted the entry of the European expeditions and Arab slavers into their homelands." It gets worse. "On other occasions," says MacLaren, "Stairs ordered his men to kill the wounded. He had the heads cut off the dead and impaled on poles as warnings to others. But it was the severing of hands which he pursued more commonly." Stairs's account of his ferocities establishes that *even* Canadians, blinded by racism, can become swashbuckling exterminators.

One might imagine that Stairs's behaviour was aberrant. Yet Canada's December 1992 deployment of peacekeeping troops to Somalia, and the resultant incidents of lethal Negrophobic violence, suggests it is a racialized imperialism itself that mandates the agony of the disempowered and the disarmed.[122] African-Canadian sociologist Sherene H. Razack, in her brilliant 2004 study, *Dark Threats, White Knights: The Somalia Affair, Peacekeeping, and the New Imperialism*, argues that "empire is a structure of feeling, a deeply held belief in the need to and the right to dominate others *for their own good*, others who are expected to be grateful."

Razack maintains that "modern peacekeeping is constructed as a colour line with civilized white nations standing on one side and uncivilized Third World nations standing on the other." This division engenders war crimes: "Men who understand themselves to be on colonial terrain, as some Western peacekeepers seem to have done, have humiliated, raped, tortured, and killed the local population they came to help." Reflecting these tendencies, Canadians in Somalia felt "invited to 'act white'—that is, to come to know themselves as men from the land of clean snow whose presence in the hot desert of Belet Huen was a civilizing one." Believing thus, these troops could exercise a "policing violence," one required to exorcise "the perils white bodies encounter from Black mobs when they attempt to keep the peace." The result? This short, grim tally of Canadians' victims in Somalia:

On 4 March 1993, two Somalis were shot in the back by Canadian soldiers, one fatally. Barely two weeks later, on 16 March, a Somali prisoner, sixteen-year-old Shidane Abukar Arone, was tortured to death by soldiers of the Canadian Airborne Regiment.[123]

The racialist and masculinist psychologies that enabled such homicidal sadism were later illuminated by the apparition of a videotape depicting the hazing rituals of the Canadian Airborne Regiment. Here one witnesses "a Black soldier being smeared with faeces spelling out the words 'I love the KKK,' then tied to a tree and sprinkled with white flour." This blanching of black flesh was also practised in Somalia, where black children, accused of theft, were "bound with hands painted white."

Intriguingly, the rationales that the Canadian news media, government, and military voiced to explain away the torture "our boys" visited upon Somalis repeat those employed by Stairs and, a century later, by his editor, MacLaren. These explanations support a raced environment-alism (white "Nordic" men cannot cope with "tropical" climates and their dark-skinned inhabitants) and a rank Manichaeism ("civilized" whites are degraded by long, close encounters with "beastly" non-white *others*). Razack confirms this perspective: "the everyday context of peacekeeping is a colonial one, where Europeans think of themselves as bringing order and civilization to a darker race." The drawback is that they fancy "the cruelties of Africa and Africans push Western men to violence."

Then there is the problem of too much sun (which Canadian troops experience during "a six-hour march in heat of forty-five degree Celsius with insufficient water and loaded down with 45 kilograms (100 pounds) of equipment." Trying to explicate the Somalia debacle, Canadian journalist Peter Desbarats comments that "there must have been times when the heat and dust made [Canadian troops] long for [winter]." Given the conditions their soldiers faced, Canadians asked themselves this telling rhetorical question, "In Africa, who can be a saint?"

Spookily, Stairs advances similar justifications for his hacking, hanging, and gunning down of African men, his chaining of African women and children, and his leering at African females. He warns us, in September 1888, "Never believe that any man as you know him in *civilization* will be the same man in mid-Africa. Let success go as it may and that man will [still] be as different in disposition in every way, as day is from night." April 1889 finds Stairs complaining, "How wild these natives make one sometimes with their jabbering and yelling!" In August 1889, Stairs remarks that "long marches without water terrify [my men]. The hardships and the weariness cause me such endless cares." On his return to the African interior, Stairs figures that "a starving man is no longer a human being.... He cheats and robs the locals. The name of the white man, who thus acquires, through no fault of his own, a terrible reputation." It is Africa and Africans who cause whites to regress to animalistic praxis, Stairs contends. In fact, European force is necessary to impose discipline—government—upon the Africans:

Everyone who has visited Africa knows that the black is selfish, boastful and a great lover of talk

199

and *pombe* [palm wine]. He considers himself the elect, the chosen, beyond whom there is nothing else. He retains this good opinion of himself until he has received a sound thrashing from someone whom he then recognizes as his superior.

Without bloody, but sanguine, European intervention, "petty chiefs" will continue to "govern (badly) territory the size of a good Canadian farm." Viewing a cemetery where three Catholic priests have been interred, Stairs states that they "gave their lives in cause of salvation of the African from barbarism."

Given his background, Stairs *should* hold such views, but, surprisingly, so does MacLaren. Yet, as a superior Canadian diplomat (High Commissioner for Canada in the United Kingdom from 1996 to 2000 and a member of the Canadian Privy Council, appointed in 1983), MacLaren really should know better. Instead, he packages Stairs's story as the hoary one of "progression from an open innocence to a spiritual corruption." Gullibly, MacLaren accepts Conrad's *Heart of Darkness* as an "analysis of the transformation black Africa wrought in Europeans" and applies this magically exculpatory reading to Stairs: "Nothing in Stairs's life had prepared him for such ruthless and ultimately corrupting encounters with aboriginal people as he experienced on the Congo."[124] MacLaren also warrants that "most Europeans, if not all, on Congo expeditions behaved irritably, irrationally and even hysterically."[125]

While conceiving that Stairs's immorality is a function of "corruption" occasioned by the avails of "absolute power,"

MacLaren's judgment is uninformed by any notion of race and racism. MacLaren does not appreciate that Stairs's status—a white Canadian of Anglo-Saxon heritage, reared in the most militaristic of Victorian Canadian cities, and entering adulthood at the high-tide of Anglo-Canadian support for British imperialism—more than "prepared him for...ruthless actions."

No, MacLaren blames Africa and Africans for Stairs's inhumanity: "The penetration of Africa corrupted Stairs." MacLaren's ideas verify Razack's insights that "white innocence depend[s] on Black culpability" and that "the story of an encounter with unfathomable evil is only intelligible through race." MacLaren's note, regarding Stairs's enjoyment of a pit-stop among European missionaries, reveals the editor's ascription to an inadvertent racialism: "[Missionary A. M.] *MacKay's kindness* [to Stairs and his expedition] *acted as a reminder of the need to begin to adjust themselves to the values of white communities.*" MacLaren seems oblivious to the glaring irony that it was "*the values of white communities*" that were leading Stairs to devastate every African settlement he breached. MacLaren fashions one more example of what Razack calls a "biblical narrative of a First World [citizen] overwhelmed by the evil of the Third World." Like Europeans in the Congo a century earlier, Canadian war criminals in Somalia saw themselves exonerated by the identical mythology that MacLaren articulates for Stairs: they could not help it; they were, as Razack puts it, "pushed to the brink by the savagery of Africans and Africa itself."[126]

In her fine long poem on the Somalia intervention, "Sister (Y)Our Manchild at the Close of the Twentieth Century,"

African-Canadian poet Claire Harris meditates on one of the most striking aspects of the calamity, namely that some of the torturers and murderers of Somalis were, themselves, "of colour," in this case, Indigenous. One was Cree; one part-Cree; another served with the Americans. Razack wonders, "Why are two Aboriginal men beating a Black man [Shidane Arone] so mercilessly," then reflects, "Somewhere on the edges of memory in Canada, the bodies curled in a fetal position are Aboriginal ones as often as they are Black."

In her poem, Harris narrates the maturation of a Prairie Aboriginal, his decision to join the US Marines, his participation in the Persian Gulf War, and his eventual dispatch to Somalia, where his anti-African attitudes echo those of his fraternal white solders. Employing a feminist-stentorian voice, one addressing "Sister," Harris's persona, after cataloguing US escapades of the 1980s and the early 1990s ("Iraq Panama Grenada Somalia Bosnia"), informs her addressee, "we suffer race war / we who midwife evil call it realism." Her persona remembers what the "Amerindian" Canadian hero does not:

> five
> ten
> million Africans trapped branded transported
>   twice five
> ten dying
> in the attempt the three hundred years of slavery
> rape its terrible
> aftermath.

Next, the speaker recalls "the depopulation of vivid teeming Americas brown people wrenched / from the circle to vacancy the land despoiled." Now, death dines on "the innocent mountains of dark / dead the growing mountains of dead." This fact inspires dread, a "collected"—if not collective—memory of imperial-settler violence against Plains Nations and imperial Europe's enslavement of Africans:

> dead babies grim water warrior sons my
> sisters behind her scalped Blackfoot Crow
> their raped tortured women and the babies'
> brains pinkish grey moss on virgin pines
> behind her my mothers my little sisters
> chained above deck divided
> > from brothers fathers
> > earth
> (a) pleasure of those captains
> tools of gentlemen owners

Tellingly, Harris blends the Aboriginal and African experiences of epic, pseudo-genocidal violence, so both groups suffer at the "pleasure" of "captains" or "gentlemen owners." Significantly, subjugated women—whether African or Aboriginal—endure rape and torture and the slaughter of their children.[127]

While sexual assault is concomitant with imperial expansion (*Lebensraum*) and economic exploitation, it is also *de rigueur* in racialized conflicts. Razack understands that, in a patriarchal, nationalist context, "the ideal man is one who is superior to both women and racial minorities."

Applying like wisdom to her analysis of the situation of Canadian Army Aboriginals in Somalia, Razack asserts, "Membership in the Armed Forces of a white, Northern nation on duty in Africa—enables such men to engage in acts of subordination (in this case, violence against Somalis) to compensate for the devaluation they experience." In this way, these minority-group males, oppressed at home by white Canadians, obtain (temporarily) the exhilarating position of elite white males by treating other males of colour *like women*, that is to say, subject to abuse.[128] Harris highlights this irony. The Indigenous Canuck soldier, the "baby boy man," serving his white "master" and striving to be as empowered as *him*, decamps to Africa—"with his good Canadian buddies our Airborne"—and exhibits the macho racism that is his Canadian heritage.[129]

Yet the continent seems to welcome, Harris's speaker hints, "my sister's son": flamingos "rise a brisk whispering cloud"; there is "happy chatter" and "gossiping houses." Africa is defined as "that various surprising complexity that black / wine," a site of "ancient majesty" and of "frequent, original hells" that are, importantly, rich with "surprise." But the Indigenous soldier tells a British reporter, "*I think every marine came here with the idea that he might get / a chance for a confirmed kill*" (62). Harris hints that his refusal of solidarity with Somalis marks a failure of imagination, a loss of memory, and a rejection of his own mother. But the statement is purely logical, given his engagement with rapacious imperialism. He becomes, in essence, a "Half-Breed" version of Stairs, or the grown-up version of the boy-babe featured in Canadian poet Duncan Campbell Scott's 1898 sonnet "The Onondaga Madonna":[130]

And closer in the shawl about her breast,
The latest promise of her nation's doom,
Paler than she, her baby clings and lies,
The primal warrior gleaming from his eyes;
He sulks, and burdened with his infant gloom,
He draws his heavy brows and will not rest.[131]

This sestet of the poem charges that the child, a result of sexual intercourse between the Onondaga woman and a European man, represents the "doom" of the maternal line while his half-white inheritance ensures he will be a Métis Edmund, seething with restless violence, endless potential for treachery, and thus ready, in the end, to play a fearsome conquistador. This "baby boy" is likely, like the lad in Harris's poem, to disappoint his mother and desecrate his own people.[132]

While military invasion and occupation—Stairs's *penetration* of Africa, Harris's soldier itching to "notch his belt" by cutting down a Somali—offer clear allegories of sexual assault, this masculinized, plus racialized, victimization need not be directed against "alien" foes but can be utilized at home, against women and children, to keep them mute and pliant. Razack suggests a connection between household brutality and peacekeeping violence:

> For one, [this violence] is most openly practiced with several witnesses and participants. Second, the soldiers document many of the violent incidents by taking a number of videotapes and trophy

photos to visually record the violence they enact and by writing descriptions of it in their diaries.[133] A third feature is that the victims of the violence are often children and youth. Fourth, the violence is sexualized with rape and sodomy occurring.

A prime example of home-grown torture occurs in Elly Danica's searing 1988 incest-survivor memoir, *Don't: A Woman's Word*. A Dutch-Canadian immigrant to Canada, Danica speaks from the perspective of a girl-child, an older girl, an adolescent, and an adult. She details her experiences of paternal rapes, behind closed doors and in a basement, but with the full knowledge and complicity of her mother and authority figures—a lawyer, a doctor, a judge—in Moose Jaw, where they have settled. Her father, an amateur pornographer, snaps "trophy photos" of his daughter, and he abuses her verbally as much as he does physically. She endures her subjection for eleven years, until age fifteen, before fleeing her home—albeit into an appalling marriage—at age eighteen.

Publishing *Don't* just after her fortieth birthday, Danica appreciated, by then, as she later states, "As a woman, I am always a foreigner in, and never a citizen of, the patriarchal country."[134] Her memoir is thus a story of alienation and violation: "I knew as a girl that a war was being made against me, against my body, against my budding sense of who I was or might become, against my being, because I was young, female, vulnerable, and unprotected." In *Don't*, she spurns the patriarchal preachments she imbibed as a terrorized child:

And what did we learn? We learned that power is respected, that violence is respected, but that such respect is prompted by fear for the consequences, which, as far as I am concerned, has nothing to do with respect and everything to do with terrorism.

Indeed, as an "abused child," she had been expected to be a "selfless slave whose sole purpose [was] to serve the interests of the master, even at the cost of his or her life." Her subjection at her father's hands is equivalent to Africa's at Europe's, Somalia's at Canada's.

In *Beyond Don't: Dreaming Past the Dark*, published in 1996, Danica registers that her "parents refused to speak about [World War II]." However, she writes,

> My father told me once, as he held me down and forced me yet another time to do what he wanted, that he had used his hands to kill before and that it would be no hardship to do so once again and remove me from the face of the earth.

One does not know whether the father's extra-mural violence was, in inspiration, pro-Nazi or pro-Resistance, but his oppression of his daughter replicates the *feel* of the German invasion and occupation of the Netherlands. Whatever the father's feelings about the German conquest of Holland, pro or con, he visits the fury of this past aggression upon Danica, forcing her to know war trauma as rape.[135] The toxic horror of Nazi aggression is transmuted into the Gothic experience of sexual violation:

Nightmare. I am being swallowed up by a hole in the dining room floor. First, somebody touches me, then I am swallowed up. I land in a swamp. Everything I touch is sticky. Darkness. There is no place to put my feet. I slide in ooze. I am surrounded by black slime hanging from trees.

The war in Holland was similar. A 1952 novel, *Turvey* by Earle Birney, narrates a Canadian's wartime sortie to Nijmegen, Holland, offering a glimpse of the nation's vast destruction and mass pain:

The main street, either by bad luck or some diabolical aiming, was hit a few minutes ago by a V-Two. And these are two Dutch bodies lying half revealed by the acrid wind that has blown askew the sacking thrown over them. Some kind of bomb has torn up a hundred foot of paving, and there are three heaps of slaggy asphalt, sweepings from some other bombing, dumped here to repair the road. Each heap is clustered with children, some with naked blue legs, thin as willows. With frayed gloves or bare hands, they are fingering the heaps for nuggets of tar or burnable flakes of asphalt, and stowing their loot in shopping bags. No, Turvey could not fall into gaiety on the road to Nijmegen as the mist thickened to rain and then to sleet.

Danica, as a girl in Canada, is just as fragile and as vulnerable as the children Turvey spies atop the broken bits of Nijmegen pavement. Yet the protective responsibility that overseas Canadian troops felt, apparently, for Dutch children was not extended "at home" to Danica herself, a Dutch-Canadian immigrant preyed upon by her father.

No thorough student of Canadian literature may retreat from its constant barrage of tales of crisis, mayhem, rebellion, executions, war measures, incidents of fanatical misogyny, pacification exercises, crusades against First Nations peoples, naval blockades against voyaging immigrants, and popular subscriptions to superpower campaigns that feature Canadians either as fierce killers ("shock troops"—said the Huns) or as peacekeepers. In his diaries, Stairs pursues a *Pax Canadiana* for Africa that is just a licence for white and European plunder, pillage, rape, and massacres.

Harris and Razack warn that the *Pax Canadiana* ideal of peacekeeping is a mask for imperialist aggression by First World nations versus the Third. They also reveal that even First World men of colour may feel compelled to employ their vicious prerogatives of racist and sexist authority against their own oppressed peoples or those elsewhere. Finally, Danica's memoir-*cum*-slave-narrative recognizes that the *Pax Canadiana* demands that even white (in her case, Dutch) immigrant girls and women to Canada endure sexual assault—the "home" war of patriarchy—in silence.

To truly scrutinize Canadian literature is to come face to face with a subtext of war and rumours of war that nixes any pretext of peace. When Canadian scribblers speak of peace, expect arsenic in your maple syrup.

[*Building Liberty: Canada and World Peace, 1945-2005*, edited by Conny Steenman-Marcusse and Aritha van Herk. Barkhuis Publishing, 2005]

∼

I agree: Canada is a liberator, not a conquistador (except at home, versus Indigenous peoples). I, too, salute the successful campaigns to liberate Holland and Italy from the Hitlerians and to triumph by outwitting this devious foe, so their lairs became their graves. Yet courage can regress into brutality on the battlefield and oppression at home. But what if such violence, held at the ready until unleashed, results from the psychological pressure arising from our need to serve unstintingly as foot soldiers for the two Great Anglo Powers (the US and UK), because we confuse democracy with white supremacy?

∼

Canada: The Invisible Empire?

OF THE GROUP OF EIGHT—or G8—highly industrialized northern-hemisphere nations[136] that determine much of global trade rules, environmental attitudes, economic development, and foreign policy, only two lack a brazenly imperialist past: Canada and the United States. The other G8 members—the United Kingdom, France, Russia, Germany, Italy, and Japan—all erected empires, though those of the former Axis trio were short-lived. One may object that the Russian Federation's predecessor—the Soviet Union—was not, officially, an empire; yet we should remember that the Soviet Union succeeded the Russian Empire. Another objection may be made regarding the US, which although it has never formally constituted an empire has nevertheless enlarged its territory through conquest and annexation, and which possesses protectorates (such as Panama) and dependencies (such as Puerto Rico) just like any self-respecting imperial power.[137] (Note also that the 2001 decision of president George W. Bush to create a Department of Homeland Security enacts a de facto recognition of America's imperial status: only empires, which by definition exist in transnational space and exercise international power, may possess "homelands.")

Although four other historically imperial powers—Spain, Portugal, Belgium, and Holland—are absent from the G8, they are represented through their membership in the European Union, which also participates in meetings of the "octovirate," to coin a term. Of all the G8 member states and their European Union satellites, then, only Canada may legitimately be said to lack a history of imperialism. It has not conquered and settled other nations, and it holds no offshore colonies. No less an intellectual than John Ralston Saul has pointed out that Canada failed to fulfill, unlike the United States, "the model of the monolithic frontier-conquering nation-state." Historians, political scientists, and postcolonial literary critics tend to think of Canada as having been, rather, a clutch of imperial French and imperial British colonies that, having accepted a constitutional union in 1867, has been trying ever since to determine its own identity vis-à-vis Europe and America.

This vision of Canada is eminently sensible and is succinctly articulated by late Canadian political philosopher George Grant, who opined, in 1965, "To be [an English] Canadian was to build, along with the French, a more ordered and stable society than the liberal experiment in the United States." Clearly, for him, Canada is a nation, one that engages in a wary bilateral relationship with what he terms the "American Empire." But Grant also advises that "English-speaking Canadians had never broken with their origins in Western Europe," meaning that they had remained tied to the British Empire and the British Monarch and Anglo-Christianity, at least until a certain point in the twentieth century, when they began to buy into America's "homogenized culture." For his part, André

Siegfried, an early twentieth century French commentator on Canada, finds that the English and French populations in Canada constitute, together, a "colonial civilization."

Anticipating Grant, Siegfried also warns, "It is not the American nation that threatens the Canadian nation; rather, it is the American form of civilization that threatens to supplant the British." These political readings of Canada—a colony (or several) that formed a nation, under British tutelage, with European ties, which struggles against economic and cultural absorption within the US—are backed by facts. The head of state is a British native who is, constitutionally, the King or Queen of Canada; the nation utilizes the European metric system; it employs two *official* European languages; its legal system is based on both the English common law and the pre–French Revolution *code civil*; the bulk of its trade is with the US; and much of its popular culture is literally imported from the latter. Arguably, and for good reasons, these données of history and constitutional law have shaped much Canadian and international thinking about Canadian politics, history, and culture.

However, I want to trouble this relatively passive image of Canada as being an entity only gradually gaining its independence from Britain and only slowly fixing its identity as a work-in-progress while facing, next door, the distorting funhouse mirror that is America. I think that, if we scrutinize Canadian history and geography, a different, more difficult, and more challenging image of Canada emerges. What if Canada is not the lovechild of Britain and France but is, rather, a British Frankenstein's monster, so to speak, cobbled together not just for defensive purposes against a million-man US Union Army interested in teaching Britain a lesson for having backed the losing Confederacy in the Civil War but for an implicitly offensive purpose instead. What if Canada is not "America's attic" but a buttress against American expansionism during the period of naked American aggression westward? What if the world's longest undefended border is really an invisible barrier against American continentalism? What if Canada was not designed to be a country *per se* but to be a shadow empire, a sub-empire, to the British parent?

My own wondering along these lines is indebted to the indecently overlooked 1852 booklet *A Plea for Emigration, or Notes on Canada West,* a propaganda tract authored by that marvellous African-American bluestocking Mary Ann Shadd, who, while serving the Abolitionist cause from her base in Canada West (or Ontario), also undertook extensive public lecture tours. Shadd's booklet, published in Detroit, urges African-Americans to emigrate from the slaveholding republic to the province of Canada, where, thanks to Queen Victoria's just rule, they will finally know peace, equality, prosperity, literacy, and liberty.

That "plea for emigration" is remarkable in and of itself, but Shadd goes further. As if foreseeing today's geopolitical talking-head strategists, she positions herself before a globe and begins to comment on the choicest sites for African-American emigration. She rules out Africa (too hot), Canada East (Quebec) and South America (too Catholic), and several other potential refuges, but solidly favours Canada West, British Columbia, and Jamaica. Moreover, her reasons for doing so may anticipate Britain's own strategies for imping along Canadian

Confederation in 1867. Righteously, she calls for mass African-American settlement in the Canadian territories to buttress them against what she sees as an aggressively expansionist slaveholding power, namely the US. In other words, she argues that it is in the African-American interest to "garrison" (her verb) Jamaica in order to protect the newly slavery-free West Indies, as well as Cuba, from potential American aggression to expand slavery; to ensure that Vancouver Island and Canada West do not fall prey to American expansionism; and to "keep up the balance of power."

Given that an African-American public intellectual was musing about these sorts of purposes in stimulating African-American movement into British imperial Canada, so must have colonial overlords in London and their thoughtful white Canadian underlings also entertained necessary speculations. See, for instance, John Richardson's 1832 *Wacousta; or, The Prophecy: A Tale of the Canadas*, a novel that replays the War of 1812 (of which Richardson was a veteran), and not only the strife between Briton/Canadian and American but also between Europeans and Natives. This conflict is doubly racialized, however, for Richardson often describes his Aboriginal characters as black in colour, thus giving the trilateral struggle among British North American, American, and Aboriginal peoples a fourth and racial dimension. This manoeuvre is important, for, in his fine 2006 study, *White Civility: The Literary Project of English Canada*, Daniel Coleman holds that the debates about "American liberty" versus "British [Canadian] law and order" are merely "a struggle between men over degrees of whiteness."

Indeed, the question of whose white supremacy is most

superior lies behind the question of whose imperialism leads best: American or British. Or *Canadian*? Colonial Nova Scotian poet Oliver Goldsmith lauds the latter. His poem, *The Rising Village*, published in 1834, calls in its conclusion for the rise of Acadia as a Western Empire to rival Britain. Goldsmith salutes Britain as being "matur'd and strong", and shining "in manhood's prime, / The first and brightest star of Europe's clime." But he goes on to hope that Acadia's "glories rise, / To be the wonder of the Western skies.... / Till empires rise and sink no more." Clearly, while Britain may dominate "Europe's climes," Acadia should, thinks Goldsmith, "star" in "Western skies." For his part, Coleman explains, "Canadian imperialists...represent a peculiar progeny of British imperialism in that they advocated loyalty to Britain at the same time as they believed Canada's newly acquired wealth of resources (once it had annexed the northwest) would cause the young, giant nation to supplant Britain as the centre of the British Empire."

The most famous—and arguably most accomplished—author of nineteenth-century Canada, Thomas Chandler Haliburton, as of 1835, began publishing slapstick satirical sketches to promote industry in Nova Scotia, defend slavery and black oppression, denounce democratization as being opposed to the principles of monarchy, hierarchy, and law and order, and lobby for greater colonial Canadian participation in the running of the empire. For Haliburton, "first principles" meant feeling "attached to the mother country [Britain] and [desiring] to live under a monarchical form of government."[138] That Haliburton died in 1865 as an elected member of the British Parliament provides some testimony to the extent to which he tried to put his beliefs into practice. But Richardson, Goldsmith, and Haliburton were not alone in musing about the future of colonial Canada within the British Empire and seeking greater power, or, as in Goldsmith's case, dreaming of the day when Acadia/ Canada would actually displace imperial Britain.

In a May 29, 2008, article in *The New York Review of Books*, Geoffrey Wheatcroft acknowledges that, in the pre– Second World War era, "the real enemy of Great Britain and its empire was the United States." (True: expecting eventual war with the British Empire, the United States developed, in 1930, a scheme to invade Canada, titled "War Plan Red," which, according to Floyd Rudmin's 1993 book *Bordering on Aggression*, called for "the first-use of nerve-gas, at the earliest possible time.") Thus, loyalist British Canadians were quite right to look askance at the United States and to trumpet the virtues of the British connection (or, in the case of Goldsmith, to envision and plump for Canada's ascendency over its English-speaking parent). It is for these reasons that, as Rudmin reminds us, a Canadian colonel, James Sutherland "Buster" Brown, promoted a strike-first strategic attack on the United States, calling for a type of Canuck *Blitzkrieg* into the US heartland, wreaking havoc and mass carnage, until the British could sail and march to the Dominion's rescue.

Then again, the great twentieth-century Caribbean intellectual C. L. R. James has opined, "There is nothing so fierce as an imperialist in the colonies." Too, Coleman holds that "settler colonies are founded on a paradox in that 'they simultaneously resisted and accommodated the authority of an imperialist Europe.'" According to Canadian literary theorist Northrop Frye, "The imperial and the regional are both inherently anti-poetic environments, yet they go hand in hand; and together they make up what I call the colonial in Canadian life." In 1907, English-Canadian humourist Stephen Leacock feels, "Imperialism means but the realization of a greater Canada, the recognition of a wider citizenship."

Taken together, these comments suggest that English Canadians suffered a kind of schizoid psychology, both before and after Confederation, in 1867: they were Canadian and colonial—derivative but also British and imperial, that is to say, empowered to co-manage the British Empire. Grant upholds this point, asserting, "The collapse of nineteenth-century Europe automatically entailed the collapse of Canada": his statement suggests that he sees no separation between being Canadian and being British (or French). Those who sought a nationalist Canadian or un-British identity were condemned, thus, to perennial self-doubt, asking, as Frye does, "Where is here?" Or, with even more abject sorrow, "Who am I?" Fascinatingly, it is Frantz Fanon who acknowledges, in his 1961 book, *The Wretched of the Earth*, that "colonialism forces the people it dominates to ask themselves the question constantly: In reality, who am I?"

Too, one can apply to Canada the observations that Lloyd King offers Latin America and the Caribbean, namely "its colonial and neo-colonial situations, its New World idiosyncracies of geography, the impress of the language[s] and the traditions of [Europe], and the results of the encounter between [European] imperialism and colonization on Indian and transported African peoples and their cultures." These factors result, mandates King, in "a search for definition which [is] simultaneously a quest for recognition" as well as the production of "cultural nationalism along with an obsession with the new" and "a fascination with the archaic or traditional aspects of one's native ground." While shared whiteness allowed English Canadians to imagine a trans-Atlantic solidarity with real Britons, their imperialism helped feed the same kind of self-questioning that non-white British subjects experienced in nations/colonies that were never given a self-governing or semi-imperial status.

In Canada's case, this unitary double-citizenship (so to doublespeak) did facilitate British interests. Leacock's aspiration for a "greater Canada" had already been set in motion by Confederation, wherein four colonies had been united, more or less by imperial fiat, into one larger, semi-autonomous nation, whose head of state was also, simultaneously, the Queen of Great Britain and the Empress of India. Furthermore, this "greater Canada" of Nova Scotia, New Brunswick, Canada West, and Canada East, would expand further by adding the western colonies of Manitoba and British Columbia, in 1870; the eastern colony of Prince Edward Island, in 1873; the so-called North-West Territories of Alberta and Saskatchewan, in 1905 (while simultaneously enlarging the territories of Ontario and Québec); and Newfoundland, a British colony bestowed upon Canada (perhaps via Machiavellian legerdemain), in 1949.

Although Leacock had in mind a Canada enhanced by increased participation in, say, running Africa and India, in concert with Britain, the British daughter, Canada, became geographically grander, expanding by accumulating new territories and colonies to the point that it matched the transcontinental reach of the United States. Sherene H. Razack registers that Canadians believe they "never [have] been a colonial power or engaged in aggressive occupations," but she knows it is a myth, calling attention to "internal colonialism [against Indigenous peoples]."

Indeed, intriguingly, while commentators have recognized the implicitly imperialistic growth of the US at this period of time, Canada's quieter but just as insistent expansion has seldom been recognized as also being imperialist. Hence, the Martiniquan-born Algerian anti-imperialist Fanon is able to write, in *The Wretched of the Earth*, "Two centuries ago, a former European colony decided to catch up with Europe. It succeeded so well that the United States of America became a monster, in which the taints, the sickness, and the inhumanity of Europe have grown to appalling dimensions." Yet Canadians—and especially English Canadians—who saw no break in continuity between themselves and Europe or Britain (and, thus, no globe-straddling need to "catch up") were active participants in oppressive imperial(ist) campaigns, both at home and abroad. While it is true that French philosopher Jean-Paul Sartre refers collectively to "that super-European monstrosity, North America" in his introduction to *The Wretched of the Earth*, it is not at all clear that he is including Canada and Mexico in this condemnation. For both Sartre and Fanon, the possibility of a specifically Canadian imperialism seems remote.

Even so, as Shadd foresaw in 1852, the only real threat to British North America was the empire-building US, whose principal bard of the era, Walt Whitman, penned rhapsodies—as in his screed *Democratic Vistas* (1871)—predicting the eventual enclosure of the Canadian colonies within the freedom-loving Republic.[139] Cross-border Irish nationalist Fenian raids in the 1860s underlined this danger, as did the reality of a post–Civil War US government irritated by tacit British support for the erstwhile Confederacy. True: scholars have often noted these circumstances as reasons for British support of Canadian Confederation. But I think there was another, equally salient reason, one that would allow Canadian subjects to help preserve and extend the Empire in a passive-aggressive fashion: namely, by blocking the north-ward continental extension of the United States.[140]

It is helpful here to recall a poetic cognomen historians have bestowed upon colonial Canada. "The Empire of the St. Lawrence" is a term that underlines the role of the fur trade in the rise of New France, pinpointing Montreal, which remained, until the 1970s, the financial capital of Canada. (See Donald Creighton's *The Empire of the St. Lawrence*.) Just as vital, though, has been the nationalist romance of Canada as the land of the "North-West"—a Shangri-La of potential. The Canadian "North-West" refers to the Prairies and the Arctic, romantically, as a single, undifferentiated region and confers upon it the fabulous sense that here is Canada's Promised Land of ungodly wealth and divine heft. (Here, I want to trouble Saul's notion that colonial Canada did not proceed as a "frontier-conquering nation-state" by reminding us that the sponsors of British North America and New France—the British and French Empires, respectively—did so. Canada is the result of the armed pacification and occupation of the northern reaches of North America by the emissaries of these two imperial powers.)

If we think of central Canada as "The Empire of the St. Lawrence" and western and northern Canada as "The Canaan of the North-West," we may imagine that one reason for the continued western-eastern cultural-political split in Canada has to do with competing imperial inheritances, including the signal fact that two western provinces—Alberta and Saskatchewan—were governed as colonies from the eastern-dominated capital, Ottawa, until 1905. Ottawa is still the controller—imperial, I will say—of three entities, namely, the Yukon, the Northwest Territories, and Nunavut. To upset Canadian political scientists, it may be more logical to refer, in general, to provinces as colonies and the federal government as imperial.

Certainly, the Riel or North-West Rebellions make better sense viewed in this regard. Canadian literary scholar Frank Davey argues that Louis Riel became "a symbol of the Catholic-Protestant and French-English conflict in Canada." But he was also a mystical Métis in an age of *Lebensraum* imperialism trumpeting "blood purity." Thus, his rebellion had a racial element: it was an insurrection of Indigenous people against white settler overlords and their hunger for territorial enlargement in the so-called North-West. Moreover, Riel's erection of a provisional government constituted a threat to the imperial authority of Ottawa. After the defeat of Riel's forces and his execution, Ottawa borrowed a strategy of the British Empire in attempting to settle the Prairie provinces—or the "North-West"—with peoples who would be loyal to itself: in this case, British settlers and Eastern European serfs. However, as these "North-West" territories obtained provincial self-goverment, they became more and more assertive of their relative sovereignties, frustrating whatever pan-Canadian nationalism and identities the federal government had sought (or seeks) to inculcate.

But a further result of the British imperial consolidation of British North America as an expressly east-west expansionary Canada, and what may have been its motivation, is, again, its blocking of the northward thrust of the American Republic. John Milton's proverb "They also serve who only stand and wait" applies here, I think, to Canadian Confederation: it was a passive, non-militaristic means of frustrating American Manifest Destiny while also legitimizing the expansion of the empires of the St. Lawrence and the North West, with a constitution giving Ottawa the power to admit new colonies. (Interestingly, Ottawa created a special constabulary—the North-West Mounted Police— to oversee the settlement of that territory.) The formation of the Dominion of Canada was a British imperialist gambit to blunt American imperialism (or continentalism). Perhaps one reason why Canadian imperialism has gone unremarked is that it was (and is) a counter-imperialism to that of the United States. (Remember Frye's pithy definition of a Canadian: "A Canadian is an American who rejects the Revolution." Here is one source of Canadian strategic—or counter—imperialism.)

One may surmise this counter-imperialism from the enthusiasms of English Canadians, especially, following Confederation and the deliberate, persistent bulking up of the

Canadian state in terms of territory and authority, but also in terms of a fanatic passion for British conquistador imperialism, at least up until the election of Wilfrid Laurier as prime minister, in 1896. It is a poignant irony indeed that, even before Confederation, an Africadian—or African Nova Scotian—sailor, William Hall, won the Victoria Cross, the British Empire's highest honour for military valour, by almost single-handedly serving to suppress the Indian Mutiny, at Lucknow, in 1857. Thus, a black man, descended from Africans brought to the Americas on a European slave vessel, assisted Europeans in maintaining their oppression and exploitation of India even while he faced, undoubtedly, white racism in British North America and from his British military superiors.

Born in Halifax in 1863, William Grant Stairs was one of the first graduates of the Royal Military College in Kingston, Ontario, and soon found himself stationed as a surveyor in the North-West Territories. According to Stairs's latter-day editor, Roy MacLaren, "young Canadians such as Stairs" thought of the whole globe-girdling British Empire "as part of their natural birthright, just as Canada itself was." Stairs himself believed that "authority [over the negroes] should be exercised by whites to the exclusion of all, and the sooner the better." After accepting a commission in the British Army, Stairs accompanied British explorer Henry Stanley to the Congo in 1887, where he was to record in his diaries, not published entirely until 1998, that he cut off natives' heads and spiked them on poles, a scene that may have inspired Joseph Conrad's *Heart of Darkness*. (Indeed, on his second trip to Africa in 1891, Stairs records, in his diary, his impression that he is "back on the road to the heart of darkness," a phrase that may have turned up in the 1891 serialization of parts of his diaries in *The Nineteenth Century*, a British magazine. In his classic work, *How Europe Underdeveloped Africa*, Guyanese intellectual Walter Rodney writes, "Unilever factories established in... Canada were participants in the expropriation of Africa's surplus and in using that surplus for its own development."

In *Passport to the Heart: Reflections on Canada Caribbean Relations*, published in 2001, Barbadian lawyer Trevor A. Carmichael notes that Great Britain mused, during the Great War, that Canada should "secure its colonies in the tropics." Hence, Canadian prime minister Robert Borden commissioned Joseph Pope to "study and report on the subject of the annexation of the West India islands to the Dominion of Canada." Pope's report, titled "Confidential Memorandum upon the Subject of the Annexation of the West India Islands to the Dominion of Canada," concluded, "Annexation would be advantageous." Authoritative historian of African Canada Robin W. Winks monitors these waxing-waning Canadian imperial aspirations in the Caribbean (a region subcontracted to Canada by Britain) in his 1968 *Canadian–West Indian Union: A Forty-Year Minuet*. From a Canadian imperialist perspective, annexation of—or union with—the British West Indies made geopolitical sense, for it would, according to Carmichael, serve Canada's "role within the British Empire as well as fulfilling its perceived North American responsibilities."

As far back as the 1870s, the Canada First movement called for "closer trade relations with the West Indies, with a view to ultimate political connexion." In the late nineteenth-century, Nova Scotia–born prime minister Charles Tupper said, reportedly, "The day is coming when Canada, which has become the right arm of the British Empire, will dominate the American continent." If the Dominion of Canada's invention and expansion into the North-West was intended, in part, to blunt American aspirations in that section of the continent, the proposed expansion into the Caribbean would have accomplished the same—on behalf of the British Empire. In *The History of Canadian Business, 1867–1914*, R. T. Naylor writes that, due to a "profound depression in the sugar islands" in 1884/85, "inside Canada some pressure for outright annexation existed, especially after Britain announced it had no objection to Canada annexing Jamaica." Naylor also states that, as a result of the Spanish-American War, "Prospects of political union between Canada and Jamaica…improved." In 1911, "Canadian financiers…began a campaign for the annexation of the Bahamas."

It is worthwhile to notice that, customarily, when the word *annexation* is voiced in relation to Canada, it is in the context of fear of American aggression. (Even the atrocious Adolf Hitler thought this event was likely, suggesting in a September 2, 1942, dinner conversation that, if America believed the British Empire was disintegrating, it might occupy Canada.) Here, however, one encounters the proposal that Canada annex—in the ready imperial fashion—another foreign territory. This notion may seem surprising, but, arguably, the Dominion of Canada was already engaged in annexing its own North-West Territories, and, in 1949, instead of annexing the British West Indies, it annexed Newfoundland. (One might even perceive the

British-engineered takeover of Newfoundland by Canada as a kind of consolation prize for its reluctance to aggressively confront US influence in the Caribbean by annexing West Indian colonies.) It is perhaps because Canada was acting in a manner similar to its sponsor, the British Empire, that French Canadians lauded fascist Italy's invasion (or annexation) of Ethiopia (Abyssinia) in 1935 as "a lesson taught to the British Empire by a Catholic and Latin country," or so claims Filippo Salvatore in his 1998 oral history *Fascism and the Italians of Montreal*.

Oui, Canada did not annex the British West Indies—mainly due to its ascription to late-nineteenth-century views of race. Cultural historian Petrine Archer-Straw recognizes that "Darwin's suggestion that the white race was superior in the human species had the impact of providing a pseudo-scientific justification for European expansion and imperialism." Coleman asserts that Canadian imperialism has always been invested in "race, Britishness and the ideology of 'enterprise.'" Due to its imbrication with racist, white supremacist philosophies and practices, Canada's designs on the Caribbean foundered. The *Monetary Times* reported, "Annexation would bring us [a large black] population which it is not desirable to have" (see Naylor).

In this context, we must recall that the Ku Klux Klan, or the Knights of the Ku Klux Klan, and other varieties of this American Negrophobic terrorist organization, billed themselves as constituting an "Invisible Empire." (See Anthony Karen's 2009 work, *The Invisible Empire: Ku Klux Klan*.) This nomenclature was not an exaggeration, for, at the height of its strength, in the 1920s, the Klan was the de facto government of Indiana as well as a significant force in Tennessee, Oklahoma, and Oregon. In 1924, the year of its zenith, it had six million members, including Canadians attracted by its anti-Catholic message. The connection between the Klan's "Invisible Empire" and that of Canada is that both are predicated on the informal promulgation of white supremacy. However, Canadian white supremacy can operate in both an explicitly imperialist political mode and a subtle commercial mode.

Hence, although Canada never organized a political empire within the Caribbean, its capitalists have been perennially present there. Naylor records that, in the early twentieth century, "Trinidad had Canadian capital in its telephone system,…and in its electric light and tramway company." Another Canuck syndicate was "responsible for utilities in Demerara and Kingston." In 1912, according to an essay by Kathryne V. Lindberg, "a Winnipeg securities firm began a big advertising campaign to sell banana lands in central America for $20 an acre." In Jamaica, Lindberg writes, "the Canadian firm, West Indian Tramway Company…raised fares and refused to increase the wages of the conductors and motormen who were forced to do more work, including policing those who refused to pay the increased fare." The Canadian company's "intransigence" led to "a confrontation that pitted Jamaicans against a foreign [monopoly] and implicitly against colonial rule itself." In 1971, Carl Lumumba wrote this protest paragraph:

It seems obvious that Canadian exploitation of the West Indies is deep-rooted in history. The salted pig offal—ears, snout, neckbone, rib bones, knuckles, feet, and backbone—which fed the negro slaves were supplied by Canada. Supplied under similar cicumstances were third-rate, dried salted cod, herrings, and mackerels. These forms of food which white Canadians disdain to eat, are still supplied to the West Indies, in keeping with these three-hundred-year-old depraved trade agreements.

African-Canadian historian Afua Cooper is less bitter about this long commerce between Canada and the Caribbean: "There was a brisk trade between the capitalists of eastern Canada and the slaveholders of the Caribbean. Fish from Newfoundland and eastern Canada fed the enslaved people in the West Indies. The maritime products were then exchanged for slave-grown products: sugar, rum, molasses, tobacco, coffee, and the like. West Indian slaves were also bought by Canadian slaveholders and merchants." Several of Canada's transnational corporations—Rio Tinto Alcan, the Bank of Nova Scotia (Scotiabank), and the Royal Bank of Canada (RBC), to name but a few—are major regional players in the Caribbean. Too, the Canadian people—as tourists—carry out their own annual occupations of Caribbean beaches and resorts, often with utter gringo disregard for local cultures. Finally, in both 1974 and 1985, the Turks and Caicos Islands sought admission to Canada as a province but were rejected by the Pierre Trudeau and Brian Mulroney governments, respectively. Trudeau opposed the idea because it seemed neo-colonial; Mulroney feared the acquisition of what might become, in sum, a black Newfoundland—a welfare dependency.

In reviewing this history of Canadian military and economic intervention abroad, we may conclude that one reason these ventures have seldom been labelled "imperialist" is because they have been undertaken on behalf of greater self-declared empires, such as Britain's and, nowadays, the United States'. It would be an interesting project, then, for an art historian and cultural critic to document the statuary erected in various Canadian cities and towns in honour of our deadly missions on behalf of one empire or the other. In Halifax, one finds the only memorial to the Crimean War in North America, a monument to two Haligonians slain in the Battle of Sebastopol. In Montreal, the only equestrian statue in the city honours the slain of the Boer War. Also in Montreal is a statue of Norman Bethune, an Ontario-born doctor who died in China while providing medical services to the People's Liberation Army of Mao Zedong. In downtown Ottawa, within sight of Parliament Hill, stands a grove of busts of colonial and post-Confederation Canadian war heroes. On the Niagara Escarpment, near Niagara Falls, a statue of General Brock, a hero of the War of 1812, peers at the US from atop a column reminiscent of London's Nelson's, staring down defiantly at the adjacent cliffs of New York State.

Such statuary bears mute testimony to the historical lust of Canadians—English Canadians—to serve as cannon fodder in the voluptuous wars of larger, more certain empires.[141] Assuredly, Canada—the deputy empire to Great Britain and the counter-empire to the United States—has sought to prove its allegiance to its French and British parents through indulgence in Norman or Gothic architecture. But it has also, arguably, domesticated the influence of the British

Raj, thus legitimizing British imperialism, a point apparent, I think, in the designs of the provincial legislatures of British Columbia and Ontario. (That arch observer of empire and its minions, spy novelist Ian Fleming, in his James Bond thriller *For Your Eyes Only*, observes of the building then housing the Department of Justice in Ottawa, "Like most Canadian public buildings, [it] is a massive block of grey masonry built to look stodgily important and to withstand the long and hard winters.")

Despite Canada's history of imperialism—at home and abroad—very few authors have commented upon it, and even fewer have criticized it. Introducing the third[142] African-Canadian literary anthology, *Canada in Us Now*, which appeared in 1976, editor Harold Head, born in South Africa, argues that the rhetoric of black consciousness and anti-imperialism is the rallying point for black—and brown (Asian)—intellectuals displaced in(to) Canada. Yet, while contributors to the anthology attack white Canadian racism and Western imperialism, none tackles the Canadian version, except, obliquely, Arthur Nortje, a South African native who immigrated to Canada in 1967, then left for England in 1970, where he committed suicide. (Note that, in his poetry, Nortje attacks South African apartheid, British imperialism, and Canadian anti-black and anti-Indigenous racism. But he also excoriates Canada for accepting racist white South Africans as immigrants and for the weakness of what he terms its "bulldozer civilization." For Nortje, every part of the putative Anglo-Saxon Union—South Africa, Britain, and Canada—proves hostile to black and mixed-race peoples. In his tramps around London's Trafalgar Square, Nortje would surely have noticed that Canada House and South Africa House—the two nations' embassies—flank this centre of the old empire and are as oppressive as their mentor.)

One of the few African-Canadian authors to attack Canadian imperialism directly is Jamaican-born Dub poet Lillian Allen, who notes with scathing irony, in her poem "I Fight Back," that Canadian corporations are welcome in the West Indies while she and other immigrants of colour are not welcome in Canada:

> ITT ALCAN KAISER
> Canadian Imperial Bank of Commerce
> These are privileged names in my Country
> But I AM ILLEGAL HERE

Later on in the poem, Allen's persona sets the black immigrant's plight against the context of white Canadian "romantic" racism:

> And Constantly they ask
> "Oh Beautiful Tropical Beach
> With Coconut Tree and Rum
> Why did you Leave There
> Why on Earth did you Come?"
>   AND I SAY:
> For the Same Reasons
> Your Mothers Came.

I would be remiss not to also mention, here, African-Canadian apologists for Anglo-Saxon imperialism: the first

African-Canadian lawyer, Abraham Beverley Walker (1851–1909), and the first African-Canadian woman to publish a book of poetry, Anna Minerva Henderson (1887–1987), whose sole chapbook of self-published verse, *Citadel*, appeared in 1967, when she was eighty. Both Walker and Henderson address British imperialism, although Henderson does so from a seemingly raceless Canadian position while Walker views it from a black-nationalist perspective.

Surely, it is best to describe Walker as a neo-British imperialist, whose discourse is intended to counter the white supremacism and Anglo-Saxon chauvinism of the Canadian Imperial Federationists of the day, who wanted white British-descended Canadians to help white Britons, Australians, New Zealanders, and South Africans police and administer the empire. (D. R. Owram records that, "When British imperialists founded the Imperial Federation League in 1884, Canadian supporters established branches. They sought a way for Canada to develop beyond colonial status without separating from the empire." Mixing "Christian idealism and anti-Americanism," they believed that the dominions "should participate in foreign policy at the imperial level.")

Walker's Pan-Africanist-*cum*-anglophilic imperialism is a deliberately blackened ancillary to the white Anglo-Saxon fetish of Canadian Imperial Federationists. In a 1903 article in his literary journal, *Neith*, Walker espouses his dream of African "uplift," to be accomplished by African acceptance of "the advanced institutions of Christendom," by its being "brought within the pale of Christian civilization," and by its submission to the leadership of African Diasporic intellectuals like Walker himself, so as to effect "the ultimate, triumphant nationalization of the race." Walker's model administration for his African Civilization Movement is British:

> To have everything about it and in it British. To adopt British laws and traditions. To have the system of education British. To follow British ideals of life. And to pattern after British models of society.... And our common schools will be copies of the best common schools in Anglo-Saxon countries.

Walker's answer to aggressive British and European imperialism in Africa is the African Diasporic embrace of a British brand of imperialism to govern Africa in its own name. Yet its precepts, had they succeeded, would also have justified the ferocious repression of Indigenous Africans and their cultures, religions, languages, and civilizations. But Walker was willing to undertake this task in order to lay "the foundation of nationhood and empire in the land of [our] forefathers." No wonder his publication contradictorily fuses New World African imperialism to the global white supremacy enthused in by backers of what John Daniel Logan in 1923 called an "Anglo-Saxon union" between Great Britain and the United States. Then again, as Nova Scotian historian Barry Cahill reports, Walker believed that "the white race was deteriorating so badly that a little admixture of Negro blood would be good for it." Perhaps he really did envision a black-white partnership in ruling Africa.

Henderson's pro-British attitude is more Canadian than African-Canadian. In her poem "Corner Grocery Store," her persona discovers a London shop that reminds her of a corner store she knew in her hometown of Saint John, New Brunswick. She exults, "Oceans do not divide us, but unite. / It was like coming home when all was said." The "us" envisioned here is Canadian and British. Yet the London "grocery store" also reflects the empire, "with its goods from everywhere," thus yielding "a jolly place to learn geography!" The London shop is a locus of British imperialism (now translated into a global supply of consumer goods for "home" consumption) and of the global reach of English civilization. But the London store is also reminiscent of the Saint John one, thereby indicating that Saint John is a partner in British imperialism or, rather, a proponent of the Canadian, British-derived version. Bearing in mind that the British Empire was a maritime one, it was under its blood-coloured banner (the British naval flag—or Red Ensign—Canada's official flag until 1965) that the world's oceans were, metaphorically, united. In this regard, Henderson's "us" refers to all who speak English—the global language, one promulgated by imperial (British) domination. Arguably, though, Henderson's poem seeks to render British imperialism more palatable as a kind of multicultural liberalism: its flag and cannon/canon unify humanity.

In moving toward a conclusion, I want to suggest that the hidden history of Canadian imperialism carries profound ramifications for how we configure the nation's literature. To say that Canada is postcolonial is too reductive, especially if we think that the term implies, to cite Stephen M. Finn, "the overthrow of the colonial"—which is fallacious, for "the major former occupying power might have been physically removed, but another is still hanging on." This point is abjectly true for Canada, where British occupation has been long gone but where British symbols and a British head of state not only remain but are entrenched.

Reed Way Dasenbrock questions the applicability of "postcolonial" to First World settler-regime economic powers like Canada as opposed to Indigenously controlled ex-colonies. Yet Canada is postcolonial in terms of its origin in the power struggles between discrete empires (first British and French, then British versus the uppity American colossus, and *always* the conflicts between settlers/colonists [and descendants] and Indigenous peoples). Understood in this way, "postcolonial" describes an ongoing process of complex interchanges between ex-empires and the territories they annexed, exploited, conquered, settled, and then were expelled from or permitted to exit quietly. But Canada is also quasi-imperial in terms of its relationship to its own "territories," its original organization and expansion vis-à-vis the United States, its political and economic relationships with Africa and the Caribbean, its latent authority to welcome new provinces and territories into its union, and its deputy imperial intervention in (once-)established empires' wars. In sum, we need more political sophistication and less innocence in reading Canadian literature, history, political science, jurisprudence, and geography. Canada is not the "Peaceable Kingdom" but an empire-sized nation with occasional (if nuanced) imperial ambitions.

Moreover, the memory of its deep engagement with British imperialism is evident in a landscape littered with war memorials to the Canadian dead in conflicts materially irrelevant to Canada. Canada's heritage of violent, racially charged intervention in foreign conflict is an inheritance of its British-fostered—and now US-affianced—imperialism.

[*The Canadian Mosaic in the Age of Transnationalism*, edited by Jutta Ernst and Brigitte Glaser. Heidelberg: Universitätsverlag, 2010]

∾

Because Canada misunderstands itself, thus acting as Britain's extension into the Americas (despite persistent francophone objection), so have our authors—from Thomas Chandler Haliburton to Conrad Black—proposed our constant solicitude of American or British regimens and policies. In studying the works of poets Ralph Gustafson and Rita Joe (as do the pursuant two essays), one sees how Gustafson arrived at a love of the local only after attempting a cosmopolitan utterance that was vapid when it was not opaque; in contrast, Joe, grounded in her Indigenous identity, never felt the anguish of having to kowtow to alienating traditions.

∾

The Road to North Hatley:
Ralph Gustafson's Postcolonial Odyssey

In memory of John Pengwerne Matthews (1928–1995)

IN THE AUTUMN OF HIS CAREER, in a 1981 memoir titled "Some Literary Reminiscences of the Eastern Townships," Ralph Gustafson reflected on his first dreams of literary success: "As a neophyte, how I longed to be thought one of this valour of warbling authors indigenous to the summer waters and winter snowdrifts of the Eastern Townships!" The words carry a scintilla of emotion, illuminating the extent to which the rural anglophone *Cantons-de-l'Est* of Quebec, the "inscape" which nurtured the tyro poet, informed his vocation. Accordingly, following a genteel three-decade-long exile involving shuttling among Oxford, London, and New York City, Gustafson returned, in 1963, to the demesne of his childhood, settling with his wife, Elisabeth, in North Hatley, beside Lake Massawippi. Here, he wrote the poems that won him distinction and the poems that should accord him immortality.

But the rah-rah nostalgia of Gustafson's memoir obscures the truth that the road to North Hatley had not been an obvious one for the ambitious younger poet to take. The "warbling" of a local tradition did not come naturally to him. For this reason, Gustafson's career exemplifies the (post-)colonial dilemma that Tobago-born Canadian poet M. NourbeSe Philip sketches in the introduction to her collection of poems, *She Tries Her Tongue, Her Silence Softly Breaks* (1989): "To come upon an understanding of language good-english-bad-english english, Queenglish and Kinglish—the anguish that is english in colonial societies."[143] This "anguish" arises from the difficulty of attempting to domesticate an imperial English—its legislated grammar, diction, and traditions—that is to say, to make it one's own. The necessary emancipation, or rather decolonization, must be won in the forum of form. Problematically, Gustafson had to publish poetry for some two decades before he could arrive at this solution.

One of the last important pre-1914-born English-Canadian poets to commence his career with a sense of colonial anxiety in regard to both the British poetic heritage and the seemingly manifest American destiny, Gustafson had good reason to worry. Neither the British nor the American canons had much room for Canadian interlopers, and a commanding Canadian canon, as such, did not exist. Hence, starting out, Gustafson faced the possibility of winning either an annihilating obscurity within the dominant Anglo-American canon (the fate of Bliss Carman) or, worse, a celebrated mediocrity within the local (the fate of Frederick George Scott.)

Though high modernist techniques signalled a way out of this quandary, Gustafson seems to have presumed, at first, that their adoption mandated the disappearance of the local (save for token, revocable moments). Indeed, by juxtaposing Gustafson's 1944 poems with those published in 1960, one becomes conscious of a sharp schism in his work, between the high modernist, orthodox poems of the Fierce Forties—with their distracted imagery—and the downhome-in-North-Hatley lyrics of the Seditious Sixties and later. Arguably, the wispy universality toward which Gustafson strove in 1944 gave way to a grounded localism in his later poetry. Significantly, it is these plainer pieces that occasion his unassailable grandeur. Because his oeuvre, in its first decades, evinces philosophical wrong turns and poetical dead ends, it is instructive to examine the ideological barriers that Gustafson encountered on the twisting road, via Europe and New York, to North Hatley. Gustafson's odyssey and final homecoming reveal the perils that beset a lynchpin of Canadian literary modernism.

A shooting war was devastating Europe, North Africa, and the Pacific Rim when Gustafson, a debonair thirtyish litteratus-about-Manhattan with two respected books of respectably Romantic poetry to his credit, trained critical fire upon the provincial philistines occupying English-Canadian poetry. In his preface to his apprentice 1942 Pelican-published *Anthology of Canadian Poetry,* Gustafson sounds militantly peremptory as he outflanks his parochial foes:

> A Canadian poet can no longer consider that his poem derives importance solely because it is written; his increasing individuality has outgrown a

former imitativeness of the pre-1914 English poetic convention; he has a critical familiarity with poetic advances in the United States and England; a kinetic sensitivity to his social environment—these factors have produced a Canadian poetry which is urgent, which can exist as poetry while remaining (not only geographically) distinguishable as Canadian.

Perhaps the *citoyen du monde* rhetoric—"increasing individuality," "critical familiarity," and "kinetic sensitivity"—is more like A. J. M. Smith, another Manhattanized Canuck, whose theories sculpted Gustafson's forties' poetics. In any case, Gustafson's preface, first inked in January 1941, exudes the clairvoyant passion of a Canadian determined to avoid the hacking cough of a rheumatoid provincialism. The preface is neither the *Regina Manifesto* nor *What Is to Be Done?*, but it does imply a yearning to sweep away the trashy maple leaf patriotism that too many English-Canadians thought requisite for a *Canadian* poetry. Gustafson lectures his readers, "'Canadianism' is not a poem." His selections for his anthology were judged, he warns, "not by historical significance nor by 'Canadianism,' but in terms of vitality: is it *alive* or *dead*?" Colonialism was, it seemed, dead. Paradoxically, though, Gustafson was imbibing the modernist-*cum*-aestheticist tenets of Smith and the new wave in American and British poetry. His preface suggests an adherence to what Smith termed a cosmopolitan tradition[144]—and to metropolitan schools in New York and London. Nevertheless, Gustafson remained a partisan of Canadian poetry:

Most non-Canadians will be surprised to learn that Canadian poetry exists at all. It is my hope that this anthology will persuade them to an eager acknowledgement.

His prime interest, however, was poetry, its national origins excised: "I am hoping, above all, that the poems herein will become synonymous with *pleasure*—startle with fine excess of beauty." This point recurs in his third-party memoir, "The Story of the Penguin," published in 1983, where, recalling his internship in poetry as Bishop's University, near his hometown of Sherbrooke, Quebec, he expresses admiration for his then poet-professor Frank Oliver Call, who combined "the conventional world of poetry with the coming world of modern poetry." As a youth, he suspected that his Canadianness provided a vantage point from which to wage ink-stained guerilla war upon legions of Babbitts. He planned, as an undergraduate, "to make a book of modern Canadian poetry that would shake the literary ignorance of the English-speaking world." He would oppose poetic "wrongheadedness" wherever it appeared.

Strange it is, then, that after landing in jostling, rumours-of-war New York, his brain bristling with chivalric schemes for tilting at wrong-thinking poets, Gustafson concocted a curious blend of nationalist assertiveness—"Canadians can write fine poetry"—and liberal worldliness—"individualism extirpates hokey localism." Yet this premiere contradiction within Gustafson is responsible for his likewise divided achievement. By cleaving to cosmopolitanism to elude the late-colonial present, Gustafson was tempted to compose, in his first mature book, *Flight into Darkness*, in 1944, a poetry that occludes the quotidian, the referential, the homely. It was not until the appearance of *Rivers Among Rocks*, in 1960, that Gustafson, at last addressing native terrain, began to realize his true potential. If he had set out in the forties to conquer *le monde des Anglais* by demonstrating an anchorless mastery of modernist poetics, by 1960 he seemed to realize that these poetics would have to be enacted in service of the local. He would have to dump metaphysics and dish up meat and potatoes, eh?

This conflict between local/provincial and universal/cosmopolitan orientations could not be dodged. It was the precise crisis confronting all English-Canadian critics and poets of the war years. Perhaps Gustafson was doomed, then, to embrace the Medusa of universality and watch it turn a portion of his oeuvre to stone. For one thing, his edited *Anthology* reached an English Canada whose literary critics were deciding that its intellectual subservience to Great Britain (and, for some, the United States) entailed literary mediocrity. Hence, B. K. Sandwell in a *Saturday Night* review in 1942 asserts that the collection, given—as Gustafson quotes in "The Story of the Penguin"—"its sustained high level of accomplishment together with its extreme accessibility, will go a long way to check the occasionally insufferable condescension of the British intellectual toward the Canadian."

Though Gustafson's anthology gave writers like Sandwell reason for cheer, an academic "Gang of Four"—Northrop Frye, E. K. Brown, W. P. Wilgar, and Smith—continued to denounce the milquetoast, derivative, outmoded quality of English-Canadian poetry in a constellation of damning essays. For instance, in *On Canadian Poetry*, published in 1943, Brown deprecates the nation's "colonial spirit" and its adoption of imported standards, both "artificial and distorting." Brown complains that Canada is "colonial not only in its attitude towards Britain, but often in its attitude toward the United States." Frye, also writing in 1943, contends that Canadian colonial feeling—"a frostbite at the roots of the Canadian imagination"—fostered "creative schizophrenia"— manifestations of divided consciousness—and "prudery," namely "the instinct to seek a conventional or commonplace expression of an idea." In "Poetry and the Divided Mind in Canada," a 1944 essay, Wilgar detects "divided loyalty" and a "split personality" within the English-Canadian poet, who wavers between the "almost invariably unsuitable thought processes of the present-day British poets and the uncomfortable knowledge of an understanding for and a sympathy with the matter and manner of American poetry."

The hapless Canadian feels "pulled" toward both stultifying British metres and the rambunctious liberty of American form. Smith chased his disciple's *Anthology* with his own *The Book of Canadian Poetry*, published in 1943 in the modernist citadel of Chicago. In his introduction, Smith separates mukluked poetasters from cigarette-holder sophisticates. The "natives," in his species of imperial categorization, comprise nature poets and regional and populist poets. Cosmopolitans utilize, in contrast, "the poetry of ideas, social criticism, of wit and satire," genres representing "the universal, civilizing culture of ideas."[145] Their modernism radiates "intellectualism…and a merging of personality into a classicism of form." These dualisms—the division between poets/critics and a mass audience perceived as philistine, the colonial "double-aims" that seem to vitiate creative endeavours, the essential distinguishing between backwoods "natives" and bookish cosmopolitans—demarcate, in the 1940s, the English-Canadian poet's incessant and oeuvre-threatening marginality.

This perception had its effect on Gustafson. He had not journeyed from the backroads of the Eastern Townships to the glistening meccas of Anglo-American poetry to play a neon-veneered *habitant*. Thus, he took his place in the "cosmopolitan" section of his mentor's *Book of Canadian Poetry*, "the section the bumpkin adherence of Canadian critics deplored" (as he remarks, with a dose of caustic self-interest, some forty years later). Sensing that it would likely be impossible for a great poet to arise from the Dominion, that culture slumped in an obdurate, narcissistic inferiority, Gustafson chose to ground his poetic in an overarching intellectualism. Ironically, by doing so, he displayed calculated, even colonial obeisance to a still-imperial parent tradition, favouring its most Anglo-Saxon and Anglo-American manifestations in vers libre. Assuredly, he fuses, in his early verse, the aural, hyperstress techniques of Gerard Manley Hopkins with the hieratic, glissando eloquence of T. S. Eliot, Hart Crane, Wallace Stevens, and W. H. Auden, and he de-emphasizes the local and the colloquial—that is to say, the Canadian—until late in his career (when he imports the clarity of Ezra Pound, the jocularity of Williams Carlos Williams).

Flight into Darkness establishes Gustafson's affinity with the critiques of English-Canadian poetry extant in the forties.

Spurning the attractions of a tawdry parochialism, he exalts a chaste intellection, a studied complexity, in hermetic, well-shaped verbal icons. The local appears in these objets d'art, but prettified by a screen of Latinisms, Hellenisms, and arabesque periphrases. Three poems—"Excelling the Starry Splendour of this Night," "Mythos," and "Flight into Darkness"—typify Gustafson's heroic effort to create a nominally Canadian poetry that would resist the potentially humiliating limitations of localism. The poems stage a play of influences, with Hopkins assuming stardom and the others—Eliot, Crane, Stevens, Auden—glimmering in his excess light.

Reproduced in Gustafson's 1987 *Collected Poems*, "Excelling the Starry Splendour of the Night" offers a Hamletesque meditation, in ten quatrains, on mortality. Full rhyme is repressed, but the poem demonstrates an aggressive commitment to intricate, hide-and-go-seek patterns of half-rhyme, inner rhyme, consonance, assonance, and alliteration that almost out-Hopkinses Hopkins:

> Whereby what mortal crevice, coign of skull
> Shall man be less, than all, this whole
> And aggregate of god; snuff
> With a pinch of logic, proof?

A puzzle-solving-like pleasure may be derived from ascertaining how certain word arrangements ("crevice" and "coign"; "skull" and "Shall"; "all" and "whole"; "skull" and "whole"; "aggregate" and "god"; "snuff" and "proof") might suit a handbook of rhetorical techniques. Essentially, though, the poetic devices become poetic vices. An "instress" of technique, so to speak, darks the "inscape" of sense:

> Come cranking then, to him, test-tube, text,
> Within thy claw. No man that's sneezed
> But will from all they groans and gravings
> Pluck the paradox!

This is superficial Hopkins, artificial metaphysics. Instead of the Victorian poet's spontaneous awe before God's fierce grandeur in nature, an awe that compiles mysterious congeries, Gustafson essays a fastidious cleverness that dissolves into a prolix incoherence. The poem is unsettlingly finessed, derivative, and cold, from a writer too infatuated with an unassimilated aesthetic. Its clearest lines are, tellingly, organic, vivid: "He shall / This day surely plant turnips, // Fiddle with a shoestring: tomorrow serve / A grasp of gravel with his deeds." Regardless of their tactility, the poem's setting remains generic, the tone flat or, on occasion, falsely inflated. The work is a literary exercise, not a vision of life.

"Mythos" further reveals the deleterious impress of Hopkins upon Gustafson's sensibilities. Demonstrably, the poet still does not know that the central tradition must be altered—like light passed through gravity—by his own environment. He still seems innocent of the truth that Hopkins cannot be utilized in quite the same way by an Anglo-Québécois poet as he may be employed by a British (or, for that matter, Mauritian) poet. Because this insight has not yet been gleaned by Gustafson, "Mythos" recycles the errors of "Excelling." Its strophes display a poetic intelligence riven of a diction that it can call its own:

Spurt of crimson plunged in foam
his daring down (Star-dazed dare!
Hurl then, hurtle the headlong winds
Nor haggle joy in the gasping lungs,

Moon-managed gallant of gales! Go,
Greet the giant grapple of sun.
On cunning wax and quill let Daedalus
Limp, shaking precautious beard.)

Though it appears accentual-syllabic, the poem's metre
enacts the strong-stress rhythm of the Anglo-Saxon line: each
hemistich bears two hammer-blow beats. Greek myth is recast,
jarringly, in the metre of the *Beowulf* bard and of Hopkins.
Stridently convoluted, starkly pretentious, "Mythos" aspires
to an imagined rather than a realized cosmopolitanism. Too
unoriginal, perhaps, or too indiscriminately unoriginal, it
compacts with an obscurantist, Fallstaffian bomphiologia:

(What Theseus-love shall penetrate,
Plunge the mazing green miraculous

To monstrous centre, nor burst the green
And beast with bomb to no-solution
Wisdom list? O we have need
The other way, trammelling the heart

With faith, omphalos of globe and guerdon.)

In his 1983 memoir, "Red Wheelbarrows," Gustafson
labels "Mythos" a species of verticalism, and his fealty

to this school earned him a place in Eugene Jolas's 1940 *Vertical: A Yearbook for Romantic-Mystic Ascensions* "along with international names."[146] The romantic-mystic rubric does not redeem, however, the ostentatious failure of this twelve-quatrain poem, in which alliteration plods toward uneuphonious parimion. The poem represents not a synthesizing vision but a tin ear. It is a case of style over reason.[147] In fact, the work is open to the charge that J. M. Cohen lodges against Hopkins: "[The] highly conscious attention to texture...replaces concentration on the intellectual argument of [the] poem."

The ambitious title poem of the 1944 collection, "Flight into Darkness," plays homage to the cerebral, poésie pur style of Stevens. The poem's title echoes the terminus of Stevens's oft-reproduced poem "Sunday Morning": "Downward to darkness, on extended wings." Moreover, Gustafson adopts Stevens's strategy of suggestive elusiveness: "And yet, coming on sun across / An alien street, stand suddenly surprised— / As Galileo, before his midnight window." For all its seven sextets, though, "Flight" flounders in the metaphorical chaos of an attempted metaphysics:

> Was it today we fumbled spiral of spring,
> Clutched at the throat the knot of accurate winds,
> Noose and thong of beauty slung?

The third strophe is an exemplum of slavish imitation:

> Who now, regretting June with adult smiles,
> Set nodding with a finger Buddha's porcelain head:

Hearing of marvels in the township, turned
Expensive keys against the empty street,
From possible cars saw moon eclipse the sun,
Cautious glass before our eyes.

Gustafson means to achieve the beatific pathos that scores Stevens's elegant panegyric to apostasy, but, curiously, a debt to Crane also emerges due to the poem's recourse to a painstaking obscurantism. Thus, Cohen's criticism of Crane applies evidently to Gustafson: the poet's words "seem to be used only for their sound, and in order to convey the illusion of profundity." Lines of less opaque writing, especially "Yesterday yesterday! The hills were bare of snow, / The hackneyed maple broke with leaf, the bough / Sprang colour along the sweetened air," disrupt the dominant attitude of insistent preciosity. But they are not enough. In sum, "Flight into Darkness" flies from luminous immediacy into sacerdotal abstraction:

For we remembering our defense refused
The mirror's prosecution, praised the speaker
On the chairman's right: within the files,
Found brief anger for the anonymous clock,
Looking up, the calendar on startled walls –
Withdrawing truth from blundering sleep.

This poem exemplifies the debacle awaiting a poet who plumps for rhetoric over an engagé diction. What Gustafson needed was direct speech *and* the judicious adoption of local reference, but, in 1944, he had not yet found out this insight.

Notably, four decades after the appearance of *Flight into Darkness*, Gustafson insisted that he had always recognized that "poetry is in local things. I realized it then; have always realized it." But the poems contradict the poet. In 1944, the local did not entail for Gustafson the empathy with concreteness that it would entail for him later. The language, the referentiality, of the poems reviewed above eschews close observation of "local things." Rather, Gustafson is vulnerable to the criticisms that Australian poet Judith Wright aims at her poet forebear Furnley Maurice (a veritable case study of Frygian "creative schizophrenia" in the Australian context). For instance, Wright notices that Maurice swung "sometimes in the same short poem from colloquial vigour to cliché and poeticism, as though he was listening with one ear to the voice of conscience embedded in the minor Georgians and with the other to what was happening around him: an ambience which he was never quite able to trust or translate."

Gustafson may even by critiqued in the terms that the *bolekaja* critics—Chinweizu, Jemie, and Madubuike— wield against anglophone African writers, dismissing their "old-fashioned, craggy, unmusical language, obscure and inaccessible diction; a plethora of imported imagery" (as quoted in *The Empire Writes Back*, edited by Bill Ashcroft *et al*). Irrefutably, a fatal colonialism-induced split-consciousness scores much of Gustafson's forties verse. In attempting to address this mortal duality, he is too often Sisyphus, not Hercules.

But *Flight into Darkness* is not, it must be said, total darkness. Here and there, Gustafson uncovers glimmers of a native voice. Three works are crucial in this regard: "Crisis,"

"Quebec Sugarbush," and "Prologue to Summer." In all of them, there is a diction seemingly localized in provenance, a grappling with substantives, a more or less unmediated clarity.

Gustafson recognized, later, that "Crisis" marked a decisive shift in his poetics. In his 1985 essay "Reflections on a War Not Ended," he cites it as an example of his attainment of a demotic tone:

> Cherish them now for they shall not be yours:
> The lathe pressing to the hardwood maple's heart
> The whetstone and the standing corn
> The single thought.
>
> You shall harvest (moths circling the moon)
> And you shall still work a work with your hand
> But you shall say: This harvest's bitter
> The fingers blunt.
>
> And the wind shall be sickly in the Annapolis,
> On the Massawippi water...

Gustafson's appreciation of this poem is correct: its first ten (and twelve) lines are amazingly mimetic, free of cant. A dropping off into platitudes does occur in the last four strophes: "Your cities shall reap greed and there will be / Smoke above the wall and no / Word to say," and Auden's "September 1, 1939" voice bulldozes through some lines:

> The stolid labour at the sunburnt husking
> The annihilating hands of lovers and the short

Laugh, the coward dark of cupboards
Shall find you out.

Nevertheless, the poem employs successful home-bound details. Gustafson asserts, rightly, that, "for all the Biblical approximation of the poem toward rhythm and phrasing, the poem out of Europe is nothing but the Eastern Townships of Quebec in imagery." In other words, it accesses the universal through the local. It is surprising, then, that though "Crisis" dates back to the Nervous Thirties, Gustafson did not exploit its poetic truths until the twilight of his career.

"Quebec Sugarbush," like "Crisis," is half-abstract: "Something more than signature / (The huge sedition of the hills) / To sterile peace." But its other half is finely realized: "The close conspiracy of hollows / At the brittle ribs of snow, / The broken pool." Hints of elemental roughness indicate a domesticated diction. In "Red Wheelbarrows," Gustafson cites the poem to support his claim that he had always known that "poetry is in local things.... I was writing about water-barrels and Quebec sugarbushes: Where buckets are sweet with sap drives / Telesphore of the crimson tuque / His barrel from pail to tree." Even in his strophe, though, "Telesphore" (an apparent neologism cobbled from "tele," "spore," and possibly "metaphor"), seems a Hopkinsesque throwback to the vice of abstraction.

"Prologue to Summer" is, indubitably, the finest poem in *Flight into Darkness*. Its hyphenated compounds, assonantal rhymes, and three-stress accentual metre, though traceable to Hopkins, are neatly utilized, that is, *nationalized*, by

Gustafson. The landscape specifics articulated in the poem belong not just to poetry or even the Eastern Townships but to Gustafson himself. A truly original style emerges here. The diction—"garbles," "Flake of sun," "slime," "leaf-mould," "Belly-up stinking," "ice / Rotted"—is grounded, corporeal, valid:

Under the gangrened stump
Slugs drag slime,
The fieldmouse gnaws
The crust of air.

This visual clarity is a welcome advance over the opaque intellection of "Mythos." An unhesitant sensuosity, a beautiful feel for the actual, animates these lines, which foresee the openly Canadian verse of 1960 and later:

Smell!—the leaf-mould smokes,
At the water-edge flapped
By the waves a fish
Belly-up stinking.

Only in the final strophe does a throwaway disruptive rhetoric appear:

Male-naked the air. Compel!
Urgent the deed, urgent
And muscular the dream
Invaginate!

Whether Gustafson realized it or not, his reputation-preserving canon would come to consist largely of "provincial" works like "Prologue."

Gustafson progressed toward his first major poems, those of 1960, through continued attention, throughout the Fearful Fifties, to contemporary critiques of Canadian poetry and partisan devotion to new tangents in modernism. An initial devotee of Brown, Frye, Wilgar, and Smith, he had applied cosmopolitan aesthetics to his verse in order to cleanse it of any hint of English-Canadian provinciality but had also rendered it, thereby, pallid and irrelevant. The adoption of modernist poetics could not eliminate, by itself, a colonial mentality. Like Smith, Gustafson and others seem to have merely exchanged the staid romanticism of Victorian verse for the unlovely obscurantism propagated by Eliotian vers libre.

In reaction to this apparent failing, critic John Sutherland, introducing *Other Canadians*, his 1947 anthology of ostensibly socialist Canadian poetry (a corrective riposte to Smith's *Book of Canadian Poetry*), charges that Canadian intellectualism had reinforced colonialism:

> Our poetry is colonial because it is the product of a cultured English group who are out of touch with a people who long ago began adjusting themselves to life on this continent. The lack of all rapport between the poetry and the environment is one of the factors accounting for the incredibly unreal and ethereal quality of some of the new poetry.

Attacking the high-toned English-Canadian poetry of the day, Sutherland maintains that a native poetry cannot be constructed by the *virage* toward high modernism. He prefers a "hard-fisted proletarianism" (influenced by urban American poets) that will obliterate "the dividing wall between the author and the people." Similarly, in 1962, scholar John Matthews denounces the persistence of an anxious academism in Canadian poetry:

> Many contemporary Canadian poets are concerned with recording universal experience, with little reference to the local scene. Intellectual and esoteric in its imagery, their poetry sets up barriers against all but a comparatively few readers.

The estrangement of English-Canadian intellectuals from their own immediate context is, Matthews suggests, a consequence of their post postcoloniality. In addition, their obeisance to foreign taste diminishes their imaginative power: "With their eyes firmly fixed upon the parent tradition more than upon the object before them, they have been chasing, prematurely, a universal which cannot exist for them until it grows from local roots"

Gustafson was conversant with such criticisms, for, in his introduction to *The Penguin Book of Canadian Verse*, published in 1958, he does not condemn "Canadianism." Au contraire, his introduction traces a genealogy of poets whose virtue is their primordial Canadianness, a quality connected to their engagement with a northern landscape of snow and maples. Yet, in implicit reply to Sutherland's critique of cosmopolitanism, Gustafson defends the tactics of the forties:

> The poet cannot be asked to find his national identity before the factors that present it to him exist. Canadian poets identifiable as such, have had to wait for Canada.

If English-Canadian poets, including himself, had sought their legitimacy from London, New York, and Chicago, Gustafson protests, the fault had not been in themselves but in the failure of Canada to articulate itself as a nation. Even so, thanks to the forties poets, Canadian poetry had come of age:

> The Canadian poets of the forties demanded dignity, personal and social, buttressed it, defended it, and published it…. They are accomplished technically. Their phrasing is Canadian. It is becoming increasingly apparent that Canada has a poetry that is distinctly her own.

Gustafson refused to mourn the poetic practices of the forties, and he launched a covert assault on Sutherland; still, his 1957 introduction marked a shift from Smithian cosmopolitanism. For instance, nineteenth-century poets like Charles Mair and Charles G. D. Roberts earn his praise for, respectively, attentiveness to "details of homes and nature around him" and "sensitive evocation of the rural scene." In 1941, "poetry" took precedence over "Canadianism"; but, in 1957, it resided in the felt details of Canadian life:

A method of thought, pattern of feeling, distinguishes the verbal texture of the modern Canadian poem. The "phrasing," the "fingering"...is different; the Canadian "phrasing" is not the American, it is certainly not the English.

Given comments such as this and Gustafson's cataloguing of the "specifics of contemporary Canadian poetry," it is clear that his aesthetics had shifted in an inchoately nationalist direction by the late fifties. He could now value a local verisimilitude.

This point is further supported by his foreword to the 1967 version of *The Penguin Book of Canadian Verse*, where Gustafson announces that "despair is universal over the question of who everyone is. It is necessary to know." Gustafson admits, then, a nationalist concern for self-identification. Accordingly, "the dialogue of the new Canadian poets is of the greatest interest." In developing a native technique, English-Canadian poetry had veered "from the Yeats/Eliot axis to the Pound/Williams axis," from abstract superficiality to "no ideas but in things." Now, "immediacy and objectism are the demands; freedom from the traditional prosodic formalities."

As usual, Gustafson's global pronouncements apply with as much (or greater) force to himself as to anyone else. Hence, his critique of wayward turns in the new poetry is an amazing instance of oblique self-criticism of his own forties verse. For instance, he now recognizes that "poetry... carries a burden of logical meaning"; "dead" poetry is, then, "inaccessible" or composed of "unholy," unnatural phrasing. Importantly too, Gustafson insists upon the necessity of maintaining a coherent syntax and metre. "Without the drama of syntax there is no tension"; metre must consist of "instinctive physiological *and*...intellectual pacing." By 1966, then, Gustafson had rejected or radically revised his 1941 insistence upon technique over content; now "the Canadian occupation [of poetry] is distinguished and distinguishable."

Gustafson's conditional embrace of local/national themes is richly evident in *Rivers Among Rocks*, his first publication of 1960. A Smithian intellectualist ethos is still on display but is now mitigated by a refreshing Pound/ Williams-observant sensuousness. The promise of "Prologue to Summer" is, herein, fulfilled, not in all of the 1960 poems (including those of the later volume *Rocky Mountain Poems*) but in enough that one can mark Gustafson's grappling with particularized geographies, autobiographical histories, thereby forging an expansive localism conveyed with colloquial vigour.

The new approach even informs "Legend," a poem that, though dependent upon classicist machinery, employs a specific diction:

> whoever has got up,
> Standing, certainty under his adjusting heels,
> And height tugged by the tide, ocean rinsing
> From flank and belly, ravelling loins with wet

Here vers libéré—a loosened blank verse—and a demotic tone engender a poem whose universality is versed in physicality. To be sure, not quite enough of a grounding in the diurnal occurs; a degree of obscurity returns:

He, that salt upon his time's tongue,
Knows, standing the margin ocean and sand,
Ilium toppled thunder his ears, what's left
Of Helen naked drag between his toes.

Gustafson is still too literary, too stilted, but his heart is in the right place. In fact, a triumvirate of Quebec-set poems figure Gustafson's maturity: "Quebec Night," "Quebec, Late Autumn," and "Quebec Winterscene." In these works, Gustafson seeks to hallow a way of life in a memorable space and to convey this existence through sinuous diction and naturalistic imagery.

"Quebec Night" differs positively from both "Flight into Darkness" and "Mythos." Unlike "Flight," it is a poem of fine-tooled specifics, à la Williams's "Red Wheelbarrow":

The red logs
crisp on the outside,
the wood solid, being new,
are chained to the sleigh.
The runner drags a cleat for the hill up,
and the snow is pleated in the logs,
the snow in the far woods
falling

Here is vernacular speech, local rhythms. Each line exhibits an Imagist exactness, an aesthetic victory undergirded by the balance of line length and pictorial activity. Released from the enervating dualism that had once been his lot, Gustafson, reconciled to his New World/Anglo-

Québécois inheritance, wins an uncompromised, beautiful colloquiality. The two- and three-beat accentual lines spurn the tortuous stutterings of "Mythos."

"Quebec, Late Autumn," a poem consisting of seven occasionally half-rhymed quatrains, strays radically from the styles of "Mythos" and "Excelling." Eschewing the unconvincing metaphysical allegiances of the 1944 poems, the 1960 lyric records a single resonant location and life. The plotted revelation of a precisely rendered world draws the reader progressively into the poem:

> Suddenly now the ragged oak
> And maple overnight are fire,
> The green sluice falters in the elm.

The verbs derive from tactile experience—"Cider wets the wooden mill, / The rafter hangs with cobs of corn"—and express an unstinted concreteness—"The zinc pail holds a hoop of ice / Standing in the milking stall." The procession of cold-weather images recalls Shakespeare's "Winter" (from *Love's Labour's Lost*), in which "Tom bears logs into the hall, / And milk comes frozen home in a pail." Alliteration is called upon, but it is controlled. Nothing extraneous is admitted to the poem; its lines attain a photographic quality: "The morning's pulleys in the cobweb / Freeze, the pump drips icicle." The known (local) world acquires a poet, and provinciality vanishes in scrutinizing the provincial life. He is suddenly as hardy as Hardy, with Hopkins held in restraints.

"Quebec Winterscene," Gustafson's first deathless poem, reveals the revolution that had taken place in his poetics by 1960. Abandoning the old, vague language, he eyes his own environment of rural Quebec. Hopkins still haunts the poem—"harvest / Helps over, buckled"—but his ghost is an invited guest, not an incubus. A straightforward tone dominates the whole: the elitist mask is lost. Exact is the mimesis: "Dipper icy a man drinks gasping." The poet descants, sans cant, of "snow trodden round the yard" and "straw ravelled near the barn." There is room, suddenly, for the recognizable, the workaday, the familiar:

> At dusk, acres clamped cold,
> Threshold and clearing everywhere white
> To the distant scribble of alders, across
> The frozen field snakefence
> Like charred music; sky only harvest
> Helps over, buckled, with taste of tin
> Dipper icy a man drinks gasping

Here is the rasp of existence. Unforced, the poem arises from the poet's experience, the revelation of his own backyard:

> Sweat of warm barn-work a hazard
> Once out, door-to, headed for house.

Lovely, trés lovely, this clipped poiciologia, this loving attentiveness to rudimentary parrhesia and energia. The alliteration at play in the poem is largely unobtrusive, as is the four-stress metre: "The long snow of the fourfold land." Speech rhythms drive the poem, which echoes the expression of a speaker standing outdoors on a frigid day. These cadences possess an agonizingly piercing music. Vers libéré and strict statement, both elements of mastery, signal the synthesis that the poet has achieved between his environment and his inherited language. Furthermore, a hint of miraculous discovery pervades the piece. The speaker senses unfolding, "a history happening," the landscape gravid with incipient event. When a train "pulls past," sounding a "heard warning," the speaker experiences an epiphany, namely, the recognition that the only possible reply to the train is "the local heart."

The poet's identification with the local symbolizes the end of his alienation from himself. His identification with North Hatley is of a piece with Charles G. D. Roberts's annexation of the Tantramar Marsh or, nearer in time and space, A. M. Klein's domestication of Montreal: the poets locate a space that promotes the fusion of the personal, the literary, and the social. Gustafson's resolution of his former imperial/colonial "schizophrenia" permits him to sing from "the country in the heart," in Australian poet A. D. Hope's phrase.

From 1960 on, then, Gustafson exploits once-scorned "provincial" images and demotic speech patterns in his poems, obtaining a sensuality (especially in his canticles for the Gala-like Elisabeth) that had hitherto evaded his grasp. His later fine poems—even those that are latently metaphysical—build upon his initial, auspicious recognition of the apt essentialism of "the local heart." In technical terms, in "Quebec Winterscene" and his other good poems, Gustafson reconnoitres a synthesis between what Edwin Fussell designates the British tradition of order and the American tradition of liberty.[148] With "Quebec

Winterscene," then, Gustafson begins to utilize an ordered liberty—in metre, imagery, and diction. He indulges in the informal formalism that signifies the English-Canadian compromise between its UK and US influences.

Gustafson imagined that his "greatness" derived from his cosmopolitan leanings, that is to say, his having lived, like Smith, "elsewhere other than being beside the village pump." In actuality, commencing with "Quebec Winterscene," he wrote much of his best poetry about life around, near, beside the proverbial pump. Twenty-five years after the appearance of *Rivers Among Rocks*, Gustafson affirmed that local details never *necessitate* provincialism; after all, "the Eastern Townships around Lake Massawippi were 'international.'" In his 1981 essay, "Some Literary Reminiscences of the Eastern Townships," he cites F. R. Scott "exploring the countryside around the several Hatleys; to examine his wood-chopping and bird-feeding." Even Smith "shaped experience with what the landscape and the inscape of his district gave him." Gustafson even chides an early Eastern Townships poet, Frederick George Scott, for having committed the sin that Gustafson also practised, namely abstraction: "He should have nailed my attention with something within my experience and not in heaven—a road out to Lime Ridge where I was born, say, and 'the creak of a lumberman's sleigh.'" In the October of his career, Gustafson knew the value of empirical observation.

Finally, Gustafson recognized that "all great writing springs out of the writer's own intimate, experienced, loved backyard." Suitably, then, he locates the source of his poetic achievement in "the Eastern Townships I was born to and grew up in." Only after learning to observe the "'thisness' of this world, the *quidditas*, the *haecceity*" was Gustafson able to find a unique voice, one strong enough to address the larger world. Once he recognized that the central tradition is only a clutch of words, a way of seeing, that he could utilize and alter to meet his own empirical needs, he was able to carve out a place for himself in that tradition. Dissolving the self, "the local heart," into poetry, Gustafson salved the schizophrenia or anxiety of being a non-British and non-American poet who wrote in English. Thus, he moved from "Quebec Sugarbush" to "Quebec Winterscene"; he found in "Canada" the "Poetry" that he so exalted.[149]

With the foregoing analysis in mind, a *forensically* rigorous edition of Gustafson's *best* poems must now be compiled. If we privilege his concise, colloquial pieces, beginning, perhaps, with "Quebec Winterscene" (or "Prologue to Summer"), the "final" list should include "In the Yukon" (1960); "Into the Tonquin Valley" (1960); "On the Flanks of Carnarvon" (1960); "On Mountain Summit" (1960); "Aspects of Some Forsythia Branches" (1966); "Columbus Reaches Juana, 1492" (1966); "The Valley of Kings" (1969); the englishings of Alfred DesRochers and Anne Hébert (1970); "Hyacinths with Brevity" (1974); "Wednesday at North Hartley" (1977); "Red Square" (1978); "Country Walking" (1979); "The Things of This World are OK" (1980); "Among the Wheatfields" (1981); #46 from *Gradations of Grandeur* (1982); "Hearing the Woodthrush in the Evening" (1984); "'Hunter's Moon" (1984); III, V, VII, VIII, IX, and XI from *Twelve Landscapes* (1985); "Winter Arrival" (1987); "Cinquains of a Sort for E. P." (1989); "D. G. Jones" (1989); "A Window

Lighted" (1991); "Somewhat of Lilacs" (1991); "Love Poem" (1991); "Evidence for the Time Being" (1991); "The beauty of the world is not over" from *Configurations at Midnight* (1992); "That Day in January" (1994); "The Moment Is as Her Presence Is" (1994); "Winter Solstice" (1994); "At the rue de Buci One Evening" (1994); and a few dozen others culled from, especially, the later works.

These poems prove Gustafson's centrality to the Canadian modernist canon; these poems keep his name from dust.

[*Journal of Eastern Townships*, no. 9]

∾

I pray that I have not maligned or demeaned Gustafson, for only a genius is born with the voice imperishably present, already astute, righteous in diction, clarion in sense, incisive in clarity, and so authentic that all within earshot of the recited words are enthralled, enchanted, enlightened. Though Gustafson had to labour for a generation to find his Muse in his homemaker and his Parnassus in North Hatley, Quebec, to discover that *dipper* and *pump* are as vital words as are Dionysus and Pan, in contrast, the resolutely plain poet Rita Joe, electing to be a salt-of-the-earth Bard for her people, ignored the Ivory Tower in preference for the moccasin-trod Stations of the Cross of her down-home Calvary. Weighing Gustafson against Joe, one sets a pupil of high modernism versus an elder dispensing wisdom. Perhaps one would laurel the once-Manhattanite boulevardier faster than the earth-mother of quilts and bannock. But seldom do we get our divinities right, and, in the end, the critic vanishes, anyway, and the poet stands, having weathered all praise, all persecution, and all misprision.

≈

Rereading Rita Joe: A Hearing

PLAIN TALK, WITH "LOCAL COLOUR" or "ethnic flavour," is the bastard child of the British poetic tradition. Geoff Chaucer, Bobby Burns, Billy Blake, Jack Clare, all versified within the registers of vernacular, or kindergarten clarity, or backwoods idiom. However, though Chaucer and Blake broke into the canon, as did Burns (with an asterisk of excuse—or acclaim—for his "brogue"), Clare is still an eccentric, relegated to margins (despite Nobel laureate Derek Walcott's championing of the peasant-born Romantic-Victorian poet).

People poets, *vox populi* poets, poets unabashedly anti-*oppression*, all get short shrift in English Canadian poetry too, which, historically, has been aimed more at educated elites than at economically struggling classes or the racism-suffering Indigenous and "African" readership. Indeed, from Confederation up to the Conservatives (pseudo–Republican Party types) of the recent federal (Confederate) governments, English-Canadian poetry has been biased in favour of Ivy League, white-washed, Ivory Tower verse, stressing obscurity, experiment, elitism, and education (PhD poets). We English-Canadian poets are mainly downtown types (or suburbanites) who write about camping trips or the occasional portage with an e-reader in one hip pocket and a flask in the other.

So English Canada celebrates no Walt Whitman, no Al Ginsberg, no Jack Kerouac, no Chuck Bukowski, no Billy Collins: I mean, *nobody* who could recite poetry in a tavern or a diner and have it be received by scholars as meaningful or important.

We've tried—or, rather, a brave few have tried to alter this perennial status quo. Bobby Service's poems about Yukon shoot-outs and Billy Drummond's poems that make French pea soup out of English alphabet soup promote a popular poetry. Lookit: Service succeeded so well that most folks believe he's American. But Drummond has disappeared from consciousness because everyone's righteously embarrassed by his minstrel ventriloquism of French-Canadian *types* and *gars*. Some mid-twentieth-century intellectual poets—F. R. Scott and A. J. M. Smith and Duncan Campbell Scott— strove to be personable in their poesy, but F. R. stopped at satire; A. J. M. at imagism; and D. C. at (apologetic) racism.

Fast forward to the 1960s and one finds the working-class Milty Acorn (dubbed "The People's Poet") espousing his plaid-shirt-plus-stogie socialism; Al Purdy musing on geologic eras and the chronicles of Ontario pulpits; and Irv Layton campaigning for free love at home and tough-love abroad. Of this trio, Acorn was the retro-Marxist (thus spurning soap as a "luxury"), Purdy the voice of the *Maclean's*-magazine-reading RRSP'd WASP, and Layton the Georgie Byron of the boudoir and the Bobby Graves of the Greeks. I should not omit Ray Souster, who was a true-blue banker, but closer in sensibility to Doc W. C. Williams and Carl Sandburg, both Yank men-o-de-folk, than he was to once-banker T. S. Eliot, that pinstripe Prufrock.

In the Maritimes, apart from PEI-born Acorn, in the 1960s, there was only one poet who might be named as a preface to the plain-speech, simple (but not simplistic) address of Rita Joe, and that's—of course—Alden Nowlan, whose verses are heartfelt but never sentimental. (Nowlan was also a precursor to the anthemic and/or Beat-derived poetry of Africadian poet Maxine Tynes.) Perhaps the reason is that Nowlan was, like Acorn, self-taught, and found his profession as a journalist only after he escaped from the Nova Scotia asylum, where he had been jailed not so much because he was "insane" but because his family was too poor to resist the decisions of child welfare officials. (Come to think of it, Nowlan's incarceration—as a dreamy, moody teen—is not unlike the experience of too many First Nations persons, imprisoned—basically—due to running afoul of bourgeois Judeo-Christian norms.) Nowlan's upbringing taught him sympathy for the downtrodden, though he also delighted in heraldry and titles.

Still contemplating English-Canadian poets who aimed at simplicity, a special case is E. Pauline Johnson, whose Mohawk moniker is Tekahionwake and whose poems straddle the colour-line (ahem) between English gentility and Indigenous lore. Hers is a Métis poetry, really, which can be understood as seeking to introduce WASP readers to Native "reservations" (double entendre intended). But the height of her fame coincided with Vaudeville and the pre-Beat vogue of "Vagabondia" (to refer to Bliss Carman's 1894 co-authored volume of Omar Khayyam–styled verse of wine & women & song & the open road).

In other words, while Tekahionwake was down-to-earth

and accessible, she was also a safe symbol of conformist Indigeneity and leisurely wilderness "ambling." She was the reverse of the Indian-pretending Englishman Grey Owl, for she was a Native woman who could "pass" as English. No, she was the Grey Owl of the parlour-library-and-sherry set.

I say all of the above to set a context for the precedent-busting, cigar-store-Indian-splintering, quiet, icon-smashing poet who is Rita Joe. Born Rita Bernard in Whycocomagh, Cape Breton Isle, Nova Scotia, in 1932, Joe must have grown up as a disenfranchised minority (Mi'kmaw) within a disadvantaged majority (the Scots) who were themselves a minority ethnicity within Nova Scotia entire. Thus, Joe "came to voice" in a manner not unlike another major poet of minority ethnicity, A. M. Klein—who was Jewish, Anglo, a Montrealer, and a Canadian, with a love for French-Canadian language and culture, who combined his multiple heritages in inimitably layered poems. (See 1948's *The Rocking Chair*.)

Something of the same is central to Rita Joe's poetics—and thought. In her foreword to *We Are the Dreamers* (1999), she identifies herself as "Indian" and as bearing a "burden" that has an "invisible line" and that she cannot "drop" because she remains dissatisfied with the quality of her hefting. This symbolic image has many resonances, both ethnic and artistic. Her "burden" recalls Rudy Kipling's infamous 1899 poem, "White Man's Burden," with its the idea that white males have a taxing duty to support—uplift—the world's dark-skinned, unenlightened, "inferior" peoples (by simultaneously policin' 'em, preachin' at 'em, and exploitin' 'em).

In contrast, for Joe, the "burden" is one of representation, self-representation, as a poet and "Indian," to express her culture vividly by writing indelible poetry. (In a 1978 poem, she writes, "burdens follow / Out of old chronicles.") Yet "invisible line" echoes African-American scholar W. E. B. Du Bois's concern in 1903 that contemporary world history is defined by the "color-line," that is to say, the fundamental segregation between "elect" whites and subject peoples-of-colour. So Joe's burden is both race and art, or the articulation of race versus erasure. When Joe tells us her "minor self-war has turned into a mountain, I cannot reach the top. The top being my own satisfied conclusion," we hear an echo of the Greek myth of Sisyphus—condemned to never succeed in his effort to roll a boulder up a hillside. But one also detects an echo of Marty King's last speech, in April 3, 1968, about getting to the top of the mountain but only seeing—not entering—the Promised Land.

In other words, Joe subscribes to an existentialist ethos, the idea of Double Consciousness (cf. Du Bois), of being a poet and of bearing responsibility for expressing "Nativism"—not parochial nationalism but a belief system that appreciates earth and roots, ecology and psychology, geography and genealogy. Her "burden" is the necessity of reconciling her various heritages—Mi'qmaw, Anglo, Catholic, Nova Scotian—with Indigenous faith and the aloof aesthetics of modernism.

For Joe, the process of writing poetry is the process of carrying—and trying to surrender—the "burden." The complication of this dual task of representation and self-repre-sentation shows up in an early 1978 poem: "I am not / What they portray me. / I am civilized. / I am trying / To fit in this century."

Clearly, Joe resists here the Hollywood *and* Ottawa

representations of the "Indian." She is not *that* portrayal. (Intriguingly, she writes *What*, not the grammatically correct *How*, to accent, very subtly, that stereotypes render Indigenous people things, not persons.) The statement "I am civilized" is stripped and stark—almost mischievously so, for, in a single sentence, Joe eliminates centuries of European propaganda against "savages." She is also asking us to define what it means to be "civilized": she is conventionally "civilized" in writing the poem, as we are in reading it; moreover, this cultural transaction occurs in English, the tongue of the King James Version and of Shakespeare. Yet the raison d'être for the poem is—implicitly—the prior refusal of non-Indigenous persons to receive "Indians" as "civilized," preferring, rather, to reject their civilizations with utmost genocidal fervour.

Think for a moment that Joe is not the author but that an Inca or an Aztec is—someone, that is, facing the wholesale obliteration of their civilization by the "civilized" conquistadors of yore. The last lines of the quotation are woefully awful—I mean, horrific: the idea that one is trying to find space inside this "century"—to live—suggests that one's being is opposed by those who find one's people an anachronism, a living fossil, better off extinguished. (In a 1978 poem, Joe insists, "I must accept what this century / Has destroyed and left behind— / The innocence of my ancestry.") One can imagine mid-twentieth-century European Jewry making the same agonized statement for the same ghastly reason. Simultaneously, one witnesses Joe penning a modernist poem, thus flouting those who would view her Indigenous heritage as inherently retrograde, anti-modern, atavistic.

273

True: Joe does not spell out her Du Boisian anti-racism. The absolute simplicity of her utterance seems to deny the existence of philosophy, political science, and even of spiritually informed history. But they are there, needing only due sensitivity to ferret them out. A case in point is "Someday They Will Listen." In this 1999 poem, Joe's persona states, "I am a Mi'kmaw mingling with writers." At once, there is a separation between the "Mi'kmaw"—poet—and other, presumably non-Indigenous writers. Because the poet is "mingling," there is also a process of de facto representation of Mi'kmaw—to others—occurring. But this cultural trade is overshadowed by the felt sense that the others are indifferent while Joe's persona feels "discomfort...unsettled." Indeed, the "traders" are "still there," suggesting hucksters out to short-change or cheat Indigenous artists of their proper due.

Thus, the "discomfort" is distrust; a situation not settled because so many other discomforts—land claims, residential school compensation, the quest for self-government, respect for treaty rights, etc., remain "unsettled." The poet asks, "How do we bombard when only half listen? / The roar on the other side modern in its din." Once again, Joe gives us much to ponder: How can First Nations' demands for justice and equality be respected when only "half" of the oppressive settler descendants will "listen"? Not only that, but opponents to Indigenous equality maintain that the "Native Question" is really about the refusal of backward people(s) to accept white civilization, Christianity, and capitalism as the catalysts of "modern" development.

The poet is oppressed by the "many voices / The suppression adding to the loneliness"; she feels, "My nativeness

274

fighting a lost war." Again Joe speaks to an existentialist stoicism in writing the poem to confront her "small" persona's silencing "in the great ballroom of the elegant hotel." Yet the poem ends with a sense of apocalyptic triumph: "The elders on my reservation said be patient / When all else is gone / They will listen." These lines ask us to imagine the collapse of Occidental civilization, due to ecological or economic calamity (or both), and the then necessary-for-survival recuperation of traditional Mi'kmaw—or Indigenous—belief systems demanding sustainable ecology and a small-s socialist economy. Certainly, as Joe says in a 1978 poem, "While skyscrapers hide the heavens / They can fall." She is a combo of Earth Matriarch and Hebrew prophet decrying Babylon.

In rereading Joe, we must note a complex of ideas haunting lines that are prima facie plain, but this accessibility is that of Blake, a clarity that is dazzling because it is infused with the light of mysticism or spirituality. In "There Is a Hill," from 1999, Joe's persona appeals to Saint Simeon of Cyrene (usually marked as black or African) to help ease her climb of a "steep and hard" hill, topped by a "cross." The prayer gets spoken, and her way is eased to the peak, "Where we the Micmac have put a cross" and "an image of the Blessed Mother." Next, the poet suggests that non-Natives should make the climb too, "especially on Good Friday," in communion with the Mi'kmaw, so that "then maybe we may look on each other as friends / Like we wanted you to [do] since the day you came."

This hope is chased by two lines in Roman-alphabet Mi'kmaw that translate as "Our prayers will join / We will find happiness." Joe's persona proposes that shared worship on Mi'kmaw territory, before Mi'kmaw-fashioned Christian (and Catholic) symbols, will result in a transcendence of cultural (superficial) difference so that Mi'kmaq and non-Mi'kmaq may finally see each other as friends. Crucially, this prayer is rendered, ultimately, in the Mi'kmaw language. This fact suggests that, for Rita Joe, if not most Mi'kmaq, there is a fusion of their language, lore, and heritage (faith) with Catholicism (in particular). No wonder several of Joe's poems are prayers or recount visions or address a spirit (sacred or ghostly). Again, there is a connection to Blake (and/or Ginsberg) in this regard.

But it could be fruitful to read Joe in tandem with other mystical poets, such as Tommy Merton or Sor Juana or even Jack Kerouac—another Catholic who first sought his visions through sex, drugs, jazz, and the open road, and then tried Zen, and then resuscitated conservative Québécois roots. (One might read Kerouac's career as both a premonition of *La Révolution tranquille* and then its repudiation.) In this sense, Joe is constantly constructing in her poetry a wigwam cathedral—or chapel—wherein thought passes "between two minds" or is "swinging to and fro / From English to Native."

Another characteristic of poet-mystics or mystical poets is the tendency to fetishize "I," for this "I" is the eye of the visionary, the eccentric, the uniquely gifted, the genius, the seer, who is specifically empowered via vatic attributes to relate glimpses of the divine and/or the esoteric. Joe titles a book *We Are the Dreamers* (1999), but there is always only *one* oracle in her poems: herself—or her persona. This pattern repeats throughout her oeuvre: "I like to think of our native life, / Curious, free; / And look at the stars / Sending icy messages." (It is appropriate that *We Are the Dreamers* is divided into Book One and Book Two: the parallel with New and Old Testament cannot be accidental.)

Joe's tone is subtle, quiet, almost withdrawn. She whispers, muses, meditates. But she jests too: "I want my country to know / Natives are No. 1, then mounties, then finally the snow." The miniscule "m" for "mounties" is a sly cutting down to size of a police force with a history of legalized terrorism against the First Nations. Even in joking, Joe may imply an impolitic critique.

Finally, in keeping with her modernist heritage, Joe is an Imagist. See her 1978 poem about the making of moose butter: "After the meat is removed / The bones of the moose are collected, / Pounded with rocks / Reduced to powder, / Then placed in a kettle / And boiled well, / Bringing the grease atop." The poem moves as nimbly in its close-up narration as might a documentary filmmaker's camera in providing a subject its most scrupulous scrutiny.

To conclude: Rita Joe's superficial simplicity has been read too simplistically by too many scholars. A dedicated rereading, by scholars cognizant of imperial/colonial history, Indigenous spirituality, and the poetics of spoken word clarity will do much to reveal the suppressed—and just—animosities, prophecies for justice, and reclamations of civilization and beauty (ecological and aesthetic) that are Rita Joe's principled and principal interventionist sayings in Anglo-Canadian poetry. Reading—or rereading—Joe in this way, we should find our spirits moved, our hearts enlarged, our minds expanded. We should also revivify our respect for poets so masterly that they can compress volumes of intellectual argument into lines so elementary that they would seem hardly to resist the comprehension of a child. Such a poetics is humbling—nay, *civilizing*—indeed.

WORKS CITED

Allen, Lillian. "I Fight Back." *Rhythm an' Hardtimes.* Domestic Bliss, 1982, p. 15.

Ambler, Eric. *The Mask of Dimitrios.* Hodder & Stoughton, 1939.

An Anthology of Canadian Poetry (English), compiled by Ralph Gustafson, Penguin—Pelican Books, 1942.

Anonymous. *The Hidden Sight of Love.* Palladium Publications, 1958.

Anthony, Trey. *da' Kink in my Hair: voices of black womyn.* Playwrights Canada Press, 2005.

Archer-Straw, Petrine. *Negrophilia: Avant-Garde Paris and Black Culture in the 1920s.* Harvard University Press, 1998.

Ashcroft, Bill, Gareth Griffiths, and Helen Tiffin. *The Empire Writes Back: Theory and Practice in Post-Colonial Literatures.* 1989. Routledge, 1993.

Aspinall, Algernon. *The Handbook of the British West Indies, British Guiana, and British Honduras.* Sifton Praed & Co., 1931.

Atwood, Margaret. *Strange Things: The Malevolent North in Canadian Literature.* 1995. Virago Press, 2004.

——. *Surfacing.* 1972. Virago, 1979.

——. *Survival: A Thematic Guide to Canadian Literature.* House of Anansi, 1972.

Auden, W. H. "September 1, 1939." 1939. poets.org/poem/september-1-1939

Austen, Jane. *Pride and Prejudice.* 1813.

Bailey, Cameron. "Caribana: 12 Steps to a Cure." *NOW Magazine,* 28 July 2005. nowtoronto.com/caribana-12-steps-to-a-cure. Accessed September 14, 2013.

Bailey, Troy Burle. *The Pierre Bonga Loops*. Commodore Books, 2010.

Bakan, Abigail B. "Reconsidering the Underground Railroad: Slavery and Racialization in the Making of the Canadian State." *Socialist Studies*, vol. 4, no. 1, 2008, pp. 3-29.

Bannerji, Himani. *The Dark Side of the Nation: Essays on Multiculturalism, Nationalism and Gender*. Canadian Scholars Press, 2000.

Bates, Ernest Sutherland, ed. *The Bible Designed to be Read as Literature*. 1936. Simon & Schuster, 1952.

Baudrillard, Jean. *Seduction*. Translated by Brian Singer, St. Martin's Press, 1990.

Bell, F. McKelvey. *The First Canadians in France: The Chronicle of a Military Hospital in the War Zone*. George A. Doran, [1917].

———. *A Romance of the Halifax Disaster*. Royal Print & Litho., 1918.

Beowulf. Heroic epic poem by Anonymous. 700–1000 AD.

Bernath, Michael T. "'Global Whitemanism': The Capitalist Economy and Dark Dreams of the Slaveholding South." *Harvard Magazine*, vol. 116, no. 1, 2013, pp. 25–28.

Birney, Earle. *Turvey: A Military Picaresque*. McClelland and Stewart, 1949.

The Birth of a Nation. Film directed by D. W. Griffith. David W. Griffith Corp., 1915.

Borden, Walter M. *Tightrope Time: Ain't Nuthin' More than Some Itty Bitty Madness Between Twilight & Dawn*. 1986. Playwrights Canada Press, 2005.

———. "Tightrope Time: Ain't Nuthin' More than Some Itty Bitty Madness Between Twilight & Dawn." In *Testifyin': Contemporary African Canadian Drama, Volume 1*, ed. Djanet Sears, Playwrights Canada Press, 2001.

Boyd, George. *Consecrated Ground*. Blizzard Publishing, 1999.

———. "Consecrated Ground." [Teleplay] In *Fire on the Water: An Anthology of Black Nova Scotian Writing*. Volume Two. Ed. George Elliott Clarke, Pottersfield Press, 1992, pp. 98–109.

———. "Consecrated Ground" [Teleplay]. 1992. *Two, By George*, by George Elroy Boyd, Stage Hand Publishers, 1996, pp. 9-33.

Bradley, David. *The Chaneysville Incident*. Harper & Row, 1981.

Brand, Dionne. *In Another Place, Not Here*. Alfred A. Knopf Canada, 1996.

Brenner, Marie. "To War in Silk Stockings." *Vanity Fair*, Nov 2011, pp. 208–20.

Brown, E. K. *On Canadian Poetry*. Ryerson, 1943.

Brown, George W. "Have the Americas a Common History? A Canadian View." *The Canadian Historical Review*, June 1942, pp. 132–39. archive.org/stream/haveamericascomm00binkuoft/haveamericascomm00binkuoft_djvu.txt. Accessed on June 30, 2009.

Brown, Lennox. *The Captive: Snow Dark Sunday*. Ottawa: Little Theatre, 1965.

Buchan, John. *The Thirty-Nine Steps*. William Blackwood and Sons, 1915.

Bujo, Bénézet. *Foundations of an African Ethic: Beyond the Universal Claims of Western Morality*. Translated by Brian McNeil, Crossroad, 2001.

Burdick, Eugene, and Harvey Wheeler. *Fail-Safe*. 1962. Ecco Press, 1999.

Cahill, Barry. "First Things in Africadia; or, The Trauma of being a Black Lawyer in Late Victorian Saint John, New Brunswick." 1994. TS in the possession of the author.

Caldwell, Erskine. *Tobacco Road*. Scribners, 1932.

Callboard. Nova Scotian Drama League magazine. Monthly. 1951–?

Canada. 1867. Section 91. *The British North America Act*. Ottawa: Government of Canada. 5 May 2005. canada.justice. gc.ca/en/ps/const/loireg/p1t1-3.html

"Canada 2001 Census". *Wikipedia*, en.wikipedia.org/wiki/ Canada_2001_Census. Accessed October 2, 2013.

Carman, Bliss, and Richard Hovey. *Songs of Vagabondia*. Copeland & Day, 1894.

Carmichael, Trevor A. *Passport to the Heart: Reflections on Canada Caribbean Relations*. Ian Randle Publishers, 2001.

Caruth, Cathy. *Unclaimed Experience: Trauma, Narrative, and History*. The Johns Hopkins University Press, 1996.

Casino Royale. Film directed by Martin Campbell, Sony Pictures Entertainment, 2006.

Chandler, Nahum Dimitri. "The Economy of Desedimentation: W. E. B. DuBois and the Discourses of the Negro." Callaloo. 19.1 (Winter 1996), pp. 78–93.

Chaucer, Geoffrey. 1372–1400. *The Canterbury Tales*.

Chesterfield, Fourth Earl of. *Letters to His Son on Becoming a Man of the World and a Gentleman*. 1774.

Chiwengo, Ngwarsungu. *Understanding Cry, the Beloved Country: A Student Casebook to Issues, Sources, and Historical Documents*. Greenwood Press, 2007.

Cité libre. Montreal. 1950–66.

Clairmont, Donald H., and Dennis William Magill. *Africville: The Life and Death of a Canadian Black Community*. 1974. Canadian Scholars' Press, 1999.

Clarke, Austin. "Canadian Experience." *Nine Men Who Laughed*, Penguin, 1986, pp. 31–51.

———. Introduction. *Nine Men Who Laughed*, Penguin, 1986, pp. 1–7.

Clarke, George Elliott. *Beatrice Chancy*. Polestar Book Publishers, 1999.

———. "Canada: The Invisible Empire?" *The Canadian*

Mosaic in the Age of Transnationalism, edited by Jutta Ernst and Brigitte Glaser, Heidelberg: Universitätsverlag, 2010, pp. 19–35.

——. "Contesting a Model Blackness: A Meditation on African-Canadian African Americanism, or The Structures of African-Canadianité." *Essays on Canadian Writing*. 63 (Spring 1998): 1–55.

——. *Directions Home: Approaches to African-Canadian Literature*. University of Toronto Press, 2012.

——. "Frederick Ward: Writing as Jazz." *Directions Home: Approaches to African-Canadian Literature*. University of Toronto Press, 2012, pp. 190-206.

——. Introduction. *Eyeing the North Star: Directions in African-Canadian Literature*, edited by George Elliott Clarke, McClelland and Stewart, 1997, pp. xi–xxviii.

——. *Odysseys Home: Mapping African-Canadian Literature*. University of Toronto Press, 2002.

——. "Raising Raced and Erased Executions in African-Literature: Or, Unearthing Angélique." *Directions Home: Approaches to African-Canadian Literature*, by George Elliott Clarke, University of Toronto Press, 2012, pp. 78–90.

——. "Seeing Through Race: Surveillance of Black Males in Jessome, Satirizing Black Stereotypes in James." *Directions Home: Approaches to African-Canadian Literature*, by George Elliott Clarke, University of Toronto Press, 2012, pp. 68–77.

——. "Settling Africville." *Scripting (Im)migration: New Canadian Plays*, edited by Yana Meerzon, Playwrights Canada Press, 2019, pp. 107–181.

——. "Surveys." *Odysseys Home: Mapping African-Canadian Literature*, University of Toronto Press, 2002, pp. 323–448.

——. "White cops, Black corpses: U.S. and Canada have histories of police violence against minorities." *National Post* (Saturday, April 11, 2015), p. A17.

———. "Writing the Pax Canadiana: Terror Abroad, Torture at Home." *Building Liberty: Canada and World Peace, 1945–2005*, edited by Conny Steenman–Marcusse and Aritha van Herk, Barkhuis, 2005, pp. 213–36.

Cleaver, Eldridge. "The Allegory of the Black Eunuchs." *Soul on Ice.* 1968. Ramparts-Dell Publishing, 1970, pp. 145–162.

Cohen, J. M. *Poetry of This Age: 1908–1965.* 1960 & 1966. Perennial—Harper & Row, 1968.

Coleman, Daniel. *White Civility: The Literary Project of English Canada.* University of Toronto Press, 2006.

Colvin, Jeffrey. *Africaville: A Novel.* HarperCollins, 2019.

———. *Africville: A Novel.* HarperCollins Canada, 2019.

Connolly, Brian. "Intimate Atlantics: Toward a Critical History of Transnational Early America." *Common-Place.* 11.2, 2011.

Conrad, Joseph. *Heart of Darkness.* 1899, 1902. Edited by Frank Kermode and John Hollander, Oxford University Press, 1973.

Conrad, Peter. *The Hitchcock Murders.* 2000. Faber and Faber, 2007.

Constitution Act, The. 1982. (Section B, The Canada Act [United Kingdom]).

Cookson, William. *A Guide to the Cantos of Ezra Pound*, rev. ed., Anvil Press Poetry, 2001.

Cooper, Afua. *The Hanging of Angélique: The Untold Story of Canadian Slavery and the Burning of Old Montréal.* HarperCollins Canada, 2006.

———. "The invisible history of the slave trade." *The Toronto Star.* 25 Mar. 2007, A15.

Crane, Hart. *The Bridge.* Black Sun Press, 1930.

Creighton, Donald. *The Empire of the St. Lawrence.* Macmillan Co. of Canada, 1956.

Cromwell, Liz [Eliza Rebecca Cromwell], editor. *One Out of Many: A Collection of Writings by 21 Black Women in Ontario.* WACACRO productions, 1975.

Cruise, David, and Alison Griffiths. *On South Mountain: The Dark Secrets of the Goler Clan.* Viking Canada, 1997.

Cruse, Harold. *Plural but Equal: A Critical Study of Blacks and Minorities and America's Plural Society.* William Morrow, 1987.

Cunard, Nancy. *Essays on Race and Empire*, edited by Maureen Moynagh, Broadview, 2002.

Danica, Elly. *Beyond Don't: Dreaming Past the Dark.* Gynergy, 1996.

——. *Don't: A Woman's Word*, Gynergy, 1988.

Dasenbrock, Reed Way. "Why the Post in Post-Colonial Is Not the Post in Post-Modern: Homer, Dante, Pound, Walcott." *Ezra Pound and African American Modernism*, edited by Michael Coyle. The National Poetry Foundation, 2001, pp. 111–122.

Dash, Julie, director. *Daughters of the Dust.* Julie Dash, Lindsay Law, *et al.* Film. 1991.

Davey, Frank. *Karla's Web: A Cultural Investigation of the Mahaffy-French Murders.* Penguin Books Canada, 1994.

Dawson, R. MacGregor, ed. "The British North America Act, 1867." 1977.

Daymond, Douglas and Leslie Monkman, editors. *Literature in Canada: Volume 1.* Gage, 1978.

De La Roche, Mazo. *Centenary at Jalna.* 1958. Dundurn Press, 2011.

Delisle, Louise. "The Days of Evan." *Back Talk: Plays of Black Experience,* Roseway, 2005.

Desbarats, Peter. *Somalia Cover-Up: A Commissioner's Journal.* McClelland and Stewart, 1997.

Desbiens, Jean-Paul. *Les insolences du Frère Untel.* Les Éditions de l'homme, 1960.

Django Unchained. Film directed by Quentin Tarantino. Columbia Pictures, 2012.

Dr. No. Film directed by Terence Young. United Artists, 1962.

Du Bois, W. E. B. *The Souls of Black Folks: Essays and Sketches*. A. C. McClurg & Co., 1903.

Eliot, T. S. "The Waste Land." *The Waste Land and Other Poems*, Faber & Faber, 1940, 1972, pp. 25–51.

Fanon, Frantz. *Black Skin, White Masks*. 1952. Translated by Charles Lam Markmann, Grove Press, 1967.

——. *The Wretched of the Earth*. 1961. Translated by Constance Farrington, Grove Press, 1968.

Fermor, Patrick Leigh. *The Traveller's Tree*. John Murray, 1950.

Finn, Stephen M. "Transcolonial Metapoetry in South Africa." *SPAN*, no. 36, 1993.

Fleming, Ian. *Casino Royale*. 1953. Coronet, 1988.

——. *Diamonds Are Forever*. 1956. Penguin, 2002.

——. *Dr. No*. 1958. Penguin, 2006.

——. "For Your Eyes Only." *For Your Eyes Only*. 1960. Penguin, 2006, pp. 32–76.

——. *From Russia with Love*. 1956. Penguin, 2002.

——. *Goldfinger*. 1959. Coronet, 1989.

——. *Live and Let Die*. 1954. Penguin, 2003.

——. "The Living Daylights." 1966. *Octopussy* and *The Living Daylights*. Penguin, 2006, pp. 85–118.

——. *Moonraker*. 1955. Pan, 1959, 1964.

——. *On Her Majesty's Secret Service*. 1963. Penguin, 2006.

——. "Quantum of Solace." *For Your Eyes Only*. 1960. Penguin, 2006, pp. 77–101.

——. *The Spy Who Loved Me*. 1962. Penguin, 2006.

——. *Thunderball*. 1961. Penguin, 2003.

——. *You Only Live Twice*. 1964. Coronet, 1988.

Forsythe, Dennis. "By Way of Introduction: The Sir George Williams Affair." *Let the Niggers Burn!: The Sir George Williams University Affair and Its Caribbean Aftermath*, edited by Dennis Forsythe, Our Generation Press—Black Rose Books, 1971, pp. 7–21.

Fraser, John. *Violence in the Arts*. Cambridge University Press, 1974.

Freedland, Jonathan. "A Black and Disgraceful Site." *New York Review of Books*, 28 May 2009, pp. 25-29.

Frye, Northrop. "Canada and Its Poetry." 1943. *The Making of Modern Poetry in Canada: Essential Articles on Contemporary Canadian Poetry in English*, edited by Louis Dudek and Michael Gnarowski. Ryerson, 1967, pp. 86–97.

——. "Canada and Its Poetry." *Canadian Forum*, vol. 23, no. 275, pp. 207–210.

——. "Letters in Canada: 1952. Poetry." *University of Toronto Quarterly*, vol. 22, no. 3, pp. 269–280.

——. *The Great Code: The Bible and Literature*. Academic Press Canada, 1981, 1982.

Fung, Richard. [See "Gagnon, Monika Kim."]

Fussell, Edwin. *Lucifer in Harness: American Meter, Metaphor, and Diction*. Princeton University Press, 1973.

Gagnon, Monika Kin, and Richard Fung. *13 Conversations About Art and Cultural Race Politics*. Artextes Editions Prendre Parole, 2002.

Gale, Lorena. *Angélique*. 1999. Playwrights Canada Press, 2000.

George, David. "An Account of the Life of Mr. David George, from Sierra Leone in Africa, given by himself in a Conversation with Brother Rippon in London and Brother Pearce of Birmingham." *Fire on the Water: An Anthology of Black Nova Scotian Writing*, edited by George Elliott Clarke, vol. 1, Pottersfield Press, 1991, pp. 32–39.

Gibbon, Edward. *The Decline and Fall of the Roman Empire.* 6 vols. London: 1776-88.

Gibson, Mary Ellis. *Epic Reinvented: Ezra Pound and the Victorians.* Cornell University Press, 1995.

Gilroy, Paul. *The Black Atlantic: Modernity and Double Consciousness.* Harvard University Press, 1993.

Goldfinger. Film directed by Guy Hamilton. United Artists, 1964.

Goldsmith, Oliver. *The Rising Village, with Other Poems.* Saint John, NB: John M'Millan, 1834.

Goonewardena, Kanishka. "Postcolonialism and Diaspora: A Contribution to the Critique of Nationalist Ideology and Historiography in the Age of Globalization and Neoliberalism," *University of Toronto Quarterly,* vol. 73, no. 2, 2004, pp. 657–690.

Grant, George. *Lament for a Nation: The Defeat of Canadian Nationalism.* 1965. McClelland & Stewart, 1971.

Greenlee, Sam. *The Spook Who Sat by the Door.* Allison & Busby, 1969.

Grey Owl. Film directed by Richard Attenborough. Alliance Atlantic Communications, 1999.

Griffin, John Howard. *Black Like Me.* Houghton Mifflin, 1961.

Griffith, D. W, director. *Birth of a Nation.* Triangle Film Corp., 1915.

Gurney, Matt. "A report on abuse by Canadian peacekeepers in Haiti reveals a national disgrace." *The National Post*, September 17, 2019.
nationalpost.com/opinion/matt-gurney-a-report-on-abuse-by-canadian-peacekeepers-in-haiti-reveals-a-national-disgrace. Accessed on November 10, 2021.

Gustafson, Ralph. *Collected Poems.* Vol. 1, Sono Nis, 1987.

——. *Flight into Darkness.* Pantheon, 1944.

——. *Gradations of Grandeur: A Poem.* Sono Nis, 1979.

——. *The Moment Is All: Selected Poems, 1944-83.* McClelland & Stewart, 1984.

——. "Red Wheelbarrows." 1983. *Plummets and Other Partialities*, Sono Nis, 1987, pp. 125–129.

——. "Reflections on a War Not Ended." 1985. *Plummets and Other Partialities*, Sono Nis, 1987, pp. 117–124.

——. *Rivers Among Rocks.* McClelland and Stewart, 1960.

——. *Rocky Mountain Poems.* Klanak, 1960.

——. "Some Literary Reminiscences of the Eastern Townships." 1981. *Plummets and Other Partialities*, Sono Nis, 1987, pp. 130–139.

——. "The Story of the Penguin." 1983. *Plummets and Other Partialities*, Sono Nis, 1987, pp. 100–116.

Haliburton, Thomas Chandler. *The Clockmaker; or The Sayings and Doings of Samuel Slick, of Slickville.* [First Series.] Howe, 1836.

Harris, Claire. "Sister (Y)Our Manchild at the Close of the Twentieth Century," in *Dipped in Shadow.* Goose Lane, 1996, pp. 51–62.

Harrison, Charles Yale. *Generals Die in Bed.* Morrow, 1930.

Haynes, Camille, editor. *Black Chat: An Anthology of Black Poets.* Black and Third World Students Association, Dawson College, 1973.

Head, Harold, editor. "We have come." Introduction. *Canada In Us Now: The First[150] [sic] Anthology of Black Poetry and Prose in Canada*, NC Canada Press, 1976, pp. 7–12.

Hemans, Felicia Dorothea. "Casabianca." *New Monthly Magazine*, Vol. 2, Aug. 1826.

Henderson, Anna Minerva. "Corner Grocery Store." *Citadel*, [Henderson], 1967, p. 14.

Hendrix, Jimi. "Voodoo Chile." Recording. Reprise, 1968.

Henson, Guy. *The Condition of the Negroes of Halifax City, Nova Scotia.* Institute of Public Affairs, Dalhousie University, 1962.

Hersey, John. *A Bell for Adano*. Alfred A. Knopf, 1944.

———. *Hiroshima*. 1946. Alfred A. Knopf, 1985.

Hill, Lawrence. *Any Known Blood*. HarperCollins Canada, 1997.

———. *The Book of Negroes*. HarperCollins Canada, 2007.

Hogan, Ben, and Herbert Warren Wind. *Five Lessons: The Modern Fundamentals of Golf*. 1957. Fireside, 1985.

Hope, A. D. *Judith Wright*. Oxford University Press, 1975.

Hornby, Jim. *Black Islanders: Prince Edward Island's Historical Black Community*, Institute of Island Studies, 1991.

Howe, Joseph, and M. G. Parks, editors. *Western and Eastern Rambles: Travel Sketches of Nova Scotia. 1828, 1829 & 1831*, by Joseph Howe, University of Toronto Press, 1973.

Hudson, Peter. "Editor's Note: In the Country of the Snow-Blind." *West Coast Line*, vol. 31, no. 1, 1997, pp. 5-6.

Hune-Brown, Nicholas. "Mixie Me." *Toronto Life*, 12 Feb. 2013, torontolife.com/city/mixie-me/.

Hustak, Alan. *They Were Hanged*. Lorimer, 1987.

Jack, Ian. Introduction. *The Granta Book of Reportage*. 1993. Granta Books, 1998, pp. v-xiii.

James, C. L. R. *The Black Jacobins: Toussaint L'Ouverture and the San Domingo Revolution*. 1938. Random House— Vintage, 1963.

Jobb, Dean. *Shades of Justice: Seven Nova Scotia Murder Cases*. Nimbus, 1988.

Joe, Rita. *We are the Dreamers*. Breton Books, 1999.

Jolas, Eugene, ed. *Vertical: A Yearbook for Romantic-Mystic Ascensions*. Gotham Bookmart, 1941.

Johnson, Walter. *River of Dark Dreams: Slavery and Empire in the Cotton Kingdom*. Harvard University Press, 2013.

"Just-Pooh." *Lunatude, Disney*, 16 Nov. 2011, www.just-pooh.com.

Kanaganayakam, Chelva. "Pedagogy and Postcolonial

Literature; or, Do We Need a Centre for Postcolonial Studies?" *University of Toronto Quarterly,* vol. 73, no. 2, 2004, pp. 725–738.

Kaplan, William Edward. "Adrien Arcand." *The Canadian Encyclopedia.* thecanadianencyclopedia.ca/en/article/adrian-arcand. Accessed 2 July 2021.

Karen, Anthony. *The Invisible Empire: Ku Klux Klan.* Powerhouse Books, 2009.

Kennedy, John Fitzgerald. *Profiles in Courage: Decisive Moments in the Lives of Celebrated Americans.* Harper & Brothers, 1956.

Keung, Nicholas. "Mixed-race Couples Increase 33%." *The Toronto Star,* 20 Apr. 2010, thestar.com/news/canada/2010/04/20/mixedrace_couples_ increase_33.html. Accessed 14 Sept. 2013.

Kimber, Stephen. *Reparations.* HarperCollins Publishers, 2006.

King, Lloyd. *Towards a Caribbean Literary Tradition.* Lloyd King, n.d.

King, Martin Luther, Jr. *Conscience for Change: Massey Lectures, Seventh Series.* Canadian Broadcasting Corporation, 1967.

Kipling, Rudyard. "The White Man's Burden." 1899. *100 Poems: Old and New,* edited by Thomas Pinney, Cambridge University Press, 2013, pp. 111-113.

Klein, A. M. *The Rocking Chair and Other Poems.* Ryerson Press, 1948.

Kogawa, Joy. *Obasan.* Lester & Orpen Dennys, 1981.

Komar, Debra. *The Lynching of Peter Wheeler,* Goose Lane, 2014.

"L'amour est bleu." Recording by Paul Mauriat. Philips, 1968.

Lane, Patrick. "Passing Into Storm." Boundary 2, vol. 3, no. 1, 1974, p. 21.

La Rose, Lauren. "Mixed Race Marriages on the Rise." *The Toronto Star*, 22 Apr. 2008, thestar.com/news/canada/2008/04/02/mixed_race_marriages_on_the_rise.html. Accessed September 14, 2013.

Lee, Harper. *To Kill a Mockingbird*. J.P. Lippincott, 1960.

Lee, Spike, director. *Bamboozled*. New Line Cinema. Film. 2000.

Leyton, Elliott. *Compulsive Killers: The Story of Modern Multiple Murder*. New York University Press, 1986.

Lindberg, Kathryne V. "'Readers to the Right / Revolution to the Left': Ezra Pound and Claude McKay in 'The Syndicalist Year' of 1912." *Ezra Pound and African American Modernism*, edited by Michael Coyle, The National Poetry Foundation, 2001, pp. 11–77.

Lipset, Seymour Martin. *Continental Divide: The Values and Institutions of the United States and Canada*. Routledge, 1990.

Live and Let Die. Film directed by Guy Hamilton. United Artists, 1973.

Logan, John Daniel. *Thomas Chandler Haliburton*. Ryerson, 1923.

Longfellow, Henry Wadsworth. [1847] [1947?]. *Evangeline: A Tale of Acadie*. Peter Pauper Press, [1947?].

Lumumba, Carl. "The West Indies and the Sir George Williams University Affair: An Assessment." *Let the Niggers Burn!: The Sir George Williams University Affair and Its Caribbean Aftermath*, edited by Dennis Forsythe, Our Generation Press— Black Rose Books, 1971, pp. 144–191.

Macintyre, Ben. *For Your Eyes Only: Ian Fleming and James Bond*. Bloomsbury, 2008.

Mackenzie, Shelagh, director. *Remember Africville*. National Film Board 1991.

McLaren, Leah. "My Doomed Marriage." *Toronto Life,* 21 Feb. 2013, torontolife.com/city/my-doomed-marriage/.

MacLaren, Roy, editor. *African Exploits: The Diaries of William Stairs, 1887–1892*, by William Stairs, McGill-Queen's University Press, 1998.

MacLennan, Hugh. *Barometer Rising*. 1941. McClelland & Stewart, 1989.

——. *Voices in Time*. 1980. Penguin Books, 1981.

Malone, Stephens Gerard. *Big Town: A Novel of Africville*. Nimbus, 2011.

mandiela, ahdri zhina. *dark diaspora... in Dub*. Sisters Vision Press, 1991.

Mao Tsetung. [Zedong]. *Quotations from Chairman Mao Tsetung*. Foreign Languages, 1972.

Martin, Robert. "A Tale of Corrupt Halifax." *Halifax Chronicle-Herald,* 2 April 2006, stephenkimber.com/books/reparations/test-reviews/halifax-herald. Accessed 23 May 2012.

Matthews, John P. *Tradition in Exile: A Comparative Study of Social Influences on the Development of Australian and Canadian Poetry in the Nineteenth Century*. University of Toronto Press, 1962.

McKay, Sinclair. *The Man with the Golden Touch: How the Bond Films Conquered the World*. Overlook, 2008.

McKerrow, Peter E., and Frank Stanley Boyd, editors. *A Brief History of the Coloured Baptists of Nova Scotia, 1783–1895*. Afro-Nova Scotian Enterprises, 1976. Edited reprint of *A Brief History of the Coloured Baptists of Nova Scotia, and Their First Organization as Churches*, AD 1832, by Peter E. McKerrow. Nova Scotia Printing Company, 1895.

McMillan, Terry. *Waiting to Exhale*. Viking, 1992.

McNaught, Kenneth. *The Pelican History of Canada*. 1969. Penguin—Pelican, 1976.

"Melesse Spirit – Magic Card." & "Melesse Spirit – Creature – Angel Spirit."

magiccards.info/mr/en/231.html Accessed January 5,

2013. See also scryfall.com/card/mir/27/melesse-spirit?utm_source=mci Accessed November 9, 2021.

Merle, Robert. *Malevil*. Gallimard, 1972.

Michaels, Walter Benn. "'You who never was there': Slavery and the New Historicism, Deconstruction and the Holocaust." *Narrative*, vol. 4, no. 1, 1996, pp. 1–16.

Milton, John. "Sonnet XIX: When I Consider How my Light is Spent." 1655.

Minority Rights Group International. *World Directory of Minorities and Indigenous Peoples: Africa: Mauritius: Creoles.* minorityrights.org/minorities/creoles/.

Mitchell, James (John). Capital Case file. RG 13, vol. 1417, file 146A; 1880-89. Ottawa: National Archives.

The Mod Squad. American Broadcasting Corporation. Television crime series. 1968–73.

Montgomery, Lucy Maud. *Anne of Green Gables*. L.C. Page & Co., 1908.

Moodie, Andrew. *Riot*. Sirocco Drama, 1997.

Moodie, Susanna. "The Charivari." *Roughing It in the Bush; or, Life in Canada,* 1852, McClelland & Stewart, 1989, pp. 193–216.

Moody, A. David. *Ezra Pound: Poet, A Portrait of the Man & his Work, Volume III: The Tragic Years, 1939–1972.* Oxford University Press, 2015.

Morrison, Toni. "The Official Story: Dead Man Golfing." *Birth of a Nation 'hood: Gaze, Script, and Spectacle in the O. J. Simpson Case*, edited by Toni Morrison and Claudia Brodsky Lacour, Pantheon, 1997, pp. vii–xxviii.

——. *Song of Solomon*. Alfred A. Knopf, 1977.

Mukherjee, Arun. *Oppositional Aesthetics: Readings from a Hyphenated Space.* TSAR, 1994.

Mukherjee, Bharati. *Darkness*. Toronto: Penguin, 1985.

Naylor, R. T. *The History of Canadian Business, 1867–*

1914: Volume Two: Industrial Development. James Lorimer & Company, 1975.

Nelson, Jennifer J. *Razing Africville: A Geography of Racism.* University of Toronto Press, 2008.

The Nineteenth Century. 1877–1901. Monthly magazine.

Nortje, Arthur. "Autopsy." *Dead Roots.* London, Heinemann, 1973, pp. 52-54.

——. "Immigrant." *Dead Roots.* London, Heinemann, 1973, pp. 92-94.

Nuttall, Jeff. *Bomb Culture.* 1968. Delta—Dell, 1970.

"OJ Simpson—A Modern Othello?" *Modern Othello,* modernothello.blogspot.ca/.

On Her Majesty's Secret Service. Film directed by Peter R. Hunt, United Artists, 1969.

Osborne, Richard E. *If Hitler Had Won: The Plans He Made, The Plans He Carried Out, The Plans He Hoped to Achieve.* Riebel-Roque, 2004.

Owram, D. R. "Imperialism." *The Canadian Encyclopedia: Edu-Min.* 2nd ed., Hurtig Publishers Ltd., 1988, pp. 1049–1050.

Pabst, Naomi. "'Mama, I'm Walking to Canada': Black Geopolitics and Invisible Empires." MacMillan Center African Series, no. 7, 2005, pp. 25–45, isn.ethz.ch/layout/set/print/content/view/full /24593?lng=en&id=47045. Accessed September 18, 2013.

Paton, Alan. *Cry, the Beloved Country.* Charles Scribner's Sons, 1948.

Pearson, John. *James Bond: The Authorized Biography of 007.* Sidgwick & Jackson, 1973.

Penguin Anthology of Canadian Poetry (English), edited by Ralph Gustafson. 1942. Pelican, 1967.

Penguin Book of Canadian Verse, edited by Ralph Gustafson. Penguin, 1958.

Perkyns, Dorothy. *Last Days in Africville.* Dundurn Press, 2006.

Philip, M[arlene]. Nourbe[S]e. *She Tries Her Tongue, Her Silence Softly Breaks.* Ragweed Press, 1989.

Pierre, Joseph Jomo. *Shakespeare's Nigga.* Playwrights Canada Press, 2013.

Plato. *Phaedo, the Republic and other Works.* Translated by Benjamin Jowett, Doubleday Anchor, 1973, pp. 487–552.

Polanski, Roman, director. *Chinatown.* Paramount Pictures Studios—88 Productions, 1974.

Pope, Joseph. *Confidential Memorandum Upon the Subject of the Annexation of the West India Islands to the Dominion of Canada.* Dominion of Canada, 1917.

Porter, John. *The Vertical Mosaic: An Analysis of Social Class and Power in Canada.* University of Toronto Press, 1965.

Poteet, Lewis J. *Talking Country: The Eastern Townships Phrase Book.* Pigwidgeon, 1992.

Pound, Ezra. "Canto LXXIII". *The Cantos of Ezra Pound,* New Directions, 1998, pp. 438–441.

——. "Hugh Selwyn Mauberley." 1920. *Selected Poems of Ezra Pound,* New Directions, 1957, pp. 61–77.

Quantum of Solace. Film directed by Marc Forster. Sony Pictures Entertainment, 2008.

Quayson, Ato. "Symbolization Compulsion: Testing a Psychoanalytical Category on Postcolonial African Literature." *University of Toronto Quarterly,* vol. 73, no. 2, 2004, pp. 754–772.

Rajan, Balachandra. "Imperialism and the Other End of History." *University of Toronto Quarterly,* vol. 73, no. 2, 2004, pp. 707–724.

"Rampant Racism on Quebec Farm." *Canadian Employment Law Today,* 25 May 2005, employmentlawtoday.com/articleview/14608-rampant-racism-on-quebec-farm. Accessed September 18, 2013.

Razack, Sherene H. *Dark Threats & White Knights: The Somalia Affair, Peacekeeping, and the New Imperialism.* University of Toronto Press, 2004.

Regina Manifesto. Pamphlet. Co-Operative Commonwealth Federation. 1933.

Richardson, John. *Wacousta; or, The Prophecy: A Tale of the Canadas*. London: Cadell, 1832.

Rodney, Walter. *How Europe Underdeveloped Africa*. Bogle-L'Ouverture Publications and Tanzanian Publishing House, 1973.

Rose Marie. Film directed by Mervyn LeRoy. Metro-Goldwyn-Mayer, 1954.

Rothenberg, Jerome, editor. *Revolution of the Word: A New Gathering of American Avant Garde Poetry*. Seabury, 1974.

Rousseau, Jean-Jacques. *Du contrat social; ou, Principes du droit politique*. 1762. Paris, M. M. Bousquet, 1766.

Rudmin, Floyd. *Bordering on Aggression: Evidence of US Military Preparations Against Canada*. Voyageur, 1993.

Salvatore, Filippo. *Fascism and the Italians of Montreal: An Oral History, 1922-1945*. Translated by George Tombs, Guernica, 1998.

——. *La Fresque de Mussolini*. Guernica, 1992.

Sartre, Jean-Paul. Preface. *The Wretched of the Earth*. By Frantz Fanon. 1961. Grove Press, 1968, pp. 7–31.

——. "Orphée noir." *Nouvelle poésie nègre et malgache*, edited by Léopold Sédar Senghor, 1948, Presses Universitaires de France, 1972, pp. ix–xliv. Translated by S. W. Allen as *Black Orpheus*, Présence Africaine, 1963.

Saul, John Ralston. *Reflections of a Siamese Twin: Canada at the End of the Twentieth Century*. 1997. Penguin Books Canada Ltd, 1998.

Scaggs, John. *Crime Fiction*. Routledge, 2005.

Scarne, John. *Scarne on Cards*. Crown Publishers, 1949.

Scott, Duncan Campbell. "The Onondaga Madonna" (1898). *Poets of the Confederation: Duncan Campbell Scott, Archibald Lampman, Bliss Carman, Charles G. D. Roberts*, edited by Malcolm Ross, McClelland and Stewart, 1967, p. 90.

Sears, Djanet. *The Adventures of a Black Girl in Search of God*. Playwrights Canada Press, 2003.

———. *Afrika Solo*. Sister Vision Press, 1990.

———. *Harlem Duet*. Sirocco Drama, 1997.

———. Editor. *Testifyin': Contemporary African Canadian Drama, Volume 1*. Playwrights Canada Press, 2001.

Shadd, Mary Ann. *A Plea for Emigration, or, Notes of Canada West*. 1852. Edited by Richard Almonte, Mercury Press, 1998.

Shakespeare, William. The Most Lamentable Roman Tragedy of Titus Andronicus. *The Arden Shakespeare: Titus Andronicus*, edited by Jonathan Bate, Routledge, 1995.

———. Othello. The Player's Shakespeare. Edited by J. H. Walter, Heinemann Educational Books Limited, 1976.

———. The Tragedy of Hamlet, Prince of Denmark. *Three Shakespearean Plays: Hamlet, Macbeth, King Lear*. Ryerson, 1965.

———. "[Winter]." Love's Labour's Lost, Act V, Scene 2. 1598. poets.org/poem/loves-labours-lost-act-v-scene-2-winter

Shange, Ntozake. [Paulette Williams.] *for colored girls who have considered suicide/when the rainbow is enuf*. Shameless Hussy Press, 1976.

Shaw, George Bernard. *The Adventures of the Black Girl in Her Search for God (and Some Lesser Tales)*. Archibald Constable & Co. Ltd., 1932

———. *Mrs. Warren's Profession*. 1898. Archibald Constable & Co. Ltd., 1905.

Shute, Nevil. *On the Beach*. Ballantine, 1957.

Siegfried, André. *The Race Question in Canada*, 1907, edited by Frank H Underhill, McClelland and Stewart, 1966.

Smith, A. J. M. Introduction. *The Book of Canadian Poetry: A Critical and Historical Anthology*, edited by A. J. M. Smith, University of Chicago Press, 1943, pp. 3–31.

Spengler, Oswald. *Der Untergang des Abendlandes: Umrisse einer Morphologie der Weltgeschichte*. 1918. Beck, 1923.

Stairs, William G. *African Exploits: The Diaries of William Stairs, 1887-1892*, edited by Roy MacLaren. McGill-Queen's University Press, 1998.

Steeves, David. "Maniacal Murderer or Death Dealing Car: The Case of Daniel Perry Sampson, 1933–35." *The African Canadian Legal Odyssey: Historical Essays*, edited by Barrington Walker, The Osgoode Society for Canadian Legal History, 2012, pp. 201–242.

Stevens, Wallace. "Sunday Morning." 1923. poetryfoundation.org/poetrymagazine/poems/13261/sunday-morning Accessed November 10, 2021.

Stevenson, William. *A Man Called Intrepid: The Secret War*. Macmillan, 1976.

Steyn, Mark. "'Eurabia' will have to look after herself." *Jewish World Review*, 18 Mar. 2003, 14 Adar II, 5763. jewishworldreview.com/0303/steyn031803.asp

Strange, Carolyn, and Tina Loo. *True Crime, True North: The Golden Age of Canadian Pulp Magazines*, Raincoast Books, 2004.

Sutherland, John. Introduction. *Other Canadians*. 1947. *The Making of Modern Poetry in Canada: Essential Articles on Contemporary Canadian Poetry in English*, edited by Louis Dudek and Michael Gnarowski, Ryerson Press, 1970, pp. 47–61.

Talbot, Carol. *Growing Up Black in Canada*. 1984. Williams–Wallace, 1989.

Thomas, Suzanne, et al. "Mon Pays." *The Canadian Encyclopedia*, 4 Mar. 2015. thecanadianencyclopedia.ca/en/article/mon-pays. Accessed 2 July 2021.

Thunderball. Directed by Terence Young, United Artists, 1965.

Toomer, Jean. *Cane*. 1923. W. W. Norton, 1988.

Trudeau, Pierre Elliott. "The Values of a Just Society". Translated by Patricia Claxton. *Towards a Just Society: The*

Trudeau Years, edited by Thomas S. Axworthy and Pierre Elliott Trudeau, Penguin-Viking, 1990, pp. 357–385.

Trudel, Marcel. *L'Esclavage au Canada français.* 1960. Les Éditions de l'horizon, 1963.

Twain, Mark. [Samuel Clemens] *The Adventures of Huckleberry Finn.* Chatto & Windus, 1884.

United States Constitution. house.gov/Constitution/ Constitution.html

Vallières, Pierre. *Les Nègres blancs d'Amérique du nord.* Parti pris, 1968.

Valpy, Michael. "After the funeral, a look at social order." *The Globe and Mail*, 12 Apr. 1994, p. A2.

Van Creveld, Martin. *The Art of War and Military Thought.* 2000. Smithsonian Books—HarperCollins, 2005.

Van de Perre *v.* Edwards. 2 S.C.R. 1014, 2001 SCC 60, 2001, scc-csc.lexum.com/scc-csc/scc-csc/en/item/1899/index. do. Accessed September 15, 2013.

Verderbt, Verdammt, Verraten, by George Reimann, F. Decker, 1955.

Vigneault, Gilles. "Mon Pays." Recording. 1965.

Vine, David. *Island of Shame: The Secret History of the US Military Base on Diego Garcia.* Princeton University Press, 2009.

Walker, A[braham]. B., editor. *Neith: A Magazine of Literature, Science, Art, Philosophy, Jurisprudence, Criticism, History, Reform, Economics.* Saint John, NB. 1.1–5 (Feb. 1903– Jan. 1904).

Walker, James St. G. *The Black Loyalists: The Search for a Promised Land in Nova Scotia   and Sierra Leone, 1783–1870.* Dalhousie University Press, 1976.

Ward, Fred. *A Room Full of Balloons.* Tundra Books 1981.

———. *Nobody Called Me Mine.* Tundra Books 1977.

———. *Riverlisp: Black Memories.* Tundra Books 1974.

———. *The Curing Berry*. Williams-Wallace 1983.

Ward, Norman (rev.). *The Government of Canada*. 5th ed, University of Toronto Press, pp. 501–41.

What Is To Be Done?: Burning Questions of Our Movement. By V. I. Lenin. 1901. Foreign Languages Press, 1975.

Wheatcroft, Geoffrey. "Churchill and His Myths." *The New York Review of Books*, 29 May 2008, LV.9.

Whitaker, Forest, director. *Waiting to Exhale*. 20th Century Fox, 1995.

Whitfield, Harvey Amani. *Blacks on the Border: The Black Refugees in British North America, 1815–1860*. University of Vermont Press, 2006.

Whitman, Walt. *Democratic Vistas*. Walt Whitman, 1871. xroads.virginia.edu/~Hyper/Whitman/vistas/vistas.html. Accessed November 10, 2021.

———. *Leaves of Grass*. Walt Whitman, 1855.

Wilgar, W. P. "Poetry and the Divided Mind in Canada." *The Dalhousie Review*, no. 24, pp. 266-271.

Williams, Dawn P. *Who's Who in Black Canada 2: Black Success and Black Excellence in Canada*, D.P. Williams & Assoc., 2006.

Williams, Mark. "On the Discriminations of Post-colonialism in Australia and New Zealand." *University of Toronto Quarterly*, vol. 73, no. 2, 2004, pp. 739-53.

Williams, Stephen. *Karla: A Pact with the Devil*. Random House—Seal Books, 2004.

William Carlos Williams. "The Red Wheelbarrow." 1923. poetryfoundation.org/poems/45502/the-red-wheelbarrow

Winks, Robin W. *Canadian-West Indian Union: A Forty-Year Minuet*. Institute of Commonwealth Studies and Athlone Press, 1968.

———. *The Blacks in Canada: A History*. 1971. McGill-Queen's University Press, 1997.

Woolf, Virginia. *Three Guineas*. 1938. Harcourt, Brace, Jovanovich, 1966.

Wordsworth, William. "The Character of the Happy Warrior." 1807.

Wright, Judith. *Because I Was Invited*. Oxford University Press, 1975.

Wyile, Herb. *Anne of Tim Hortons: Globalization and the Reshaping of Atlantic-Canadian Literature*. Wilfrid Laurier University Press 2011.

You Only Live Twice. Film directed by Lewis Gilbert, United Artists, 1967.

ACKNOWLEDGMENTS

I begin where I must. My mother, Geraldine Elizabeth Clarke (1939–2000) was a leading educator to North End Halifax (Nova Scotia) marginalized, racialized, and working-class kids, 1960s–1970s. She employed the Montessori method to waken children's imaginations—strictly among the struggling classes—long before such became the prestigious practice of bourgeois daycares. I was pre-school-educated by her, and Alexa McDonough, who, working for and alongside "the original G. E. C.," was my kindergarten teacher (and later a provincial and federal New Democratic [democratic socialist] Party leader). My father, William Lloyd Clarke (1935–2005), was an autodidact intellectual, railway worker, and weekend artist of some talent. (He would apply oil paint to glass, then place tinfoil between the back of the glass and its cardboard backing, thus creating shimmering works akin to stained glass.) My mother and my father modelled for me the vitality of argument and the verve of art-as-craft.

In my later teens, Africadian activists Rocky and Joan Jones, Africadian poet and actor Walter Borden, Africadian filmmaker Sylvia Hamilton, then-Marxist-Leninist feminist Jackie Barkley, and community activist Bev Greenlaw piled me up with books, had me don headphones and *listen* (to jazz, folk, 1960s pop), encouraged me to write poetry, and *forced* me to go to university. What a phenomenally seditious sextet! They took a drifting North End Haligonian street kid and turned him into an intellectual.

Through my university educations, the professors who were most challenging, but who then became my champions, were Paul Beam (University of Waterloo), *The* John Fraser (Dalhousie University), and John Pengwerne Matthews (Queen's

University). Beam taught me how to write essays (in a thirteen-week bootcamp that was his lit-criticism course in fall 1980); Fraser improved my reading (and thus my writing) of poetry; Matthews introduced me to the criticism of "Commonwealth" or "Post-Colonial" literature, catalyzed my fanhood for Red Tory philosopher George Grant, and supervised my dissertation. Once I began teaching at Duke University (1994–1999), Ted Davidson, a Canadianist, and Cathy Davidson, an Americanist, enmeshed me in schools of thought that soon had me articulating the existence of African-Canadian literature. Once hired away to the University of Toronto, I came under the tutelage of *the* postmodernist and *the* postcolonialist, Linda Hutcheon, who also championed me, not only as a scholar, but as a poet—and as an opera librettist.

Now, to come to these essays, I have to thank Peter Hudson, an African-Canadianist, who solicited "White like Canada" (1998) and applied his invisible (man) hand to the editing. "An Anatomy of the Originality of African-Canadian Thought" benefited from Harvard University travel funds that took me to Baia Mare, Romania, in September 2013, and then back to Harvard itself (from Montreal), in April 2014, to face the hard questions and face the (cocktail bar) music. (And strange it was to return to Queen's University—on my birthday—in 2013 to give the first version of this paper—in the place from which I had to wrest my PhD.)

"Toward a Pedagogy of African-Canadian Literature" was one of those necessary essays—an essential demarcation of the field of Black Canadian writing. I thank the audiences—from Queen's University to conference attendees at Malta, etc., for hearing this paper. Travel funds were provided by the E. J. Pratt Chair at the University of Toronto, which means that I owe vast thanks to Sonia Labatt (1937–2022) and Victoria College, my benefactors.

"Ten African-Canadian Plays to Watch (Catch) Thus Far This Century" was solicited for a volume of essays on Canadian drama assembled by professors Albert Rau and Martin Kuester. Lookit: when I examine the course of my quarter-century career as a prof, I marvel at the truth that my work has brought me supporters from Germany and Italy—and China—but so very, very few from the African Diaspora. Pity! (Despite a 2007 reading and lecture tour to UWI campuses in Jamaica and Barbados.) Similarly, "Reading the 'Africville Novel,' or Displacing 'Race,'" was solicited by professors Klaus-Dieter Ertler and Patrick Imbert.

I will always treasure the hospitality of the German and Italian universities that hosted my lecture tours and poetry readings (Germany: December 2016; Italy: September 2012 and May 2017.). But I also have a warm spot for mainland Europe's oldest university: the University of Salamanca!

"White Judges, Black Hoods: Hanging-as-Lynching in Three Canadian True-Crime Texts" was a command perform-ance lecture to an assembly of Canadian Law Librarians in Moncton in May 2015. How sanguine we were in discussing a sanguinary justice system!

"Halifax, Hiroshima, and the Romance of Disaster" was called for by Atlantic Canadian governments and academics seeking ways to increase the region's cultural visibility and economic viability. My paper was a strange one to give, for never would I want to see a theme park devoted to the Africville relocation (and just as perverse would be a Disneyfied "Hiroshima"). And yet even the crimes and calamities of history must be marked, whether or not anyone should profiteer from the displaced bodies and the buried corpses. (The best part of the 2010 conference for which the paper was prepared was my interaction with fantastic academic Herb Wyile, who perished far too young and far too suddenly in 2016.)

"Ian Fleming's Canadian Cities" was—I admit—a frivolous paper, written partly out of my devotion to my late father's fanboy love of Bond novels and their bon-vivant author. I suspect that the wondrous academic Ana Maria Fraile-Marcos needed to ask me to justify the inclusion of the essay in her edited volume on the "Glocal" city as viewed in Anglo-Can Lit by having me write my introductory appeal for "realism" in postcolonial criticism. Well, I was glad to do it—and I stand by its insistence on the recognition of the continuation of power politics, no matter what would-be pacifying theories seem momentarily persuasive to lit-crit types.

"Writing the *Pax Canadiana:* Terror Abroad, Torture at Home" was prepared for a presentation at Middelburg, Holland, in 2005, to celebrate the sixtieth anniversary of the liberation of Holland by Canuck grunts. I thank the Dutch-Canadian academic Christl Verdun for requesting the paper, which I hope both honours gutsy Canadian veterans while critiquing Canadian praxis of racism abroad and sexism at home (or—really—of both vices in perpetual exchange).

"Canada: The Invisible Empire?" is another of those essays that *had* to be written—and which also occasioned an odyssey among European universities: Finland, Iceland, Germany, 2008–2010. I think this essay will always be necessary because of the Canadian tendency to sham and fake and deke—on the world stage—as "independent," though we continue to buttress Anglo and Americo policies—even the most vile and pernicious ones (such as making the napalm that showered upon Vietnam while we condemned, with a straight face, US aggression against the nation). Canadian imperialism must be critiqued for itself—even if it's often camouflaged as mere "do-gooderism."

"The Road to North Hatley: Ralph Gustafson's Postcolonial Paradox" was sought by the *Journal of Eastern Townships*. Betty

Gustafson came to meet me in Montreal as I finalized the paper, and I fear that she feared that I would be disrespectful or disapproving of her late husband's achievement. Truly, I hope the paper does not seem dismissive of Gustafson. I meant it— mean it—as an act of homage.

"Rereading Rita Joe: A Hearing" was commissioned by publisher Ron Caplan. I thank him for the "ask." But Rita Joe's work requires no endorsement.

Several of these essays were retyped by Christine Dagger so that they could become part of the manuscript. However, Orla Schätzlein, a former Black British student of mine in African-Canadian literature (at the University of Toronto, 2019–2020) was my editorial assistant in the summer of 2021, formatting the essays, correcting typos, noting the repetitions, figuring out how to manage the footnotes and endnotes, and then assembling the bibliography. She represents a new generation of African Diasporic intellectuals who will further change conceptions of *blackness*, so that the Ivory Tower becomes a Rainbow Tower—at last.

I thank Carmine Starnino and Simon Dardick of Véhicule Press for welcoming these essays—despite any flagrant and boisterous flaws of my cavalier making. They keep alive the tradition of the printing press and the publisher: to provoke.

Finally, I thank Giovanna Riccio for her love and patience in seeing me complete this work—the editing—in Point Pelée, Ontario. She is a formidable philosopher and *the* poet of *le mot juste*. We have debated many of the ideas in this volume, and if, dear reader, you have found them persuasive, it is because they were first tested by her rigorous critique.

White like Canada

1 See John Porter, *The Vertical Mosaic* (1965), which hypothesizes that Canadian society is structured in a racial/ethnic hierarchy wherein white Anglo-Saxon Protestants are at the summit, followed (as a distant second) by white francophone Catholics, and then various white Europeans (Nordic favoured over Southern and Eastern), and then Asians, and bottomed by Indigenous and Black.

2 See Pierre Vallières's memoir and screed, *Les Nègres Blancs d'Amérique du Nord* (1968).

An Anatomy of the Originality of African-Canadian Thought

3 Brycen Edward Clarke, born in Nova Scotia, deceased in British Columbia, was my nephew. Though he lived half of his short life in the twenty-first century, he still encountered racism in school, racism on the streets, racism in the courts: all-Canadian racism.

4 Peter Hudson gestures in this direction in a 1997 journal preface.

5 For more on these personages, see Cooper's (2006) history, and also Troy Burle Bailey's (2010) poetry collection.

6 The Canadian ideology of colour-blind multiculturalism, in its urge to forestall a discourse of anti-racism, seeks to "disappear" the very concept of "race." Discussing a similar rhetorical strategy at play in the United States, African-American writer Toni Morrison alerts us that 1) only whites are deemed "unraced, neutral" and 2) that "declarations that racism is irrelevant, over or confined to the past are premature fantasies" (Morrison xx). Another analysis of the African-American context determines that the post–World War II classification of blacks as a "minority" group rendered them merely one "minority" among many, even though it was their civil rights crusade that "led the way for the broader American minorities question to be reasserted in a fashion never before argued." In the

1970s, then, the original "black-versus-white civil rights encounter, sponsored by the judiciary, wound up...as a black *and* minority issue leavened by the 'woman question,' which took *center stage* on the domestic minority front" (Cruse 52). Arguably, this evolution of race discourse also unfolded in Canada, save that, here, it was displaced onto the crucial French-English divide as well as into the "Third World" immigrant versus European settler tension. This displacement had the effect of transforming non-Gallic and non-Anglo-Saxon European Canadians into "multicultures" seconded, according to geographic location, to either a Gallic or an Anglo-Saxon norm (with these two ethnicities holding "official" linguistic—and thus—cultural power), while the communities of colour, mainly derived from ex-colonial "developing" countries, became "*visible* minorities." African-American intellectual Harold Cruse holds, "In America there are minorities, but then there are other minorities; some minorities are equal; but some are more or less equal than others" (52). He also perceives that "white ethnics, of whatever European origin, are de facto 'assimilables' by virtue of skin color and racial origins, and are therefore candidates for intermarriage into the dominant White Anglo-Saxon Protestant (or Catholic) group" (53). Clearly, a like stratification structures—and fractures—Canadian pluralist society, with whites of British or French national derivation dominating the ruling class, with bilingual or trilingual allies drawn from "ethnic" European-Canadian elites, along with a smattering of "people"—no, "persons"—"of colour" appointed so as to flummox accusations of racism. South Asian–Canadian scholar Himani Bannerji observes, "This inscription of whiteness underwrites whatever may be called Englishness, Frenchness, and finally Europeanness" (2000, 107). The political dominance enjoyed by only a few ethnicities in Canada is accompanied by economic and cultural dominance (which is further buttressed by police forces), so pervasive that it seems natural. Let us hear Bannerji here: "An unofficial apartheid, of culture and identity, organizes the social space of 'Canada,' first between whites and non-whites, and then within the non-whites themselves" (2000, 108). Hence, impolitic folks who talk of "race" and racism speak, virtually, of treason—against the ethnic sovereign and her [*now* his]enthroned ethnicity.

7 See also my *Beatrice Chancy*: "*Slavery Is Global Industry and Trade—The Future*" (G. E. Clarke, *Beatrice* 25).

8 There is some evil irony in the fate of a poor African trying to jump ship in Spain or to stow away in the wheel well of a jet bound for America or to paddle a rough dinghy from Haiti to Florida: their very ancestors might have been brought to Europe or the Americas in chains.

9 Yes, I know, there's been "progress": today, in 2014, a Black man is in the White House. I also applaud. Yet that same African (American) president bombed an African nation (Libya) in 2012 and was unhelpful to democratic forces during the Arab Spring of 2011.

10 Euro-Canadian writer Stephen Williams observes that, for the Dominion of Canada, "Immigrants represented a kind of slave labor" (37). To immigrate to Canada was better than being shipped here as a slave, but only because, eventually, as an immigrant, one could be free of one's status as peon or serf. The fiction and non-fiction of Austin Clarke (1934–2016) is acutely conscious of the interlocking relationships, in Canada, among class, ethnicity, colour, and immigrant/citizenship status. What he terms "prepossessiveness" (A. Clarke, Introduction 3) aligns Canadian white supremacy to a sense of primordial privilege: "we" got here first, "got the good stuff while the getting was good," and don't want to share the gain with (visible minority) "newcomers" or "Johnnys-come-(too)-lately."

11 That Negroes arrived at different times, in different eras, and settled—or got settled—in different places, means that African Canada developed as—and remains—a set of discrete (and discreet) settlements: There are a "lot" of Blacks in Toronto, then, but far fewer in Thunder Bay. I'm moved to pun: In Canada, there's no "Black Belt," just "pockets."

12 The beauty of our diversity is, a just-landed, English-speaking Trinidadian of Indo-African heritage, also Muslim, can find himself, say, in Montreal, attending a carnival with a francophone

Afro-Acadien, whose roots date back centuries in Canada, and whose faith is Catholicism cut with Haitian *Vaudou*. To be Black in Canada is to negotiate constant border-crossings, so to speak, among our *cultures*. (Note the plural.)

13 A clue to this very un-Martin-Luther-King-Jr. conun-drum appears in an unselfconscious comment in a 2013 article by white Euro-Canadian writer Leah McLaren. She opines, "liberal middle-class values...have made *us* more tolerant of minorities" (54, emphasis added). Although one desires to read "us" as denoting all Canadians, McLaren's comment most likely flatters white (em-powered) Canadians, well-raised and good-intentioned ("liberal" and "middle-class"), for "tolerating" the (visible) "minorities" in their midst. In this context, liberalism means politesse; it does not mean anti-racism.

14 That history begins, says Dennis Forsythe, in "the almost universal general plight of Blacks...resulted from the socio-economic development of western society rather than from some divine plan." This history consists of "exploitation without recompense, service without thanks, promises without fulfillment: bluntly, lies and thievery" (Forsythe 15). Forsythe insists, "if anything deserves to be regarded as the 'original sin' of modern history, it is the complete reduction of black men [*sic*] to the level of private property" (20). Given that slavery was practised in colonial Canada and that, once free, African persons received little land and few letters (also true in the Caribbean), the African-Canadian community remains in deficit when compared with the wealth and (political) power of practically *any* white ethnicity. No, the reality is "the old sham white supremacy forever wedded to and dependent upon faux black inferiority" (Morrison xxvii). Bannerji agrees: in Canada, "whiteness extends into moral qualities of...possessive individualism and an ideology of capital and market" (107). In Canada, those who are ignorant of Canadian history are condemned to suffer the repetition of its unpleasantries.

15 Cf. Austin Clarke's eponymous short story ("Canadian Experience").

16 40.6 percent of Black Canadians marry non-Blacks, declare the 2006 Canadian Census results (La Rose).

17 See Section 35 of The Constitution Act, 1982 (Schedule B of the Canada Act 1982 [UK]). Canada is the world's only nation to *endorse*, constitutionally, a mixed-race identity.

18 Euro-Canadian scholar Naomi Pabst allows this obser-vation: "Canada's heritage project…espouses color-blindness, and yet [Canada] constitutes itself as the 'great white north.' What arises, then, is a brand of disavowed racism, in which black people are perceived as 'cultural' rather than 'racial' others" (31).

19 That Indigenous Canadians and Métis are considered "Status" or "Non-Status" underlines the truth that, in our Canadian (British) monarchy, race and ethnicity are arranged hierarchically.

20 In 2005, African-Canadian film critic Cameron Bailey deemed Toronto "an Asian migrant city with a white ruling class."

21 Sometimes the Lone Ranger's sidekick, Tonto, and the Green Hornet's pal, Kato, are just white guys' flunkeys.

22 The Ottawa Black-oriented monthly tabloid *The Spectrum* (1984–2013) advertised itself with the slogan "Making Minorities Visible," to answer to the issues of polite erasure and colour-blind dismissal.

23 Sharon Fernandez warns, "Elitism, cronyism, and racism continue to be forces in the struggle for plural, cultural symmetry [in Canadian arts organizations]" (Gagnon and Fung 73), and, I will add, in other institutions too.

24 Wole Soyinka, Toni Morrison, and Derek Walcott, look out! We's right behind yas!

Toward a Pedagogy of African-Canadian Literature
25 I know that other scholars are gracious enough to deem African-Canadian literature "black writing in Canada." But this alternative nomenclature robs the literature of both its continental heritage and its historical connection to the clutch of invasive British/French colonies-turned-provinces we now call Canada.

26 See King's *Conscience for Change* (Massey Lectures, Seventh Series; Canadian Broadcasting Corporation, 1967).

27 But that is not to say we will hear a cascade of positives when we begin to allow African-Canadian voices to enter our heads and our classrooms. French philosopher Jean-Paul Sartre warned, way back in 1948, "What would you expect to find, when the muzzle that has silenced the voices of black men is removed? That they would thunder your praise?"; Sartre, *Black Orpheus*, translated by S. W. Allen, Présence Africaine, [1963], p. 7; original as "Orphée noir," introduction to *Nouvelle poésie nègre et malgache*, edited by Léopold Sédar Senghor (1948, Presses Universitaires de France, 1972), p. ix ("Qu'est-ce donc que vous espérez, quand vous ôtiez le bâillon qui fermait ces bouches noires? Qu'elles allaient entonner vos louanges?"). No, no, we have too much to remember, too much to forgive, to unthinkingly lavish paeans and elegies upon a civilization that found it just to seize foreign peoples, imprison and transport them across seas, and extract their labour without pay, and then to sell their offspring into bestial servitude.

28 See Article IV, Section 2, Clause 3, and then Note 11 (regarding its repeal).

29 See Marcel Trudel, *L'Esclavage au Canada français*. 1960. Les Éditions de l'horizon, 1963.

30 Although they may have been ignorant of the sources of their own racism, the two or more young white men in—excuse the irony—a souped-up black car, who leaned out a window and screeched "NIGGER!" at me while I was walking one night, in July 1993, back to the Queen's University Graduate Residence in Kingston, Ontario, felt assuredly some claim of ownership upon me. My reaction, however, contradicted my dissertation-writing, doctoral-candidate persona: I dropped the two bags of groceries I was carrying and went running down the middle of the street after the speeding car in an attempt to hurl a rock at its rear window. I had gone straight from the end of the twentieth century back to the Stone Age.

31 I cannot resist noting that the first global industry was slavery. See also my play *Beatrice Chancy*, p. 25.

32 Fascinatingly, Stairs's diaries, published wholly in 1998, are edited by the then High Commissioner of Canada in the United

Kingdom, Roy MacLaren, whose editorial asides sometimes update the ethnocentric assumptions of Stairs. (See my article "Writing the Pax Canadiana: Terror Abroad, Torture at Home," which is reproduced in this volume.)

33 "La Négritude…est, en son essence, Poésie. Pour une fois au moins, le plus authentique projet révolutionnaire et la poésie la plus pure sortent de la même source"; Jean-Paul Sartre, "Orphée noir," *Nouvelle poésie nègre et malgache*, edited by Léopold Sédar Senghor, 1948. Presses Universitaires de France, 1972, pp. xliii–xliv. Translated by S. W. Allen as *Black Orpheus*, Présence Africaine, [1963], p. 64.

34 "À chaque époque sa poésie; à chaque époque, les circonstances de l'histoire élisent une nation, une race, une classe pour reprendre le flambeau, en créant des situations qui ne peuvent s'exprimer ou se dépasser que par la Poésie"; Sartre, "Orphée noir," xliv; translated by Allen, p. 65.

35 For a working history and bibliography of African-Canadian literature, see my "Surveys" section in *Odysseys Home: Mapping African-Canadian Literature*, University of Toronto Press, 2002, pp. 323–448.

36 In the interest of concision, I do not include the "Provisional Syllabus" here. But it is available as part of the original essay.

Ten African-Canadian Plays to Watch (Catch) Thus Far This Century

37 Not yet published, the fourth instalment of the play is now titled, "The Last Epistle of Tightrope Time." Email from Walter Borden to GEC on September 14, 2021.

38 When I worked for him as a constituency liaison, I recall Howard D. McCurdy (1932–2018), then Canada's second Black member of Parliament (1984–1993), telling me of similar episodes involving his then-teen children undertaking nocturnal liberations of "racially offensive" lawn ornaments in rural Essex County, Ontario, in the 1970s.

39 Yet, counters Oscar Wilde, "There is no essential incongruity...between crime and culture," qtd. in Peter Conrad, p. 67.

40 Canadian anthropologist Elliot Leyton affirms, "No single quality of American culture is so distinctive as its continued assertion of the nobility and beauty of violence—a notion and a mythology propagated with excitement and craft in all popular cultural forms, including films, television, and print."

41 Every murder suspect, on trial, faces the King or the Queen, the allegorical representations of the Canadian state.

42 Yes, I realize that "British justice" frowns upon mob-enacted lynching. However, such scruples have not prevented the railroading of some unfortunates fairly straightforwardly to the gallows (nixing the strong limb of a nearby tree), thus achieving a constructive lynching, if not merely a veritable one.

43 See G. E. Clarke, "Raising Raced and Erased Executions." My claim acquires irresistible force if the libraries of black and white crime and punishment, in fiction and non-fiction, of Canada and the United States are viewed side-by-side. That the United States has a larger population and a higher incarceration rate (and possibly more criminals per capita) are not the only reasons for its mania for the annals of what Scotland Yard terms "The Black Museum."

44 Komar notes that newspapers then tended to label "all swarthy men" as "Spaniards or Portuguese." This identification suggests that some European cultures were deemed less white than others and, thus, inferior.

45 Cf. Shakespeare's *Othello* (1603).

46 See e.g. "OJ Simpson—A Modern Othello?" online: <modernothello.blogspot.ca/>. The site also reproduces the notorious *Time* magazine image of a digitally "blackened" Simpson.

47 See Michael Valpy, "After the Funeral—A Look at Social Order," [Toronto] *Globe & Mail* (April 12, 1994), p. A2, for columnist Valpy's *blanket* criminalization of the speech and styles of Jamaican-Canadian youth because of the thuggish acts of a few individuals.

48 See the Mitchell, James (John) Capital Case file. RG 13, vol. 1417, file 146A; 1880–89. Ottawa: National Archives. James (John) Mitchell, a "Colored" man sentenced to death for murder of a white man in 1880. The context for the "murder," as divulged in court testimony, was a riot involving black men and white men at the roadway entrance to the Bridgetown-adjacent Africadian community of Inglewood. The culprit stabbed his victim, who later died as a result of infection of the wound. Crucially, the only evidence that this riot occurred is in the trial transcripts of the accused.

49 Minority Rights Group International, *World Directory of Minorities and Indigenous Peoples: Africa: Mauritius: Creoles*, online: <minorityrights.org/minorities/creoles/>.

50 Such language is suggestive of incest. Intriguingly, David Cruise and Alison Griffiths, in *On South Mountain: The Dark Secrets of the Goler Clan* (1997) at pp. 55, 77, find that a notorious family of intergenerational child molesters and incest practitioners, not brought to "justice" until the mid-1990s, lived quite insular lives and had done so for generations. Cruise and Griffiths cite an unpublished Acadia University study that found "ten or twelve people [living] in a few drafty rooms,…obviously sexual relationships between close family members, [and puzzlement due to] the thick [South] Mountain accents and [bemusement] that many of the women smoked pipes." Cruise and Griffiths express a racialized genetics only somewhat more sophisticated than that available to the stereotype-iterating press of a century ago. Thus, they submit that the Black War of 1812 refugee Munday Goler's "black genes are so diluted they're all but invisible in the faces of the clan he founded. But every now and then his legacy shows up in the richer skin colour or the thick, wiry hair of his descendants."

51 See also G. E. Clarke, "Seeing Through Race: Surveillance of Black Males in Jessome, Satirizing Black Stereotypes in James." *Directions Home: Approaches to African-Canadian Literature*, University of Toronto Press, 2012; G. E. Clarke, "White cops, Black corpses: U.S. and Canada have histories of police violence against minorities." *National Post*. (Saturday, April 11, 2015).

52 Tellingly, Jobb's narration of the Farmer case follows the story structure that Strange and Loo identify in the Canuck true-crime pulps: to chronicle "the police chase, [skip] quickly through the trial and [move] toward its inevitable outcome: the guilty verdict, which [restores] social harmony and [resets] moral values" Strange and Loo, *supra* note 16 at 6.

53 I'm reminded of a Malcolm X speech in which he shouts, regarding alleged white malfeasance, "You haven't done the right thing!"

54 Every cinema action-hero (James Bond *et al.*) enacts a repudiation of *Hamlet.*

55 Jobb describes Farmer's midnight trek to the police chief's home as constituting "his last taste of freedom" (103).

56 I am moved to note that suspicion directed toward blacks because they happen to be in the vicinity of a crime is really an expression of the deeper feeling that they do not belong here, anyway, or, if they are to be here, must endure constant surveillance—if not incarceration.

57 Williams, Dawn P. *Who's Who in Black Canada 2: Black Success and Black Excellence in Canada*, D. P. Williams & Assoc., 2006 at 168.

58 The Shakespeare play the Sampson case evokes? *Titus Andronicus*: therein a sly black villain, Aaron, with near impunity, arranges rape and murders and disfigurements.

59 Because racism is so ineradicably an element of law enforcement, I move that we now understand "money laundering" as representing the attempt of the "criminalized" ethnic or racial minority to achieve respectability—to "pass," as it were, as a bona fide member of the WASP ruling class.

Reading the Africville Novel

60 Nelson denounces "Relocation" as a "politically benign" term. She prefers more realistic terms like "destruction," "removal," or "forced relocation" (153, n. 22).

61 This historical overview is indebted to the works of James Walker, Harvey Amani Whitfield, and Robin W. Winks.

62 Whitfield insists, "The Black Refugees wanted to become independent landowning farmers" (51). However, he is also aware of the arguments that the colonial government "hoped to use the Refugees as a captive labor force tied to uneconomical land, with their only option being to work on the larger farms of white neighbors or as domestic servants" (55). I do maintain that the hope for subsistence-wage employment drew Black Refugees (and Black Loyalists and descendants) from the countryside to the closest rural site near central Halifax, namely Campbell Road Settlement, which by the 1900s was being identified as Africville.

63 Sociologists Donald H. Clairmont and Dennis William Magill determine that "the original Africville settlers were... former residents of the [Black] refugee settlements at Preston and Hammonds Plains [Nova Scotia] who moved to Africville in order to escape the economic hardships encountered on rocky and barren land" (32).

64 In his travel journalism of 1828, Joseph Howe speaks of meeting, on the shores of Bedford Basin, "a goodly bevy of sable beauties" (55). One cannot state for certain that the women were from Campbell Road/Africville, but they most likely were.

65 Clairmont and Magill state that "Africville" displaced "Campbell Road" by the early 1900s—or at about the same time that McKerrow was writing his history. They show that one community resident used "Africville" as early as 1860, while the railway described it as "African Village" in 1861 (38). On Halifax Harbour charts, the location of Africville was demarcated as "Negro Point."

66 A fuller treatment of Ward's biography appears in my essay, "Frederick Ward: Writing as Jazz" (2012).

67 The novel is even dedicated "to my daddy and mama / cause they know" [5], a sentence that forwards memory as a constitutive element of the fiction.

68 See the documentary film by Shelagh Mackenzie, *Remember Africville* (1991).

69 This term, my coinage, refers to historically settled African-Canadians in Nova Scotia, New Brunswick, and Prince Edward Island, *and* their historic—and historical—communities or "land-

base." See G. E. Clarke, *Directions Home* (207, note 3). It is vital to respect the truth that, as Nelson advises, "the lands allotted to [Africadians] were neither within the rightful jurisdiction of the British to distribute, nor in possession of the black settlers" (11). Yet we must remember that blacks arrived in Nova Scotia (and the Maritimes in general) as, "variably, exiled or escaped peoples struggling for survival. Many blacks came unwillingly, and those who selected Nova Scotia as their home did so within a severely limited range of choices" (Nelson 11).

70 The Robin Hood–style bureaucrat's name, James Joseph Howe, is itself resonant within provincial—and Canadian—history. Joseph Howe (1804–73) was a prominent Nova Scotian politician, journalist, author, and civil servant, and a powerful opponent of colonial Canadian Confederation in 1867. Howe is cited above, but historians also rate him as favourable to the Africadian struggle for equality, education, and prosperity. See Whitfield, for instance, who cites Howe's 1832 defence of Black Refugees from their detractors, even arguing that "black people had both intellect and ambition and questioned if any harm could come from 'a gentle infusion of black blood into those dignified orders [law, medicine, business, and government] of the state?'" (88). Kimber himself allows an explicit connection between "J. J." Howe and Joseph Howe (346).

71 Melesse is also the name of a spirit, winged creature, or angel in a deck of "magic" cards. See magiccards.info/mr/en/231.html. The significance of this factoid to Kimber is open to speculation.

72 Nelson also holds, "The liberal rhetoric of integration and renewal, never realized, was in fact a discourse and a practice of erasure from sight and site" (115).

73 Ngwarsungu Chiwengo is succinct: "*Cry, the Beloved Country* is a social novel, influenced by Abraham Lincoln's writing, which advocates a Christian, race-free South Africa. It is a Christian narrative of love, compassion, and forgiveness" (10).

74 I also detect the lurking presence of Roman Polanski's neo-noir film *Chinatown* (1974) in the scenario of *Reparations*. In the Tinseltown film, private detective J. J. "Jake" Gittes bears a name

that echoes those of Kimber's "J. J." Howe and Crown Prosecutor Henry Gettings. Moreover, the plot of Polanski's film turns on a dispute over water rights as well as the tempestuous relationship between the detective and a woman who is also the incestuous lover of her father, Noah Cross, a foe to the private eye. If *Chinatown* sites the Los Angeles Chinatown as a place where vice "just happens," Kimber produces Africville as a site of similar—if *blacker*—Orientalism.

Halifax, Hiroshima, and the Romance of Disaster

75 MacLennan's heroine in *Barometer Rising* is described, at one point, as resembling "a little girl who has just discovered that a major catastrophe can be only a minor incident to grown-ups" (98): catastrophe is in the eye of the beholding (or beholden) writer.

76 The former Africville site is situated between two "reckonings"—the Halifax Explosion originating point and Fairview Cemetery, where some of the *Titanic* victims are interred—while being itself a memorial ground.

77 This adjective merits a stiff Freudian reading!

78 The consonantal correspondence between *Warrington* and *Warren*, *Vivie* and *Vera*, cannot be coincidental.

79 One must read these consequences into Tom's [Bell's] laconic statement, "Peaceful acquisition in America was forbidden according to the Monroe Doctrine" (4).

80 Opines Ian Jack, the writer of reportage "gives the initial process of *finding out* an equal, or even a greater, priority to the later process of shaping the information discovered—the scene witnessed, the words spoken—into sentences fit for a page" (xiii, italics in the original).

81 *Hiroshima* appeared first as the contents of the August 31, 1946, issue of *The New Yorker*. Presumably, more than one Manhattan reader found *himself* able to identify with the good doctor's *Playboy*-like lifestyle.

82 Ironically, post-bombing, German priests are mistaken for enemy Yanks. They escape harm by claiming to be "German—allies" (63). But they are Christians and neutral.

83 MacLennan is reticent on this point, but one may speculate that this ancestral Wain likely imported and exported more than a few slaves—as status symbols if not as living capital (or chattel). Historically, it was the practice of his class—and not only witnessed in Jane Austen, *bien sûr*, but also in colonial Canada's Thomas Chandler Haliburton.

84 This "expansion" need not be verifiable. Jonathan Freedland writes, "Following the lead of the Romans, London once dreamed of coloring the map pink, ruling the world by conquering as much territory as it could. But the US successor seeks to rule by holding, directly at least, as little territory as it can" (27).

85 As I edited this chapter in late August 2013, America, Britain, and Canada (the ABCs of the old-fashioned Anglo-Saxon global alliance imagined a hundred years ago), plus France, plus Arab states armed and patronized by the West (for the sake of oil), were preparing to "strike" or "punish" Syria for its alleged detonation of chemical weapons. The more things change, the more they stay the same. Oh, yes, the democratic aspirations of the Arab Spring are now rolled back, throughout the region, and most strikingly in Egypt, where the US-supplied, -trained, and -financed Egyptian Army has slaughtered hundreds of members of the Muslim Brotherhood and imprisoned the democratically elected president of Egypt (Mohamed Morsi). For those who think these "news stories" are merely news, I would say, think again—but in the spirit of Fanon!

86 Yet, along with Albert Broccoli, it was a Canadian, Harry Saltzman—"who once worked in a circus" (McKay 6)—who brought the Bond books to the big screen (McKay 6). Another Canadian (McKay 256), Lois Maxwell, played Bond's flirtatious but lovelorn MI-6 contact, Moneypenny, in the first fourteen "official" (EON productions) films. Presumably, neither Saltzman nor Maxwell pushed to utilize Canadian locales and characters.

87 Macintyre agrees that Fleming and Stephenson had close contact (54) but cautions that Stephenson may have exaggerated aspects of his knowledge of Fleming (56). Yet Macintyre also records Fleming's admission that his fiction is based on "wartime memories" (20).

88 Incidentally, Winston Churchill dubbed Canucks "leopards" because they knew "silent methods of killing" (Stevenson 194).

89 Bond also owes much to his creator. Macintyre insists that author and character had much in common (18) and that, "above all, Fleming and Bond share an interest in things, the rarer and more exclusive the better" (188).

90 Fleming says, "Facts are clearer than people" (Macintyre 118), and British novelist Kingsley Amis calls the referencing "of real information in a fictional world 'The Fleming Effect'" (Macintyre 123). Bearing these quotations in mind, one may credit Fleming with having borrowed some of his fantasies from the reality of Stephenson's—and his own—employ.

91 Macintyre notes that Fleming wove facts and real people into his fiction (62); Fleming himself says that his Bond character is "a compound of all the secret agents and commando types I met during the war" (Macintyre 65). Macintyre agrees that Stephenson is a "possible Bond" prototype (72), who was praised publicly by Fleming as being, as a spy, "the real thing"(Macintyre 73). Still, Macintyre feels that Stephenson's "memoir" should be "taken with large quantities of salt" (74).

92 Bond gives the gory details of his first two kills in a later conversation (Fleming, Casino 141–142).

93 Maybe even wartime Canadian prime minister William Lyon Mackenzie King (1874–1950).

94 Stephenson himself sought espionage recruits who exhibited traits that describe Fleming's spy. He recruited those who exuded "'a love of productive peril' or a certain flamboyance if there was a moral force behind it…. The good agent starts out as a man who chose action over inaction but who learns to control his impulses… in order to resume abstract thought" (Stevenson 195).

95 Algernon Aspinall (1927).

96 Fleming took "a close interest in French pornography, and assembled an impressive personal collection of erotica, which he liked to show to visitors, especially female ones" (Macintyre 147–148).

97 In *On Her Majesty's Secret Service* (1969), Bond is seen,

forty-one seconds in, leafing through an extant *Playboy*. It likely doesn't count as "reading."

98 This Fleming novel may be the most literary. The conversation between Bond and a Japanese agent, Tiger Tanaka, canvasses "Shakespeare, Homer, Dante, Cervantes, Goethe," and Basho (100). Later, the malefactor, Blofeld, catalogues "Poe, Lautréamont, de Sade" (154). However, Russian novelist Mikhail Lermontov drops into *From Russia with Love* (138), and, in *On Her Majesty's Secret Service*, British writers Laurence Sterne, James Boswell, "Johnson, Reynolds, Goldsmith," and "Dean Swift" are named as once-upon-a-time denizens or explorers of Bond Street, London (73). In *Moonraker* (1955), British prose writers Horace Walpole and Edward Gibbon merit mention (24), as do the Prussian-German military strategist Carl von Clausewitz (71), the British reference annual *Whitaker's Almanack* (101), and American author Edgar Allan Poe (175). The sentence "The boy stood on the burning deck" (Fleming, *Moonraker* 169) refers to the poem "Casabianca" (1826) by British poet Felecia Dorothea Hemans.

99 Macintyre is right that "books are hardly mentioned in Bond's world, save for a few, including Hogan on Golf, Scarne on Cards and a few books written (inevitably) by Fleming's friends...as well as JFK's *Profiles in Courage*" (188). Even so, the Bond novels emerge from a literary universe that includes the seminal spy novel *The Thirty-Nine Steps* by John Buchan (Macintyre 28), the later Lord Tweedsmuir, Governor-General of Canada (1935–40); British novelist W. Somerset Maugham, who befriended Fleming (Macintyre 170) and praised *Casino Royale* (McKay 344); and British novelist William Plomer, who also read *Casino Royale* in manuscript (Macintyre 196). Among those to praise *Casino Royale* upon publication was British poet (and later Laureate) John Betjeman (Macintyre 196). Another Fleming friend was British playwright Noel Coward, who also knew INTREPID (Stevenson 96). Coward is name-dropped in *You Only Live Twice* (Fleming 168). British poet Stephen Spender accompanied Fleming on a pilgrimage to the set of *Dr. No* (McKay 21). Fleming dubbed his Jamaican estate Golden Eye, partly after

a novel by American author Carson McCullers (Macintyre 171). In *Moonraker* , an Edgar Allan Poe story is cited (175). Although his "converted Regency house" boasts "a book-lined sitting-room" (Fleming, *Moonraker* 22), Bond seems less a reader than Fleming is a writer. Even so, the spy is a walking encyclopedia of sartorial and gourmet dos and don'ts along with eccentric—though handy— trivia, some drawn from *Playboy* and some taken from how-to manuals and tourist guides. Indeed, a frankly commercial aspect of his Bond novels is that Fleming instructs other men, through his hero, on what marquee brands to smoke, drink, and drive, and how to dress and how to impress women, lessons also transferred, with much popularity, to the screen.

100 Stevenson tells us that, as a boy, Stephenson "experimented with electricity, steam engines, kites, and crude airplanes. He rigged his own Morse telegraph" (4).

101 Macintyre notes, "The historian of Camp X, David Stafford, could find no evidence that Ian Fleming had ever attended a course there" (56). Furthermore, the courses "described by Stephenson, at which his friend supposedly excelled, were not on the curriculum" (56). Nevertheless, Macintyre concludes, "it is certainly possible, even likely, that [Fleming] visited the camp in 1943; he may even have taken part in a few training events" (56). If Fleming did train at Camp X, the gadgets that appear in the Bond films (though less in the novels) may owe a debt to the inventions it oversaw, including "explosive loaves of bread [and] fountain pens that squirted cyanide" (Stevenson 197).

102 After touchdown in New York City, Bond dines and opines, "The smoked salmon...from Nova Scotia [was] a poor substitute for the product of Scotland" (84).

103 Accepting that Fleming used Stephenson as a model for his James Bond, we should claim Winnipeg as the cradle of two British literary icons, both Bond and Winnie the Pooh—named by children's author A. A. Milne after a Canadian bear called Winnipeg, resident at the London Zoo (just-pooh.com).

104 One wonders if this international collective of forgers served to imp Fleming to assemble a multicultural cast of villains,

spies, and "exotic" women in every Bond novel, an achievement parlayed into the films. Watching *Dr. No*, the first Bond film, one sees a miniature world expo. Indeed, Bond's first cinema killing is of a black man, and his second on-screen lover, Taro, is a "two-faced" Jamaican—Black Chinese—woman. His main love interest, Honey Ryder, is a white woman—Swiss actress Ursula Andress—speaking and singing Jamaican demotic! Dining with the Eurasian—Chinese German—villain, Dr. No, Bond wears a Nehru jacket while Ryder sports a sarong. McKay tutors us in "the determinedly internationalist outlook of the films. Look at the European cast of *Thunderball*—a French leading lady, an Italian villain" (87). In *You Only Live Twice* (1967), Bond "turns" Japanese, pretending to be a fisherman and taking a Japanese bride. For its part, *Live and Let Die* is a blaxploitation film with a white male lead. Despite Fleming's between-the-lines subscription to racialist thinking, including whiffs of his era's "intense parlor anti-Semitism" (Brenner 219), white supremacy, and fine-chap, Anglo-Saxon superiority, the novels picture a globalized world. One tours the residue of ye olde British Empire (now floated by glitzy Yank capitalists and overseen by gung-ho Yank troops), in the company of a cosmopolitan and multilingual hero (Bond has Greek and Latin and Russian and a yen for other tongues) who has gals, pals, and foes of every clime and complexion. This "disciplined exoticism," in Fleming's phrase (Macintyre 164), is lent a Technicolor shimmer in the films—the "Cantos" of the cinema. One other point: although Canada and Canadians won Fleming's attention, Jamaica and the British West Indies were just as—or more—significant. All the Bond tales were scribed at Fleming's estate—Golden Eye—in Jamaica, among a rainbow citizenry that Fleming seems to view, in his texts, with equal measures of suspicion, condescension, and respect. Fleming is, really, a Caribbean novelist.

105 In this capacity, Stevenson says, "Stephenson had to explain [to Churchill] the complexities of American politics while Europe fell around British ears" (320).

106 Fleming seems to consider the Royal Canadian Navy

an extraordinarily sober and orderly enterprise. He should know better! One presumes that he is suggesting that the decommissioned cap'n was a punch-happy drunk.

107 Fleming may be basing this episode on the true story of Marshal Josip Broz Tito (1892–1980), who left the Soviet Union in 1940, "disguised as Spiridon Mekas and carrying a British passport issued in Canada" (Stevenson 209).

108 Stevenson records the theft of ciphers and equipment from the embassy of Vichy, France, in Washington, DC, through the employment of the charms of an American agent, CYNTHIA, who serially seduced embassy staff to allow the theft to occur (331–339). This gambit seems to foreshadow Fleming's *From Russia with Love*, wherein Bond, to steal the Soviet Spektor cipher system, accepts to seduce the ultra-willing Tatiana Romanova (141–143). Later, Stevenson reports, CYNTHIA "went to Canada where she was instructed in the skills of an assassin" (341). Incidentally, women assassins and would-be killers, both "good" and "bad" in character or skill, are staples in the Bond films.

109 Fleming refers to the 1954 film *Rose Marie* (directed by Mervyn LeRoy), in which, in the Canadian forest, in the west, a woman falls for a trapper, wanted by the Mounties, who in turn is loved by the daughter of a Native chief.

110 Fleming related covert operations not so much to cloak and dagger but to cowboys and Indians, a fantasy that, again, seems indebted to Karl May and Grey Owl. Significantly, Fleming referred to his wartime agents as "'Red Indians'—somewhat to their annoyance, since a number of these warriors had little time for their self-styled chief" (Macintyre 50); after the war, Fleming recalled, nostalgically, "those romantic Red Indian daydreams so many of us indulged in at the beginning of the war" (Macintyre 46). Conceivably, another forerunner of Bond is not the real Canuck INTREPID but the fake Canuck Grey Owl.

111 The Englishman Archibald Belaney (1888–1938), who posed as Grey Owl, an Anishinaabe Ojibwe elder and leading author-conservationist, was surely a model for Fleming, who, like Belaney, seems to have been fascinated by First Nations peoples in

North America. Thus, he named his wartime commandos "Red Indians" (Macintyre 56). In a nice coincidence, Irish actor Pierce Brosnan, who played Bond on-screen throughout the 1990s, also appears as Grey Owl in the eponymous feature film (1999).

112 In that same novel, Bond castigates himself for "playing Red Indians through the years" (188) and for having been "the cool secret agent with a Double O number gallivanting round the world—playing Red Indians" (188).

113 See Pabst, who identifies Canada as "'an invisible empire' as a huge geographical space, a nation with privilege, an uncentral yet certifiable member of the overdeveloped world" (27). Savvy postcolonialists appreciate such a definition.

Writing the *Pax Canadiana*: Terror Abroad, Torture at Home

114 I dedicate this essay to Norman Kester (1962–), a mixed-race, African-Canadian poet, born in South Africa and reared under apartheid.

115 See The British North America Act (1867), Section 91.

116 Sherene H. Razack points out that "a Canadian today knows herself or himself as someone who comes from the nicest place on earth, as someone from a peacekeeping nation, and as a modest, self-deprecating individual who is able to gently teach Third World Others about civility" (9). This mythology extends to the idea that "never having been a colonial power or engaged in aggressive occupations (internal colonialism [against Indigenous peoples] is once again ignored) Canadians are content to see themselves as playing a secondary, more innocent role in world affairs." (Razack 33).

117 Scoff, if you like, at the kamikaze aspect of Brown's plan. But he was not wrong to war-game as he did, for the United States had its own scheme to invade Canada, War Plan Red, first developed in 1930, then amended in 1934, "to allow the [US] army...the first-use of nerve-gas, at the earliest possible time" (Rudmin 111).

118 Fascinatingly, on his second "tour" of Africa, in 1891, Stairs records, in his diary, his impression that he is "back on the road to the heart of darkness" (332), that is to say, he is again travelling into the

interior of the continent. Of course, his phraseology is prescient of Conrad's concerns as well as the title of his novel, *Heart of Darkness* (1899, 1902). One should note that portions of Stairs's diaries were serialized in a British magazine, *The Nineteenth Century*, in January and June of 1891 (Roy MacLaren 30).

119 The poem commits British imperialists and their allies to sacrifice themselves to uphold Anglo-Saxon and white Christendom and uplift dark, uncivilized *others*:

> Take up the White Man's burden—
> Send forth the best ye breed—
> Go, bind your sons to exile
> To serve your captives need;
> To wait, in heavy harness,
> On fluttered folk and wild—
> Your new-caught sullen peoples,
> Half devil and half child. (Qtd. in Razack xi)

White Canadians were gaga for such rhetoric. Sherene H. Razack posits that, "For us [Canadians], peacekeeping is Rudyard Kipling's white man's burden, barely transformed from its nineteenth-century origins in colonialism, when it provided moral sanction for waging 'savage wars of peace'" (4). Certainly, in his own time, Stairs is convinced of white superiority to blacks, and thus the need of the "enlightened" to salvage the "benighted":

> It follows that [Africans] are even incapable of so conducting themselves as to promote their slow evolution toward a higher level of existence. Left to themselves, one would find them in the year 3000 in exactly the same state as they are to-day…the level of wild, fearful animals (333; original ellipsis).

Later, Stairs insists, in October 1891, "Nothing abases a European more than to be in an inferior role to a black savage" (354). In November 1891, Stairs states, "Authority [over "the negroes"] should be exercised by whites to the exclusion of all [other "races"], and the sooner the better..." (359; original ellipsis).

120 See this description of the "ornaments" atop the posts of Kurtz's compound in Conrad's *Heart of Darkness* (1899, 1902): "Heads on stakes. I returned [my telescope] deliberately to the first I had seen—and there it was, black, dried, sunken, with closed eyelids—a head that seemed to sleep at the top of that pole" (154). (Stairs sketches this scene of an African ruler's redoubt: "Skeletons fixed to stakes around one section of the village and a terrible pyramid of human heads and amputated hands placed on a sort of pedestal table at the door of his dwelling" [373]). Stairs records yet another moment prescient of Conrad:

> Great sport was caused in camp to-day by a Manyuema woman. This woman got herself up in feathers and flowers and with a native rattle went all about the camp singing to the devil. I believe she is quite mad at times. At night all of a sudden one hears the most blood curdling yells and imagines about 40,000 Washenzi coming on against the camp. After a few inquiries, it generally turns out to be this woman (245).

The passage summons up one in Conrad where Marlow hears, from the banks of the Congo River, "a cry, a very loud cry, as of infinite desolation, soar[ing] slowly in the opaque air. It ceased. A complaining clamour, modulated in savage discords, filled our ears" (140). Later, Marlow encounters Kurtz's lover, a better-defined version of Stairs's "Manyeuma woman":

> She carried her head high; her hair was done in the shape of a helmet; she had brass leggings to the knees, brass wire gauntlets to the elbow, a crimson spot on her tawny cheek, innumerable necklaces of glass beads on her neck; bizarre things, charms, gifts of witch-men, that hung about her, glittered and trembled at every step. She was savage and superb, wild-eyed and magnificent (157).

Conrad's invention of this woman seems indebted, at least in part, to the blazon accorded the Egyptian princess—the Bride—in the Song of Solomon.

121 Conrad's Kurtz writes a similarly expeditious comment: "Exterminate all the brutes!" (149).

122 More recently, in 2019, six Canadian peacekeepers (albeit police, not soldiers) were accused of sexual misconduct with vulnerable Haitians. Their only punishment was their recall to Canada. (See Gurney.)

123 Canadian troops also shot and killed a Somali demonstrator (Razack 77).

124 Roy MacLaren soon repudiates this comparison, stating that Stairs's "self-destruction was not that of Kurtz in *Heart of Darkness* (400). Stairs "did not 'go native,' becoming enamoured of local life and practices" (400). However, MacLaren's argument casts suspicion on "native...local life and practices" as sources of Kurtz's moral decay (a point wrapped in implicit racialism) while asserting that Stairs and other Europeans "were themselves victims of the corrupting system which they represented" (400). But MacLaren's avoidance of a politico-racial assessment of Stairs's psychology means he must blame Stairs's "rape" of Africa on a mysterious non-entity—"the system"—thus suggesting that all the bloodshed was accidental.

125 This implicit feminization of Europeans "crazed" by Africa reinforces stereotyped pathologies applied to women, a point crucial to our pending reading of Danica.

126 In a 1942 interview with Nancy Cunard, Pan-Africanist George Padmore notes, with scathing irony, that the only parts of Africa to escape the worst excesses of European and British imperialism had not humanitarianism but a lowly insect to thank: "Not the kind-heartedness of imperialists but the mosquito has rescued 28 million natives of Nigeria, Gold Coast, Sierra Leone and Gambia from the worst effects of European colonisation" (Cunard 167).

127 Harris's persona also registers "Croatian / mountain roads winding through broken babies Bosnia full horror / of rape as

policy" (59). This passage connects black, red, and white women and their subjection to rape as a matter of macho militarist practice.

128 Razack cites Euan Hague's comment on the vicious behaviour of Bosnian Serb men against Muslims in their civil wars of the late 1990s: "By raping and impregnating women and girls, watching men rape each other in prison camps, and assuming the power position of 'masculine' in all rapes, the Bosnia Serb military and its allied regulars proved to themselves their own identities as powerful, manly and *crucially Serbs*" (qtd. in Razack 63). Reading another theorist, Razack notes, "When the [Nazi] Freikorps wanted to eliminate Jews, they imagined themselves eliminating the feminine" (59).

129 Crucial here is not soldiers' innocence but their ignorance, crucially, of history: "The first American marines to set foot in Africa they land / trapped by Hollywood by their own bloody history dazzled by four / centuries of lies" (Harris 60).

130 "At the age of seventeen [Scott (1862–1947)] entered the Department of Indian Affairs where he eventually became deputy superintendent-general" (Daymond and Monkman 378). In other words, Scott was a *domestic* Canadian imperialist, who dedicated his life to the colonization and attempted assimilation of First Nations peoples.

131 In *Heart of Darkness*, Conrad plays to a similar prejudice against the bicultural or the Métis person. His anti-hero, Kurtz, is "half-English," "half-French," but "all Europe contributed to the making of Kurtz" (148). European but mixed (up), Kurtz is a perfect ally of "the International Society for the Suppression of Savage Customs" (148). When he argues that Europe should commit genocide in Africa (149), he anticipates the thought of Harris's mixed-race and subservient Kelly but follows that of the Anglo-Saxon "bosses," Stairs and Scott.

132 Scott leaves it open to speculation, but there is every chance that the boy is the result of rape. If so, his potential self-hatred may lead him to oppress his own kin *or* his lust for vengeance may drive him to assault whites.

133 Stairs's participation in various horrors is recorded in *his*

diaries. The Abu Ghraib prisoner torture scandal, in which US troops delighted in harming or humiliating (or both) Iraqis captured after the illegal US-led invasion of Iraq in 2003, was exposed in 2004, partly because the torturers took "trophy photos" and videotape footage of their crimes.

134 This claim seems indebted to Virginia Woolf's pronouncement, "As a woman I have no country" (109).

135. When *Don't: A Woman's Word* appeared in 1988, the pursuant controversy over its veracity increased when Danica described it as an "auto-fiction." Interestingly, the refusal of some readers to accept the text as non-fiction mirrors, in fact, the spurning of reports of war trauma. Razack notes that a Canadian newspaper "dismissed [Canadian General Romeo] Dallaire's [1994 Rwanda war genocide] trauma narrative as fabrication, just as it dismissed women who accused their fathers of childhood sexual violence" (20). By revealing her incest trauma, Danica experienced the same dismissals visited upon victims of war trauma.

Canada: The Invisible Empire?

136 Given its pseudo-imperial annexation of Crimea in 2014, Russia was suspended from the G8, which is currently (once again) the G7. However, it's likely that Russia saw unquestioned naval access to the Black Sea as outweighing picturesque photo-ops with G7 leaders.

137 In his review of David Vine's *Island of Shame: The Secret History of the US Military Base on Diego Garcia* (2009), Jonathan Freedland notices that, in contrast to the British and Roman Empires of yore, their American "successor seeks to rule by holding, directly at least, as little terrain as it can" (27). Yep, the US Empire be a stealth enterprise.

138 Abigail B. Bakan asks students of Canada to adopt "an approach that emphasizes the racist and pro-imperialist character of the making of the Canadian state [and so] also challenges the left nationalist emphasis that has historically been a hallmark of Canadian political economy," one that upholds instead "the progressive national character of the Canadian ruling class relative to that of the US" (16).

139 See this sentence, for instance: "The main social, political, spine-character of the States will probably run along the Ohio, Missouri and Mississippi Rivers, and west and north of them, including Canada." (n.p.). Whitman's magniloquent vision of American democracy is grandly magnanimous enough to offer Canada hearty incorporation.

140 George W. Brown witnesses, "Confederation was achieved, not in opposition to British policy but in the end with the aid of British policy and through a combination of forces running strongly on both sides of the Atlantic. So too with the extension of the Dominion westward to the Pacific. Canada gained a western empire—the vast domain of the Hudson's Bay Company—because she herself was part of an empire" (134–135).

141 These martial loyalties can take strange forms. In his play about fascist Italy's efforts to win support among Italian-Canadians, Filippo Salvatore has a character report "la formation du corps expéditionnaire italo-canadien pour la guerre d'Éthiopie" (*Fresque* 55). In this case, Italian-Canadians enlist to go overseas to help Italy construct an empire in Africa. The example may be fictitious, but it mirrors English-Canadian support for British (and occasional American) imperial ventures.

142 Editor Harold Head thought his anthology was the first to assemble Black Canadian writers, but it was actually the third, following anthologies edited by Camille Haynes (1973) and Liz Cromwell (1975).

The Road to North Hatley: Ralph Gustafson's Postcolonial Odyssey

143 Frantz Fanon asserts that "every colonized people...finds itself face to face with the language of the civilizing nation; that is, with the culture of the mother country" (*Black* 18). Gustafson's pyrrhic struggles to harness domestic rhythms to "imperial" models demonstrates this proverb's veracity.

144 Smith's concepts of separate "native" (or provincial) and "cosmopolitan" (or intellectual) traditions in Canadian poetry debuted in his anthology, *The Book of Canadian Poetry* (1943), where he categorizes poets according to these labels.

145 The categories self-destruct, of course. For one thing, the "contemporary and cosmopolitan literary consciousness" (3) that Smith accords modern poets has always been part of Canadian poetry. Moreover, Smith's modernist "natives" include E. J. Pratt, Earle Birney, and Dorothy Livesay, all of whom gleaned poetic ideas and influences from abroad. "Cosmo" moderns like Margaret Avison, P. K. Page, Gustafson, and Smith himself are represented by poems replete with imagery reflective of Canadascapes. Thus, Smith's terms denote a politics of literary judgment. "Cosmopolitan" suggests a desirable, learned assimilationism; "native" portends a doltish, essentialist provincialism.

146 In *Revolution of the Word: A New Gathering of American Avant Garde Poetry* (1974), editor Jerome Rothenberg dismisses Jolas's achievements as "spotty, & his language experiments & platforms (verticalism & trilingualism, the revolution of the word, language of night, etc.) naively one-dimensional" (148). Whatever the cogency of Rothenberg's critique, Jolas's principles offered Gustafson no enduringly applicable aesthetic.

147 Perhaps its weaknesses inspired Gustafson to omit "Mythos" from his second grouping of elect poems, *The Moment Is All: Selected Poems 1944–83* (1984).

148 Gustafson's career delineates the search for an English Canadian middle way respectively between what Fussell calls "English regularity" and the American tendency to favour a libertarian "free verse...as inevitable as the Declaration of Independence" (11–12). If the problem of the early twentieth century for Canadian poets was the pentameter, the solution was not always a Poundian "heave."

149 Gustafson prized the local in his later career, but he was still capable, in 1982, of publishing a book of poems, *Gradations of Grandeur*, modelled on Crane's highfalutin *Bridge* (1930). Furthermore, Gustafson seems never to have exploited a single localism from the Eastern Townships, not even the "by gurry!" exclamation associated with Massawippi. See Lewis J. Poteet, *Talking Country: The Eastern Townships Phrase Book* (1992): 27.

150 Head's anthology was the *third*. See the Liz Cromwell and Camille Haynes listings above.

~

We are publishing from Tiohtià:ke, the Mohawk name for a historic place for gathering and trade for many First Nations. It is unceded traditional Indigenous territory, on which there have now been non-Indigenous settlers for more than 375 years. As publishers we know we cannot rewrite our history, but we can be part of a concerted effort to contribute to reconciliation between Indigenous Peoples and Settlers.

~

The display face of this text is Filosofia—designed by Zuzana Licko and brought to market by Emigre Fonts in 1996. A refurbishing of Giambattista Bodoni's Romantic-era Bodoni font, Filosofia grants each letter its own space, to stand apart as it were, as if each incisive letter were an independent thinker.

The body type is Minion. Sired in 1990 by Robert Slimbach for Adobe Systems, the font is a homage to Late Renaissance-era typefaces that spurred along humanist literacy by guiding eyes to glide through page upon enlightening page.